For Iain and for Angela

e alla memoria di mia madre Iolanda e mio padre Silvio

Contents

Preface

To write is to find my own voice, that of the tale-teller where narrativity is stronger than truth. In fact it is truth (though it would not survive the trial of proof): inventive, paradoxical, guided by the internal rhythm of deception that builds and grows on itself. I still remember when Aunt Maria arrived. 'What are you chatting about?' she asked in her Florentine accent. The only 'pure Italian' in a solid Neapolitan-speaking family, and being a 'stranger' she had an unnerving way of arriving at odd times. How could I go on keeping my face and say 'I was speaking of when our family went to Libya and of our adventures there.' She knew only too well that we had never moved, not even gone to Rome, so I chickened out and the abrupt confession followed: 'I was inventing things.' I can still see the astonished and wounded look of my audience, girls and boys my age, 9 or 10 – the first listeners of my tales.

This book is composed of essays that drew their inspiration from diverse occasions and different events. The intersection of cultural studies with critical theory and literary analysis has guided my interest in women's narratives, and the spaces and times that narrative occupies in women's lives.

Fiction flows between life and imagination, and it is one of the most direct links between these two worlds. As de Certeau says, 'Our stories order our world, providing the mimetic and mythical structures for experience.'[1] It began with myth: the bridge between history and everyday life, underlining both the simplicity and importance of its passage. The anthropological and mythical dimensions of tale telling have been with us for a long time, while the novelistic has contributed to the ordering of meanings for the individual in society.

Fables and myth have always had a relation to gender. The narrative function has been associated with the feminine, commencing with Scheherazade. In the active role of story teller, she provided the means for the continuation of life. Laura Mulvey, in one of her films and also in her writings, has linked the motive of the Sphinx and her riddles to the enigma of sexual difference, indicating the connection between women and the narrative drive:

> Curiosity describes a desire to know something secret so strongly that it is experienced like a drive. It is a source of danger and pleasure and knowledge. . . . In the myths of Eve and Pandora, curiosity lay behind the first woman's desire to penetrate a forbidden secret that precipitated the fall of man. These myths associate female curiosity with an active narrative function.[2]

Mythical stories are fabulations of women, probably not created by women. In those narratives, as in other dominant discourses, they are used as metaphors. Still, contrary to official history, women have been important motors of mythical (hi)stories. History comes from discord, and discord comes from women. Helen, Medea, Europa, Arianna, Io, Pasifae and Phædra were objects of rape, kidnapping, abandonment and betrayal; but they were also subjects of pleasure, of movement, of revenge.

The stories that are the argument of my book invoke movement from theory to fiction, from prose to poetry, from writing to film, from sounds to stories, from an ancestral culture to an acquired one. The movement is complex, never unidirectional, and the culture on either side is neither unaltered nor constant. As Gloria Anzaldúa in her Preface to *Borderlands/La Frontera* puts it: 'Living on borders and in margins, keeping intact one's shifting and multiple identity and integrity, is like trying to swim in a new element, an "alien" element.'[3] This alien element is never comfortable but is, at the same time, familiar. As Trinh T. Minh-ha, another voice from the border, says, 'Tale-telling brings the impossible within reach. With it, I am who It is, Whom I am seen to be, yet I can only feel myself there where I am not, *vis-à-vis* an elsewhere I do not dwell in.'[4] Narrative is where woman is and is not at the same time.

Scheherazade in *The Thousand and One Nights* indicated that telling tales marks the dividing line between life and death. Angela Carter reminds us that for Walter Benjamin the narrator borrows her/his authority from death: '. . . the end of all stories, even if the writer forebears to mention it, is death, which is where our time stops short . . . We travel along the thread of narrative like high-

wire artistes. That is our life.'[5] On the other hand, Nicole Ward
Jouve, while accepting that a deadly exchange is the essence of story-
telling, stresses the joyful character of the bargaining.[6]
Narrative is danger, as Carter's mother warned when she found
her reading a novel: 'Never let me catch you doing that again,
remember what happened to Emma Bovary'.[7] In the narratives I
examine, other mothers try to keep their daughters from reading.
(Does that make them good mothers or bad mothers? This is one of
many enigmas that evades ready solution.) But narrative is also
healing: stories can be medicines or soul vitamins, 'to guide the way
back to *el mundo subterráneo*, the underground world, our psychic
home' (Clarissa Pinkola Estés[8]), or 'to chase the demons, to keep
them away for good' (Carter). Leslie Marmon Silko, in the epigraph
to *Ceremony*, informs us that God is three women, and that they
created the world by naming things:

> Thought-Woman, the spider,
> named things and
> as she named them
> they appeared.
>
> She is sitting in her room
> thinking of a story now
>
> I'm telling you the story
> she is thinking.

Thinking is telling tales, telling tales is creating: the importance of
stories is underlined many times in this work and others. 'You don't
have anything if you don't have stories', Silko says in another
epigraph.[9]
The place that feminist theory has occupied in the development of
the recent critical panorama finds a focus in the encounter between
feminism and postmodernism on one side, and between Anglo-
American feminist thought and continental theories on the other.
This is the subject of Chapter 1 and it informs my successive
analyses of contemporary women's fictions. In recent strands of
female narratives, I have looked for the way in which feminism and
postmodernism cross each other's paths, and find a common point
of encounter in the search for new ways of narrating; and also how

feminist theories of subjectivity are inscribed and incorporated in the strategies of women's fictions, from popular culture to post-modern novels. The formal paradigms and devices often found both in serial fiction and in more sophisticated narratives can be seen as modes of articulating practices of identification and anxieties around identity.

These encounters have been crucial in my development as a feminist, and to a great extent have shaped my analysis of female narratives in this book, in relation to my specific experience as a woman living and teaching in Southern Italy, and reaching feminism after a long-held Marxist position and a communist militancy that, without needing to, repressed whole areas of my subjectivity. My interest in stories stems from these (for me) new encounters, some-what antagonistic to my former more socially oriented interests, though not necessarily so: an antagonism as unneeded today as previous exclusions. This book means also to underline the diverse uses of 'the political' that are to be found in feminist theories and practices.

Theories and narratives arise from hybrid voices, standing on the borders between different, sometime multiple, cultures, back-grounds and languages, both within Europe and across continents. This is more evidently true in the writers from the diaspora, for whom the demarcation of the area of influence is rather blurred and nationality cannot be clearly defined.[10] Hybrid selves are translated into hybrid writing, moving on the border between memory and fantasy, fable and history, tradition and innovation: standing between essay and fiction, poetry and prose. This is the case of Trinh T. Minh-ha, Leslie Marmon Silko, Louise Erdrich, Gloria Anzaldúa, Toni Morrison, Louise Aldrich and many others.

These and other fluctuations can also be found in writers with altogether steadier national identities, such as Jane Bowles, Jeanette Winterson, Joanna Russ and Angela Carter, just as it is important to remember that what is called 'French feminism' mostly includes people who are French with a hyphen (French-Québecois, French-Guadeloupean, French-Bulgarian or, mostly, French-Algerian). But, rather than speaking about their hybrid backgrounds, I wish to recall their liminal styles of writing in between the poetical and the political register.

*   *   *

Two or three fundamental themes recur throughout the book: one is the uncertain dividing line between reality and fiction; another is the concept of hybridity and contamination; yet another is female melancholia. Connected to these themes are the motifs that traverse my writing: the flux from body to writing and vice versa; the parody of female physical stereotypes; the journey of diegetic transgressions (genre, gender, style, languages).

The theme of 'what is real and what is not' emerges in Chapter 1, and comes up again in Chapter 3, but is also present in the 'hybrid fictions' and 'monstrous bodies' of successive chapters. I have thought about the issue of reality and fiction, the concrete and the imaginary, repeatedly, commencing from my original work on television and from a critique of the notion that considered popular texts as realist texts. I have found this issue present in most of the theoretical work I have been inspired by and the narratives I have chosen for my analysis.

The second question – contamination and hybridity – leads to genre. The denial of a rigid gender dichotomy (the move from in-difference to difference, and then to differences) is connected to the refusal of a rigid law of genre through displacement, transference, ambiguity and multiplicity. Chapter 2 looks at the connection between gender and genre, at its genesis, and examines diverse examples of postmodern female fiction. In the novels I discuss, the boundaries between popular and elitist culture are hazy, and the connections between genres and genders often ambiguous. From P. D. James, Patricia Highsmith and Sue Grafton to Angela Carter, Leslie Marmon Silko and Jeanette Winterson, there is often an intended evasion of genre and gender specificities.

The third chapter deals with television serial narratives of the kind usually addressed to women (soaps and tele-novelas), but also looks at crime series with their increasingly ambiguous divide between male and female genres. If genres with distinct boundaries are disappearing (in the same way as gender and sexual dichotomies are the ground for theoretical suspicion), there are nevertheless masculine and feminine constructions – whether textual or contex-tual, rhetorical, linguistic or social – in most narratives. They are never unalloyed or sharply separate. They often intermingle and change within the same text. This important, sometime exclusive, and excluded, space of narration in women's lives can be re-viewed by inserting the televisual text into the rhythms of daily life where

[handwritten annotation at top: 1 Chapter on the 'lack of narrative closure' as a way of saying —]

gossip and television, gossip in television, provide sustenance, survival and a focus for living.

I have explored these variegated textualities foregrounding certain figures — bodies, rooms, claustrophobic spaces, romance and paranoia, couples and pairs, for example — and considering such thematics as a deferral of synthesis in favour of multiplicity, fluid 'irreducible identities' and lack of narrative closure. As Hélène Cixous says, a female textual body is always endless; it is without limits, it starts on all sides, and when it ends, it starts all over again. These are recognisable features of the novels I deal with in the successive two chapters. The necessity for women to retrace their way in the literary canon, to re-visit and look at fathers and mothers with different eyes, has brought about the blurring of genres and the transformation of models: metamorphosis and grafting have produced new hybrid forms, monstrous shapes and bodies. Temporal and spatial dislocations, non-corporeal connections, fantastic forms of narration even outside science fiction proper become essential narrative tools in contemporary women's fiction. Metanarration goes along with the hybridisation of codes, genres and languages and the proliferation of monstrous bodies, as corporeal and sexual metamorphosis underlines the diegetic multiformity. The displacements, ambiguities and pluralism of the female narrative texts lead to genre transgression and contamination. This is how female monstrous bodies have stealthily appeared in a corner, and uncannily made their way into my work, acquiring an important part in its imaginative structure. The monster at the end of it all is women's writing, writing as the female body, ink and milk and blood.

Chapter 6 on Jane Bowles — a voice from the mid-century who can be seen as a forerunner of the writers that I deal with in the central part of the book — concerns the intersection of sexuality, race and gender, and deals with travel as the encounter with the 'other', with a lesbian relationship and the difficulty of writing for women. It is a fluctuating discourse with many focuses, and its methodology lingers at the crossing of literary and film analysis with postcolonial critical theory.

Jane Bowles's stories — reflections on travel rather than travel stories — follow a metaphorical itinerary through otherness and sexual ambiguity. This is the central theme in her one finished novel, *Two Serious Ladies*, in her short stories, and in the play *In the Summer House*, but above all in her letters. The encounter with a

Moroccan woman that changed her life is narrated in these letters and was anticipated, in a disquieting premonition, in her previous works. Her vision of the other has given me the occasion to attempt to underline the complexities of whiteness, and of the white gaze on the black woman, and to refer to some writings that engage with feminism and postcolonial theory.

The gaze of woman on woman is a constant in this book. But in this particular chapter, though primarily concentrating on this, I deal also with the cinematic vision of her given by the male gaze in two films by Bernardo Bertolucci and David Cronenberg. Diversity, exclusion and monstrosity are the crucial elements of this vision, and link up with the theme of hybridity and monstrosity in former chapters.

Psychoanalysis has inevitably been an important referent in my discourse on theoretical feminisms, and in the two final chapters it achieves a more direct focus in the study of female melancholia. The thread of melancholia starts from Jane Bowles, and her voyage into otherness, towards solitary madness and death. It then takes us to Ophelia and Gertrude, two disquieting female figures who might be interpreted as the counterpoint to the first weak man of modernity. This is the argument of Chapter 7.

Contemporary female criticism has produced work on Shake-speare that occupies an essential place within feminist theory. This chapter draws on that work, and particularly on the many feminist psychoanalytical re-readings of *Hamlet*. My analysis looks at these evanescent female characters, particularly Ophelia, but does this within the more general issue of melancholy in *Hamlet*, referring it to the obsession with the female so central in the drama. The work of Julia Kristeva on depression, *Black Sun*, has been my main inspiration, though she never mentions Shakespeare or Hamlet, but I have also drawn on other important female works about hysteria and women's melancholic sexuality.

These two chapters also have a link with the contamination of genres: a sort of femininisation of the tragic in *Hamlet*, a text that first puts the boundaries of genres in question; the disquieting entwining of the 'genres' of art and life in Bowles. Another link with previous narratives is the monster that reappears in the semblance of Cherifa/Fedela in Jane Bowles's story, or the many ghostly appearances in the novels of Toni Morrison, Jeanette Winterson and Louise Erdrich on the traces of the Shakespearean ghosts.

*   *   *

I wish to return briefly to the diverse occasions and different inspirations I mentioned at the beginning. Chapter 1 partly originated at the conference on 'Cultural Studies Now and in the Future' (University of Illinois at Urbana-Champaign, 1990). The conference brought me to the task of looking at the past of cultural studies, based on my experience at the Centre for Contemporary Cultural Studies (CCCS) in Birmingham, and at the future of a non-discipline facing the institutional dangers of becoming one. It was both a historical look at theory and a personal trajectory. The debate between modernism and postmodernism gave voice to the preoccupation (that emerged mostly within cultural studies) of the abandonment of the real, particularly of the political real. My work on television and on popular culture had already posed that problem, through a series of what seemed to me artificial boundaries (evasion as against commitment, for one).

The issue comes up again in Chapter 3, an analysis of soaps and other series that started with a paper on 'Genre and Gender' at the International Television Studies Conference (British Film Institute, London 1986), and more substantially at the Center for 20th Century Studies (The University of Wisconsin, Milwaukee, 1988) with the paper 'Fe/male re-presentations', at a conference on 'Television: Representation, Audience, Industry'. In both cases the versions appearing here involve substantial revisions. A recent stay in California provided the opportunity to update my tele-visions.

The chapter on Jane Bowles originated within a research on women's travels with the interdisciplinary women's group (Archivio delle donne) at the Istituto Universitario Orientale, Naples, and found a framing perspective in the unexpected appearance of Jane and Cherifa on the screen in Cronenberg's *Naked Lunch*. It was substantially rewritten to be published in *The Postcolonial Question* (Routledge, 1996). With minor corrections this is the version that appears here.

Other chapters (4, 5 and 7) appear here for the first time but have a history. The chapter I wrote for *Storia della civiltà letteraria inglese* (Turin, UTET, 1996) started me on the analysis of female novels of recent decades. The essay on Ophelia stems from my teaching of Shakespeare and originated in my introduction to *Ombre di un'ombra – Amleto e i suoi fantasmi* (1994), a re-reading of *Hamlet* in the context of psychoanalysis and late modernity. Except for the general frame, this essay departs substantially from the previous version. These three chapters were written into the present form during periods of research and work in the years 1994–95 at the Center for Cultural Studies in the University of California, Santa Cruz, and later in 1995 at the Humanities Research Institute at Irvine, California.

LIDIA CURTI

Notes

1. M. de Certeau, *The Practice of Everyday Life* (Berkeley, CA: University of California Press, 1988), p. 87.
2. L. Mulvey, *Visual and Other Pleasures* (London: Macmillan, 1989), p. x.
3. G. Anzaldúa, *Borderlands/La Frontera* (San Francisco, CA: Aunt Lute Books, 1992), p. 2. The alien element is never comfortable but is at the same time familiar, like the Freudian uncanny.
4. Trinh T. M., 'Other than myself/my other self', in G. Robertson *et al.* (eds) *Traveller's Tales – Narratives of Home and Displacement* (London and New York: Routledge, 1994), p. 11.
5. A. Carter, *Expletives Deleted* (London: Chatto & Windus, 1987), p. 2.
6. 'Story-telling is also playing against Death: your life or your story. Your life for a story. But it is many-coloured and fun and proliferating and gameful.' N. Ward Jouve, *White Woman Speaks with Forked Tongue – Criticism as Autobiography* (London: Routledge, 1991), p. 187.
7. A. Carter, *Expletives Deleted*, p. 3.
8. C. Pinkola Estés, *Women Who Run With the Wolves – Contacting the Power of the Wild Woman* (London: Rider, 1992), p. 20. And she goes on: 'Story greases the hoists and pulleys, it causes adrenaline to surge, shows us the way out, down, or up, and for our trouble, cuts for us fine wide doors in previously blank walls, openings that lead to the dreamland, that lead to love and learning, that lead us back to our own real lives as knowing wildish women.'
9. L. Marmon Silko, *Ceremony* (Harmondsworth: Penguin, 1986), respectively, pp. 1 and 2.
10. When speaking of innovation and avant-garde, it is difficult to decide whether their languages are breaking with tradition or not: which and whose tradition? And are Western critical standards applicable anyway? The latter is the most important question to ask nowadays in debates over the boundary between high and popular literature and culture.

Acknowledgements

I wish to thank the following people and institutions for inviting me to present parts of this work at conferences or seminars, and offering the occasion for useful discussions and insights: the British Film Institute, London, UK; Kathleen Woodward and Patricia Mellenkamp at the Center for 20th Century Studies, University of Wisconsin, Milwaukee, USA; Lisa Tickner at the Graduate Seminar, University of Middlesex, London, UK; Larry Grossberg, Cary Nelson and Paula A. Treichler at the University of Illinois at Urbana-Champaign, USA; Elizabeth Tuttle and Marie Yvonne Gilles at the University of Nanterre, Paris; Alessandra Marzola at the University of Bergamo, Italy; James Clifford and Carla Freccero at the Centre for Cultural Studies at the University of California, Santa Cruz; the members of Archivio delle donne at the Istituto Universitario Orientale, Napoli, Italy.

My thanks go also to Marina Vitale and Annamaria Morelli for their reading of parts of my manuscripts; to friends and colleagues in Santa Cruz and Irvine for their encouragement at difficult moments, and also for their hospitality, warmth and good food; to Angela Gervasio, Catherine Hall and Stuart Hall who in different and important ways helped me to believe in my work, and above all to Iain Chambers for his invaluable intellectual 'presence' and his patient readings. Finally, I wish to thank the graduate and undergraduate students of the Istituto Universitario Orientale who, in the last four years, while working with me on Shakespeare and on feminist theory and women's fiction, have provided an important source of inspiration and emotional support.

I also wish to thank Mara De Chiara for her help with the proofs, Catherine Gray for her stimulating editorship, and Keith Povey for his attentive handling of the manuscript.

Chapters 1 and 3 are a largely revised version of 'What is real and what is not: female fabulations in cultural analysis', which appeared in *Cultural Studies* (ed. by L. Grossberg, C. Nelson and P. Treichler, London and New York: Routledge, 1992); Chapter 6 first appeared as 'Between Two Shores' in *The Postcolonial Question* (ed. by I. Chambers and L. Curti, London and New York: Routledge, 1996). I acknowledge the kind permission granted by the publishers, Routledge.

LIDIA CURTI

Chapter 1

Introduction: The Swing of Theory

The encounter between feminism and postmodernism is at the centre of this introductory discourse. Starting from this confrontation and returning to it in its final part, this chapter examines a series of passages and debates that from the sixties onwards trace what could be called a trajectory of crisis. The debates follow one another and at the same time they coexist in what is the substance of the discourse of and on marginalities – the marginalities created by wealth, class, race, age and gender – that are still with us today.

The debates I deal with give voice to the preoccupation, mostly expressed in cultural studies, with the abandonment of the real, particularly the 'political' real. The issue of 'what is real and what is not' will come up in other parts of this book in the form of what seem to me artificial oppositions: evasion versus commitment, the images of women versus real women, the renewal of languages as opposed to the changes in the condition of woman, to mention but a few. This occurs in the analyses both of popular literature and television and of contemporary experimentation in women's writing. I believe that these are by no means necessary oppositions or fixed, unmovable divisions, just like the genres and gender boundaries that I discuss elsewhere, though I would not be able to say whether this opinion is inspired by feminism or postmodernism, by cultural and critical studies, or by the reading of literature, present and past.

The discourse of difference, partly overlapping with the confrontation of feminism with postmodernism, is presented here and will be taken up substantially in the chapters on contemporary women's fiction. It seems to mark swings in the theoretical pendulum, giving emphasis now to essentialism, now to anti-essentialism, but actually

1

signalling a multiplicity of positions, each of them traversed by many nuances and contradictions. They are at once a historical memory and a coexistence of different moments, both constituting the present richness of feminist thought and tradition.

Further elements that are important in the shared discourse between feminism and postmodernism are the decline of a strong, steady, undivided subjectivity, the refusal of canonised forms, the opposition to a morality of consensus (it is not a question of obtaining a consensus that others have had for too long but of creating a space for dissent), the stress on the hidden and the marginal. The distinctions between subject and object, centre and margins, sameness and difference, and, ideally, oppressor and oppressed are blurred and uncertain. It might be useful to describe this conjuncture as the crisis of modernity reiterated and conjoined with the development of feminist thought.

The discourse of crisis: from cultural studies to feminism

Crisis has been the password of cultural studies from Hoggart to Williams, from Hall to Jameson and Hebdige; the crisis in English, to use Hoggart's words, fostered its start at the periphery of disciplines and subjects, speaking from the margin on margins. In literature and the social sciences, in sociology and anthropology, its space was at the edge, introducing the margins as privileged objects of study, one marginality displacing and traversing another: class and youth, race and gender. The relation has not been one of addition or succession but of intersection in which what matters is the negotiation between each of the terms, the intertwining of these elements.

The discourse of crisis touches the roles of intellectuals too, their work and research. We constantly attempt to find a sort of anchorage, to utter a temporary 'truth' on the state of affairs, while being aware, more than in the past, of the loss of that centrality which our role as intellectuals had conferred on us, and with it of the break-up of former methodological, literary and philosophical guarantees. In front of the strong narratives of a recent past – structuralism, semiotics, psychoanalysis, Marxism – we experience a sense of confusion and indecision. As Roland Barthes says in his autobiography, speaking of himself in the third person: 'His relation with psychoanalysis is not a strict one (though he cannot take the resolution of contestation, or refusal). It is an undecided relation.'[1] As researchers, teachers, interpreters of art and sometimes prophets of reality, we go through the experience of being on the margins. Today our prophecies and our readings are subjected to rhetorical analysis, like the poems we are studying and interpreting.

This sense of margins has come first of all from the experience of being women and from feminist criticism. With its reference to a divided and plural subjectivity, feminism has inspired and informed a great part of this contemporary sense of crisis.[2] Like all marginalised groups, feminism has fought and still fights against this condition but the answer does not lie in exchanging the margins for the centre; a simple inversion could only confirm old dualities and a superseded order of the world and would not be really useful to women. As Gayatri Spivak says in 'Explanation and Culture: Marginalia', 'by pointing attention to a feminist marginality, I have been attempting, not to win the center for ourselves, but to point at the irreducibility of the margin in all explanations'.[3] Margins cannot be included, or appropriated or used as tokens; the movement between centre and periphery is a narration of displacement. Similarly Luce Irigaray's '*Pouvoir du discours/subordination du féminin*' points out that subordination can become women's power, and mimicry the main instrument of this transformation, the same mimicry that is historically assigned to women: 'It is a question of assuming this role deliberately. Which already means turning subordination into affirmation, and therefore subverting it.'[4]

In the essay quoted above, Spivak had referred the discourse on margins to literary criticism, defining the desire for an explanation as a desire 'for a self and a world' (p. 105), and finally a desire for centrality, what she calls a 'masculist centralism': 'it is the center that offers the official explanation; or, the center is defined and reproduced by the explanation that it can express' (p. 107). According to her, every privileged explanation must be put in question even while it is being expressed: 'that is the question I will put on the agenda: the pedagogy of the humanities as the arena of cultural explanations that question the explanations of culture' (p. 117). In another essay included in *In Other Worlds*, she comments on her own translation and study of two stories by the Bengali writer Mahasweta Devi, and concludes by stating that a textual gap inevitably exceeds the knowledge of the textual critic:

I hope these pages have made clear that, in the mise-en-scène where the text persistently rehearses itself, writer and reader are both upstaged. If the reader clandestinely carves out a piece of action by using the text as a tool, it's only in celebration of the text's apartness (être-à-l'écart) . . . in that scene of writing, the authority of the author (writer, reader, teacher) . . . must be content to stand in the wings.[5]

The explanation of a text or a phenomenon, though necessary and I would say unavoidable, is the creation of marginality, the marginality of the critic or observer. Stuart Hall, too, speaks of margins and identity in his essay 'Minimal Selves':

Thinking about my own sense of identity, I realize that it has always depended on the fact of being a migrant, on the difference from the rest of you . . . Now that, in the postmodern age, you all feel so dispersed, I become centred. What I've thought of as dispersed and fragmented comes . . . to be the representative postmodern experience! Welcome to migranthood.[6]

This centrality of 'marginalisation' is a paradox and carries the risk that once more we become prophets, the prophets of margins. Again, it is not simply a question of moving the terms around (white instead of black, men instead of women); it is rather a substantial change deriving from this decentralisation. Stuart Hall himself, speaking about black youth in contemporary London, deprived of rights, fragmented and dispersed, observes that, in spite of all that, 'they look as if they own the territory' (ibid.)

I have had a similar experience with my students: they might be defined as people who have come from the province to town – and the town is Naples with its distinctive version of cosmopolitanism – if we had not just said that dualistic terms like province and city, centre and periphery, do not make much sense any longer. They live the conflict between the original peasant-oriented cultural tradition and this metropolitan, chaotic, postearthquake experience. The crisis is there but it is part of their territory, the substance of their experience in all its aspects: life, study, entertainment, daily choices. The crisis is an essential part, 'a way, however weak, of experiencing reality, not as an object that we own and pass on, but as a horizon, a background against which we modestly move', as Gianni Vattimo says.[7]

Cultural studies suffers from the same contradiction when having started as a non-discipline it becomes one, and from the periphery it moves to the centre. This was the contradiction that struck me at the conference 'Cultural Studies Now and in the Future' from which part of this analysis originated. There are dangers hidden in the popularity and the subsequent institutionalisation of cultural studies, especially in the USA; these same dangers are stressed as regards women's studies by Gayatri Spivak, Monique Wittig and others, in the debate I refer to below.

Gramsci at Disneyland, Brecht at the Bonaventura Hotel

A paradox has been at the centre of the debate between modernism and postmodernism: on one hand there can be no clear dividing line between the vague and ever-shifting meanings of these two terms; the *post-* announces that vagueness and shows the impossibility of uttering a new name. It puts a mark of erasure on what is superseding without really cancelling it. In spite of this, in the eighties the debate was heated and acquired the status of an autonomous discourse, a sort of genre in itself, like the *querelle des anciens et des modernes* and the dispute between classics and romantics. It finds its latest development in the discussions around the term 'postcolonial'.[8]

Like all polemic arguments, it has created an artificial and rarefied scenery in which structuralism goes out and hermeneutics enters, scientism is replaced by ethics, and so on. It can be linked with the oppositional discourse that traversed cultural studies in the previous two decades, placing structuralism and culturalism, or psychoanalysis and Marxism, on opposite sides. These theories offered different contexts for such oppositions as inside versus outside, individual psyche versus social reality, personal feelings versus collective political action. The debates of more recent years maintain some of the old terms and add new ones, such as meaning and surface, political commitment and individual hedonism. The correspondences may be inverted: feelings may be identified with social reality or with evasion and fantasy. Eventually each term seems to be claimed by all sides. In this debate, which has been mostly defensive, people like Baudrillard and Jameson have been treated as prophets of postmodernism: Baudrillard in spite of his apocalyptic vision; Jameson in spite of his defence of modernism.[9]

The British debate has been marked by a familiar suspicion towards definitions or labels, towards the *-isms*.[10] Once more, as in the past, an atmosphere of suspicion and guilt, sin and repentance, has surrounded theory and in particular the theory that comes from elsewhere. The geographical and theoretical elsewhere is often France, but sometimes Italy and Germany. The debate coincided with a difficult time of transition for the left, and for Marxist critical discourse in particular. Whether right or wrong, postmodernism has been associated with the end of ideology and the decline of master narratives, and Marxism has certainly been the latter, if not the former.

In the beginning postmodernism was seen as a pluralist, capitalist discourse opposing Marxism (and what it stood for). Things have been moving rapidly: with the great changes within socialism, oppositions are not so easily established any longer. Similarly in that first phase of the debate, the connection between aesthetics and politics was presented as quite unmediated and simplistic. I am referring in particular to an exchange of the early eighties among Anderson, Eagleton, Jameson and Latimer in *New Left Review*. Perry Anderson, in 'Modernity and Revolution', took his start from Marshall Berman's *All that is Solid Melts into Air* (1982). Though admiring its rigorously Marxist inspiration, he criticized its reading of the dialectics of modernism as a revolutionary process. In the name of a strictly Leninist conception of revolution, he condemned both modernism and postmodernism as empty terms, 'one void chasing another, in a serial regression of self-congratulatory chronology'.[11] He placed both among those 'morbid symptoms' that (according to Gramsci) appear in the interregnum between the old and the new, when the new is not yet here.

Gramsci appears here and will be invoked again on the strength of the concrete character of his work, placing him safely away from theory and underlining his political purity. Bill Schwartz sees him as the last bulwark of a totalising theory of knowledge as opposed to the informal, fragmentary world of the spectacle ('Gramsci goes to Disneyland' is the title of his essay), perhaps forgetting that Gramsci had developed the art of the fragment to perfection. The brilliant intuitions of *Americanism and Fordism* and all his work on popular culture make it difficult to view him in an anti-American and anti-popular frame. Dick Hebdige writes:

> It would be foolish to present a polar opposition between the Gramscian line(s) and the (heterogeneous) Posts. There is too much shared historical and intellectual ground . . . from the perspectives heavily influenced by the Gramscian approach, nothing is anchored to the *grand récits*, to master narratives, to stable (positive) identities, to fixed and certain meanings: all social and semantic relations are contestable, hence mutable.[12]

Gramsci, however, is not the only name standing for nostalgia. Lukács, Brecht, Benjamin are invoked both in Jameson's famous essay and in Terry Eagleton's reply to it.[13] In a recent review of the former, Franco Rella, though no fan of postmodernity, criticises Jameson's generic and constant reference to socio-economic reality motivated, in his opinion, 'by the nostalgia of Brechtian art and by Lukács' marxist theory: once more the two stumbling blocks of modernity'.[14] Rella sees such nostalgia as the 'sickness' marring the whole debate.

Jameson's essay cannot be discussed in detail here. His vision is too complex to squeeze into any simple dualistic opposition. He carries on a sustained critique of postmodernity, the new map of knowledge that it is no longer possible to ignore, while giving relief to its fascination. He describes the decline of the dialectics between substance and appearance, the latent and the manifest, the authentic and the inauthentic. Instead there are surfaces made of textual practices, discourses and games, as in pastiche, in the past revisited, in the metropolitan collage. The Bonaventure Hotel is the object replacing the work of art. Like the Beaubourg and other buildings of the kind, it is a miniaturised city, a self-referential space where movement is the emblem of movement and the roads are predetermined narrative paths, for visitors to follow. 'Here the narrative stroll has been underscored, symbolized, reified and replaced by a transportation machine, which becomes the allegorical signifier of that older promenade we are no longer allowed to conduct on our own.'[15]

This limitation to individual creativity and the lack of distance in critical discourse are the features of postmodernism that he most severely criticises, along with its links to late capitalism. His mixed feelings are confirmed in a conversation with Stuart Hall. Speaking of the 'plebianisation of culture', he says: 'That's a crucial part of postmodernism, which underscores its ambiguity. One cannot object to the democratisation of culture, but one must object to other features of it. Those mixed feelings have to be preserved in any analysis of the postmodern.'[16] He still regrets the absence of a reflexive, critical distance.

Baudrillard is much more critical, even in his less pessimistic *America*, where he extends his *'j'accuse'* to all the appliances of this postmodern world:

Is this still architecture, this pure illusionism, this mere box of spatio-temporal tricks? Ludic and hallucinogenic, is this post-modern architecture? . . . Everywhere the transparency of inter-faces ends in internal refraction. Everything pretentiously termed 'communication' and 'interaction' – walkman, dark glasses, auto-matic household appliances, hi-tech cars, even the perpetual dialogue with the computer – ends up with each monad retreating into the shade of its own formula, into its self-regulating little corner and its artificial immunity.[17]

Brecht and Benjamin are the main constellations of a lost planet, the lost planet that is at the centre of an essay written by Dick Hebdige in 1987, 'The Bottom Line on Planet One'. This successful science-fiction metaphor introduces the planet of modernism (one) as opposed to that of surfaces, simulacra, and simulations (two). Three is the planet of reality, of politics, of the underdeveloped and hungry Third World. The first is the place of nostalgia, the second of escape and evasion. The magazine *The Face*, considered by Hebdi-ge's students, to his dismay, as 'the Ur Text for Magazine construc-tion', is the emblem of this escapism.[18] The essay concludes with a call for a world in which passions still have a place.

Not very dissimilarly from Jameson, Hebdige gives a picture of postmodernism that is pervaded by an involuntary appeal. It must be recalled here that he is himself considered representative of the postmodern vogue,[19] with his *Subculture. The Meaning of Style* (1979), a fascinating analysis of the importance of style and appear-ance in reality not less than in representations, in the arts not less than in popular culture. Style is sign and meaning at the same time.

There have increasingly been contrasting voices speaking for the 'New Times', or for less rigid oppositions. Some came from the 'historical' group that had lived with the pre-eminence of the Marxist-historicist stress of the seventies at the Birmingham Centre for Contemporary Cultural Studies (CCCS): Angela McRobbie, Iain Chambers and Ian Connell have spoken in favour of the potentialities of this cultural pluralism.[20] They were all working on popular culture, and the shift that took the argument out of the strictures of a debate came precisely from that field.[21]

The magazine *Marxism Today* exemplified the increasing attention to the debate within British Marxism and the now defunct British Communist Party. Its special issue called *New Times* (October 1988) was a bold attempt to bring together Marxism and postmodernism. In *Hiding in the Light*, Dick Hebdige himself takes distance from that Marxist 'religion' that is today under attack and proposes a Marxism without guarantees: 'a marxism more prone perhaps to listen, learn, adapt and to appreciate, for instance, that words like "emergency" and "struggle" don't just mean fight, conflict, war and death but birthing, the prospect of new life emerging: a struggling to the light'.[22] These accents and contributions go beyond simple mediation; rather they indicate a shift, a move beyond rigid oppositional paradigms.

Feminism 'à St-Germain-des-Près'

This move becomes fundamental for what goes under the label of postmodernism, a label that at the end of the century and at the turn of the millennium may already be obsolete. In the previous debate, we have seen sign and meaning becoming one, movement standing for movement, margins refusing to occupy the centre, while at the same time the centre is being pushed to the edge. What really counts is the oscillating movement between the two terms, and we shall see that in the discursive confrontation of feminism with postmodernism the terms will extend to art and life, high and popular culture, aesthetics and politics.

The growing critical literature exploring the relation between feminism and postmodernism underlines the many affinities between the two. The hostility from some sections of the women's movement is tempered by these resemblances while the enthusiasm of others finds a curb in the re-affirmation of female specificities. Some feel threatened by the postmodern neglect of issues of power and political change; others see in feminism one of the main components of postmodernism, if not its strong inspiration. Rather than trying to ascertain who comes first, or who inspired whom, it is more important to remember that the 'postmodern' weakening of a unitary, universal subject may have been brought about by the very existence of a female and feminist thought.

In *Feminine Fictions*, Patricia Waugh sees common concerns in their developments since the 1960s.

> Both are concerned to disrupt traditional boundaries: between 'art' and 'life', masculine and feminine, high and popular culture, the dominant and the marginal. Both examine the cultural consequences of the decline of a consensus aesthetics, of an effective 'literary' voice, or the absence of a strong sense of stable subjectivity.[23]

Similarly Linda Hutcheon in *The Politics of Postmodernism* underlines a positive reciprocal influence between these two strains of thought.[24] Linda Nicholson gives a long list of points of overlap in her introduction to *Feminism/Postmodernism*, particularly the opposition to the supposed neutrality and objectivity of knowledge, to reason, to the autonomous self and other Enlightenment ideals that have reflected Western male values. 'On such grounds', she concludes, 'postmodernism would appear to be a cultural ally of feminism'.[25] In a curious way Nicholson seems to identify the main point of coincidence in an attention to historical concerns, clashing with the prevalent feminist preoccupation for the trans-historical character of postmodernism. Some of the essays in the collection carry out a sustained critique of postmodernism.

In 'Postmodernism and Gender Relations iń Feminist Theory', Jane Flax proposes the restructuring of the notions of identity, gender and knowledge, and the desertion of linear or binary modes of thought: 'Feminist theories, like other forms of postmodernism, should encourage us to tolerate and interpret ambivalence, ambiguity and multiplicity . . . and to operate for the recognition of an unstable, complex, disorderly reality.'[26]

Susan J. Hekman, in *Gender and Knowledge*, starts from the assumption that feminism has much to gain from an alliance with postmodernism (its deconstruction of the Cartesian logic and its attack on phallocentrism) and that an analysis of the works of Derrida, Foucault and Gadamer can be the basis of a postmodern feminism. Above all Derrida's contribution to feminism seems significant to her: 'The binary logic of western thought is removed through a supplementary logic using the concept "woman" to surpass the polarity of the metaphysics of presence.'[27]

Rosi Braidotti's position goes a step forward. In *Patterns of Dissonance*, she speaks of 'the feminization of the postmodern field of knowledge', and her book is the exploration of this aspect in Derrida, Foucault, Deleuze and Lacan, while keeping a critical distance from it. The position of critical 'nomadism' that she recommends for the feminists has the *status* of a new mode of thought, 'a female feminist way': 'all elaboration of theory today – especially for a feminist woman – can only be a play of lines which intersect only to break up at once, of breaches which open in the void, of tracks which multiply indefinitely'.[28] In this, as in other cases, there is no acritical assimilation of postmodernism, or identification with its prophets. The work of Gayatri Spivak, Rosi Braidotti, Jane Flax and Susan Hekman – and of many other feminist historians, theorists and philosophers – goes beyond a straightforward critical overview. Braidotti effectively underlines the lack of symmetry between the two: 'I shall call it: dissonance, for what interests me is the play of this irreducibility, the ultimate non-coincidence of the two objects of this study: the discourse of the crisis in philosophical modernity and the elaboration of feminist theories of subjectivity, the total lack of symmetry.'[29]

She discusses the nature of the AND linking the new feminism to the crisis of philosophical knowledge, which is certainly related to that general sense of crisis I discussed above: 'Here the conjunction AND marks not only the point at which two series converge, but also the point at which they diverge, opening into an infinite series: women and philosophy and crisis and psychoanalysis, and so on.'[30]

In many cases, these are original voices giving an essential contribution to postmodern aesthetics and opening a thoroughly new chapter in it. This is particularly true of the contribution given by women of colour, from Gayatri Spivak to Lata Mani, Barbara Smith and Michele Wallace, bell hooks, Lola Young and Cherríe Moraga. It is useful to recall that two of the major living novelists, Alice Walker and Toni Morrison, have done important work as critics as well.

From Black female criticism has come a clearer distrust of postmodern theories, not disjoined from the criticism aimed towards 'white' feminism. In *Ain't I a Woman – Black Women and Feminism*, bell hooks has analysed white female racism, stating that 'To black women the issue is not whether white women are more or less racist than white men, but that they are racist.'[31] She points at the racist contradiction within the women's movement from its foundations, polemicising Adrienne Rich's reference to a white feminist anti-racist tradition, and rightly stresses the dangers of separating race from sex: 'The assumption that we can divorce the issue of race from sex, or sex from race, has so clouded the vision of American thinkers and writers on the "woman" question that most discussion of sexism, sexist oppression, or woman's place in society are distorted, biased, and inaccurate.' In spite of such drastic judgement, she still wishes to call herself a feminist, choosing to reappropriate the term in its authentic meaning of liberation from oppression and domination: 'it is a contradiction that white females have structured a women's liberation movement that is racist and excludes many non-white women. However, the existence of that contradiction should not lead any woman to ignore feminist issues.'[32] In 'Toward a Black Feminist Criticism', Barbara Smith had drastically asserted the necessity of establishing a separate critical voice: 'A Black feminist approach to literature that embodies the realization that the politics of sex as well as the politics of race and class are crucially interlocking factors in the works of Black women writers is an absolute necessity.'[33] This separation is tied to the specificity of black writing that can constitute 'an identifiable literary tradition':

> The way, for example, that Zora Neale Hurston, Margaret Walker, Toni Morrison, and Alice Walker incorporate the traditional Black female activities of rootworking, herbal medicine, conjure and midwifery into the fabric of their stories is not mere coincidence . . . The use of Black women's language and cultural experience in books *by* Black women *about* Black women results in a miraculously rich coalescing of form and content and also takes their writing far beyond the confines of white/male literary structures.[34]

Black criticism gives a decisive contribution to the issue of gender difference, breaking former boundaries and introducing new differences: those between black and white women, black women and black men, and within feminism itself, the difference within sameness.

Theory and anti-theory

There were other voices expressing a strong suspicion of postmodernism, mainly due to an initial anti-theoretical component within the Women's Liberation Movement, especially in Britain. The denunciation of the male character of theory – from psychoanalysis to structuralism – reflected the need for differentiation in a first phase of the movement, within a more general hostility to theory. There was a minor resistance towards Marxism, due to the strong presence of socialist feminists, and an inversely greater one towards poststructuralism, due to its stress on languages and its neglect of the social.

In *Women's Oppression Today*, Michèle Barrett conducted a rigorous study of gender relations within capitalism, starting from the assumption that 'female sexuality, and the general endorsement of compulsory heterosexual monogamy, can be explained not by reference to patriarchy, or male supremacy, but by the functional requirements of the capitalist mode of production'.[35] Her accent, however, was often placed on how the perspective of class was mostly privileged to the exclusion of gender (and race) issues. She concluded with the necessary connection between 'the struggle for women's liberation and the struggle for socialism'.[36]

In the same decade the many analyses of female popular literature and culture, by critics such as Rosalind Coward and Judith Williamson (among others), tempered Marxism through the influence of structuralism and semiotics. An important intervention came from the Women's Studies Group at the CCCS in Birmingham, mainly through their *Women Take Issue*. This collective book tried to invert women's invisibility in the intellectual work done at the Centre and elsewhere: 'We were constantly trying to understand the *experience* of the absence of women, at a theoretical level . . . to see how gender structures and is itself structured.'[37]

The book gave attention to the articulation of sex/gender with class, and looked at women's oppression through economic and

psychoanalytic approaches. The latter were very cautious and
rigorously referred to a Marxist framework, but were still a break-
through in British cultural studies. The second part offered very
interesting essays on working-class teenage girls, and on housewives;
on women's magazines and novels. In her analysis of *Woman*, Janice
Winship insists on the importance for feminism of not dismissing
such magazines and the definition of femininity that they give:

> We may be struggling against such a definition, but none of us,
> though we might like to, can eliminate the modes of subjectivity in
> their patriarchal form by disparagingly ignoring them . . . As
> feminists we frequently negotiate the tension between our secret
> reading of magazines for their 'useful' diets and zany fashion, and
> our attempts to break with the modes of femininity they repre-
> sent.[38]

She underlines how certain aspects of that femininity (with its
contradictions) can become sites of political struggle. At the same
time she wants to show the links with the contradictions of
masculinity: 'the mode in which "masculinity" structures "femininity" is complicated by the position of men as a site of coincidence
between patriarchal and capitalist relations'.[39]

All these intellectuals were not afraid of theory, from Althusser,
Kristeva and Barthes to Freud and Lacan, but among them Marx
was a constant. The same allegiance to wider social contexts comes
later from those British feminist critics who have more directly
engaged with postmodernism. The absence of a social discourse
seems a stumbling block to Chris Weedon, one more voice from the
Centre. Although her *Feminist Practice and Poststructuralist Theory*
(1987) actually commences with the assumption that poststructuralism offers a useful framework for feminist struggle, she regrets the
neglect of the historically specific context of reading and writing in
deconstructive textual analyses. Sabina Lovibond maintains that
feminism must distance itself from Nietzsche's anti-feminism and
reminds us that the postmodern negation of any narrative prevents
all systematic political approach.[40] An even more radical opposition
comes from Elizabeth Wilson in her support – not without contradictions – of a materialist vision.[41]

Similar reservations are sometime expressed by those same critics
who had defended the postmodern contribution to feminism.

Waugh herself reaffirms the importance of identity politics for women:

> During the 1960s, as Vonnegut waves a fond goodbye to character in fiction women writers are beginning, *for the first time in history*, to construct an identity . . . As male writers lament its demise, women writers have not yet experienced that subjectivity which will give them a sense of personal autonomy; continuous identity, a history and agency in the world.[42]

Similarly Hutcheon doubts that feminism could identify itself with the oscillation between complicity and critique inherent in post-modern politics. In her first book on the subject, *A Poetics of Postmodernism*, she had concluded with a reply to Habermas on the positive contents of postmodernism in varied fields, from the novel to drama and video, and from cinema to painting and photography. Her successive book, though exemplifying the many affinities between the two modes in the works of Barbara Kruger and other female artists, ends on a more pessimistic note: 'Feminism is a politics, postmodernism is not . . . It has not theorized the active role of the historical subject; it does not have strategies of resistance corresponding to those of feminism. Postmodernism manipulates but does not transform signification; disperses but does not (re)construct the structures of subjectivity. Feminisms must do it.'[43]

These reservations partly explain the feminist delay in entering the postmodernist debate. Andreas Huyssen, while emphasising the common aspects of postmodernism and feminism (stress on the hidden and the marginal, denial of canonised forms, fragmentation of the subject), regrets that feminist criticism has not engaged in the debate. In 'The Discourse of Others: Feminists and Postmodernism', Craig Owens observes: 'The absence of discussions of sexual difference in writings about postmodernism, as well as the fact that few women have engaged in the modernism/postmodernism debate, suggest that postmodernism may be another masculine invention to exclude women.'[44]

He is here echoing a complaint coming from some feminist critics (particularly African Americans) who note that it is no coincidence if, just when women's power appears on the horizon, male philosophers start deconstructing the concept of power. It is also true that the wide discussions of, and attempts to define, postmodernism have ignored gender or denied its relevance; as an example of the latter, Patricia Waugh quotes Frederick Karl peremptorily asserting that the deconstructionist emphasis on the eradication of the ego and on the all-importance of language 'would be a form of death for the female experience'.[45] On the whole, the debate has been, as Owens notes, 'scandalously indifferent' to feminist issues.

While all this was (or was not) discussed, feminism was developing its own creative voice, whether one wants to call it postmodern or not. The encounter between European (particularly French) and American thought has given interesting results in such differentiated scholars as Gayatri Spivak, Alice Jardine, Teresa de Lauretis, Naomi Schor, Shoshana Felman, Barbara Johnson and Trinh T. Minh-ha, whose work can in no way be simply identified with that of Derrida, Lacan or Barthes. The same is true of Francophone thinkers (even more diverse), such as Michèle Montrelay, Luce Irigaray, Hélène Cixous, Julia Kristeva, Nicole Brossard and Assia Djebar.

In an interesting essay, Herman Rapaport looks at the relationship between feminist theory and deconstruction, in particular comparing the work of Trinh T. Minh-ha to that of Derrida. He convincingly shows how the Vietnamese film-maker and poet, in confronting and appropriating deconstruction, succeeds in posing herself as its 'other':

> Trinh has allowed herself to put deconstruction aside without being tempted to invent some new and improved theory in its place. And to that extent, she has allowed for something to come in the wake of deconstruction that others have not seen, namely a certain return of metaphysics on the hither side of deconstruction's critical dismantlings.[46]

The dark lady

The discourse of man is the metaphor of woman. (G. Spivak)

The female character of postmodernism has been asserted by quite a few male critics. Among the philosophers and the seers of this 'cultural dominant' (Jameson), there are those who use woman as a metaphor of postmodernism. In *Les stratégies fatales* (1983), Baudrillard places woman at the centre of the universe of seduction and metamorphosis characterising postmodernity. He slowly perfects the picture of his – or rather her – apocalypse:

> What this woman wants, what we all want as objects . . . is not to be hallucinated and exalted as a subject in her own right, but rather to be taken profoundly as object, just as she is, with her senseless, immoral, supersensual character . . . What makes for her power is, on the contrary her triumphal in-difference, her triumphal lack of subjectivity.[47]

Such positions continue a long poetical tradition that goes from the 'dark lady' of Shakespeare's sonnets to the *femme fatale* of decadent poetry and theatre, and make feminist resentment in front of such equations justified. Baudrillard's postmodern catastrophe lies in the fatal power of female seduction, 'the heaven that leads men to this hell' of Shakespeare's Sonnet 129.[48] In the wake of Dante and Petrarch, Nietzsche and Lacan, women go on being used as the instrument of male theoretical and philosophical discourse.

In a different key, deconstructionist thought is heavily enmeshed in the metaphor of the feminine. Derrida's thought, though external to all apocalyptic visions, owes much to women, as they occupy a crucial space in his metaphorical web of terms, from *hymen* to *invagination*. The concept of woman has inspired his consistent critique of the European phallocentric structure, as he himself says in an interview given to *subjects/objects* in 1984, and then republished in *Men in Feminism*. He immediately proceeds to say (even people like Derrida 'proceed', and it is uncanny how the idea of progress insinuates itself in the following quotation) that this first strategic position must be superseded: 'We need to find some way to progress strategically. Starting with deconstruction of phallogocentrism, and using the feminine force, so to speak, in this move and then – and this would be the second stage or second level – to give up the opposition between men and women.'[49]

Alice Jardine, in *Gynesis,* analyses this new semiosis of 'woman', this rhetorical space that is to be found in Derrida as in Lacan, in Lyotard as in Baudrillard, and wonders if it is not 'a new ruse of reason':

Might there be a new kind of desire on the part of (Modern) Man to occupy all the positions at once (among women, among texts?) Are we here only brushing up against a new version of an old male fantasy: that of escaping the laws of the fathers through the independent and at the same time dependent female? . . . Do they hope to find a way of depersonalizing sexual identity while maintaining the amorous relationship through women?[50]

The deconstructionist position has been criticised by Teresa de Lauretis in *Technologies of Gender*. She points out that Derrida, in his critique of phallocentrism, uses women as mere instruments for theoretical discourse. Just as Nietzsche positioned woman as the symbol of Truth, the discourse of woman becomes the discourse of male philosophers, and her problem becomes man's problem. Philosophers speak about 'woman', never about real women.[51] In spite of her 'deconstructive' positions, Spivak similarly observes that deconstruction defines its own 'displacement' through woman, and woman becomes its figuration.[52] And Rosi Braidotti, though defining herself a 'follower of Nietzsche and of contemporary neo-Nietzschian thought', refuses woman as metaphor of the unrepresentable and of the undecidable: ' "the praise of the feminine" is confused with the apology of shadow, dispersion, silence, mystery, of the eternal wandering'.[53]

Difference deconstructed

The debate on difference has occupied an important space within feminist theory and is connected to the one for and against postmodernism that I have summarised above. Bringing forward previous oppositions between sex and gender, nature and culture, essentialism and relativism, the debate has seen the opposing fronts of those who see difference as non-renounceable, and those who defend the existence of multiple differences. It is possible to identify the position asserting gender difference as a 'strong' one (with an emphasis on women's social and economic subordination and on the struggle for emancipation), and its 'weak' counterpart (the accent here is on the displacement of the subject and its subsequent fragmentariness) as coinciding with postmodern suggestions.

Luce Irigaray is commonly placed in the first group. In *This Sex Which Is Not One* (1977), she describes the 'apartness' of being a woman, even in language:

> I am a woman. I am a being sexualized as feminine. I am sexualized female. The motivation of my work lies in the impossibility of articulating such a statement; in the fact that its utterance is in some ways senseless, inappropriate, indecent . . . In other words, to articulate the reality of my sex is impossible in discourse. (p. 148)

She quotes the female linguistic tendency to dialogic forms aimed at subject–subject relations, at the expression of more than one subject.

In 'This Sex Which Is Not One', the essay that gives the name to her book, she insists on the bodily difference, referring to women's genitalia as being not one, as her title recites: 'Woman touches herself all the time and moreover no one can forbid her to do so, for her genitals are formed of two lips in continuous contact. Thus, within herself, she is already two – but not divisible into one(s) – that caress each other . . . no possibility of distinguishing what is touching and what is touched' (p. 24). She is the mystery in a culture that enumerates everything, catalogues everything in unities: 'She is neither one nor two. She cannot be counted as one person or as two. She resists any adequate definition, she does not have a "proper" name. And her sex that is not *one*, is counted as a *non* sex' (p. 26).

In her wake, the Italian feminist group of philosophers called Diotima set out, in the eighties, to elaborate new concepts and epistemological categories within the thought of difference. Adriana Cavarero, the most authoritative voice of the group, spoke of 'the essential and originary differing', while defending the absence of universal truth. 'The philosophy of sexual difference abandons the whole and the universal . . . It is manifested in the experience of separatedness in the word from the word, everyday, everywhere.' And she goes on:

> By essential and originary differing I mean that for women to be sexed in difference is unrenounceable; for anybody who happens to be born as a woman, it is an already given and not otherwise . . . As sexual difference is in this sense an originary, it must be kept as a difference that is not preceded by any category of previous understanding.[54]

In the same spirit but with different ends, Monique Wittig observes that the possibility of conceiving themselves as total subjects through the exercise of language was stolen from women. Men have a right to 'the abstract form, the general, the universal', while women are by birth confined to the particular. Women expressing themselves in the subjective form are obliged to proclaim their sex and abandon the abstract 'I', especially in English where there is no grammatical agreement. Wittig maintains that gender denies women as absolute subjects, steals their subjectivity from them, and compels them to enter speech backwards, 'particularizing themselves and apologizing profusely'.[55]

In her works she takes up the strategy of using the neuter or even the feminine pronoun to indicate the whole of humankind. Here it is the masculine that has to be specified. In *L'Opoponax* she uses the indefinite pronoun *on* for the narrator. The enigma of the narrative lies in the locutor's sexual identity, which at the end of the novel is uncovered as a lesbian identity.[56] In a later novel, *Les guérillères*, Wittig adopts a more radical strategy and uses the feminine plural pronoun *elles* for people. The masculine – as the exception – has to be signalled by 'man', 'he', 'his', in the same way as up to now 'woman', 'she', 'her' had always to be specified within (or outside?) the universal and neuter references.

Difference as such cannot be given utterance. Wittig proposes the substitution of one term by the other (either . . . or), while Irigaray insists on the impossibility of expressing femaleness in language. She is seen by many as holding an essentialist position but while speaking of 'woman' she insists on the elusiveness of this term:

> I cannot answer either *on* or *of* woman. If I pretended I could do it – if I accepted or maintained I could do it – I would do nothing but once more bring the female question back to the discourse that keeps it displaced, banned, at best ignored . . . Femaleness cannot be signified by proper meanings, by proper names or concepts, not even that of woman. (p. 129)

As we have seen, the importance of female mimesis for her lies in its deliberate excess; the pretence to speak like the male 'subject' is for women an attempt to find the place of their own exploitation: 'repeating/interpreting the way in which, within discourse, the feminine finds itself defined as lack, deficiency, or as imitation and negative image of the subject, they should signify that with respect to this logic a disruptive excess is possible on the feminine side' (p. 78).

On the other side, there is a group of thinkers who oppose the discourse of essence in feminism. Gayatri Spivak, following the deconstructive lesson, polemically declares that essentialism is a trap: 'no rigorous definition of anything is ultimately possible, so that if one wants to, one could go on deconstructing the opposition between man and woman, and finally show that it is a binary opposition that displaces itself'.[57] She argues mainly with a certain 'white' feminism, particularly with the essentialist positivism predicated by American academics involved in *women's studies*; once out of this controversy, her position becomes more articulate, as we shall see later on.

Teresa de Lauretis has stressed that the paradigm of a universal sexual opposition keeps feminist thought anchored to Western patriarchal thought and makes it impossible to articulate the difference among women: 'I see a shift, a development . . . in the feminist understanding of female subjectivity: a shift from the earlier view of woman defined purely by sexual difference (i.e. in relation to man) to the more difficult and complex notion that the female subject is a site of differences.'[58] The difference extends to a range of aspects (economic, racial, cultural and sexual, the last not necessarily referring to men) transversally crossing the community of women.

Julia Kristeva insists on the importance of not creating a new totalitarism in which the female universe is considered to be made of 'equals', and to valorise the differences instead. It would only be a mechanical and useless substitution of one universal for another. She refers to women's writing in particular: 'Who is interested in asking a woman to write like (all) other women? That there is such a generalisation as woman's condition should be the lever to allow each woman to utter her singularity.'[59] In some of her essays, she goes a considerable way in the refusal of feminist positions, raising the protests of those thinkers who, like her, oppose any rigid binary, among them Gayatri Spivak and Rosi Braidotti. In *Patterns of Dissonance*, the latter dissociates herself from Kristeva's ambivalence towards feminism: '. . . it seems to me that the dutiful Lacanian daughter takes the upper hand over the critical feminist theorist'.[60]

The difficult play on difference and sameness is an important corrective to overly rigid oppositions and becomes crucial in the discourse of identity. The difference between one woman and another has been neglected in the first triumphal phase of the discovery of woman as the same, and has become necessary in the reflections of the *post-*. The relation among women of different generations and different power has been the object of feminist reflection in Italy in the eighties; in particular, the periodical publication *Sottosopra*, produced by the Libreria delle Donne, Milan, has dealt with the difficulty and the importance of relating to *la donna più*, the woman with more power or better knowledge.[61]

A recent issue of *Sottosopra* (January 1996) underlines the importance of reinforcing the presence of women in the world *not* in the name of equality with men, but in the name of female difference: 'Feminist positions have never been uniquely (or principally, as far as Italy is concerned) directed to the confrontation with the male condition, but to *the free sense of a female difference*, that has been conquered, step by step, *not* through legal means, but through the practice of relation among women.'[62] It is the primacy of such relation that transforms female difference into 'female authority', based on the work of mediation. The insistence on the concept of mediation as the figure of exchange, fundamental in the symbolic pact, has been crucial in Italian feminist theory, starting from Carla Lonzi's *Sputiamo su Hegel* (1974).

Rosi Braidotti, though accepting the experience of separateness, has emphasised the importance of the 'infinite richness of our singular differing the one from the other'.[63] She uses the example of the inequality between herself as a teacher in women's studies and her pupils to underline the complexity (necessary in the elaboration) of the female symbolic world. Gayatri Spivak too, in the essay quoted above, perceptively deals with the problem of being a feminist teacher, a problem that is an important part of my own life and work.

The refusal of a binary opposition comes not only from feminist deconstructionists but also and mainly from those closer to psychoanalysis, working with and sometimes against Freud's and Lacan's acquisitions. In addition to Irigaray, Kristeva and Cixous, Jacqueline Rose represents an important voice. In *Sexuality in the Field of Vision* she says:

feminism, through its foregrounding of sexuality (site of fantasies, impasses, conflict and desire) and of sexual difference (the structure towards which all of this constantly tends but against which it just as constantly breaks) is in a privileged position to challenge the dualities (inside/outside, victim/aggressor, real event/fantasy, and even good/evil) on which so much traditional politics has so often relied.[64]

This challenge to the dualities of Western logocentrism has involved an important convergence between feminism and postmodernism, and has been particularly strong in cultural studies.

The swing of a pendulum

In the great battle between essentialism and anti-essentialism, Irigaray is to essentialism what Derrida is to anti-essentialism, which means among other things that their complex texts have been ripped from their contexts and each in its different ways has been made to say what it never said. (Naomi Schor)

I could now conclude with the vision of contrasting moments, oscillating between the belief in an essential difference and the articulation of a complex range of differences, but the antagonism seems mostly artificial to me, as the above quotation underlines. The two positions have often coexisted and need to coexist.

In the mid-eighties, when the warning on the risks of essentialism was reiterated, Mary Russo was already arguing that overstating anti-essentialism might constitute 'the greatest inhibition to work in cultural theory and politics at the moment, and must be displaced'.[65] Though historically there may be phases tied to one aspect or another, theoretical developments are marked by unevenness no less than the history of a struggle, and at any given moment it may be necessary to make recourse to previous stages. The many phases of the feminist movement and the elaboration of thought accompanying them are part of a tradition that finds its strength and richness precisely in the lack of homogeneity. The movement is variegated and will be further explored in this book, from Irigaray and Cixous to Kristeva and Gilbert; from Virginia Woolf to Showalter and Toril Moi, up to the recent developments of the nineties.

'Another Look, Another Woman' is the title of a special issue of *Yale French Studies*, a review that has often given attention to French influence on the Anglo-American political and intellectual scene.[66] The issue takes a fresh look at the encounter between the two feminisms, stressing its dynamic development made of repetition and change. Revisions and re-reading – in this case even re-translations – are directed to the works and theories not of masters but of mothers or elder sisters. In this case the re-reading has an additional filter in the perspectives from Quebec, Guadeloupe and Algeria.[67]

The theoretical discourse unavoidably centres around Luce Irigaray and Hélène Cixous, but not without a side look at the contribution of rebellious daughters (among them Judith Butler). In the opening essay, 'The Question of the Other', Irigaray returns to a favourite notion of hers: 'The question of the other has been poorly formulated in the Western tradition, for the other is always seen as the other of the same, the other of the subject itself, rather than an/other subject (a subject which is other), irreducible to the masculine subject and sharing equivalent dignity' (p. 8). In contrast to Simone de Beauvoir, she does not refuse to be the other gender, the other sex, but asks to be considered *apart from,* not as a reflection of, the male political and philosophical subject. In the essay she drops all suspicion for the number two and takes the risk of substituting one essentiality for the other: 'This historic movement from the one, singular subject to the existence of the two subjects of equal worth and equal dignity seems to be rightly the task of women, on both a philosophical and a political level' (p. 18).

Here she joins theory and politics together as she does repeatedly in her 'militant' writing, and to this utopian *relation à deux* Peggy Kamuf returns in her critique of some feminist views – particularly Sandra Gilbert's and Toril Moi's – on Hélène Cixous, suggesting the use of the prefix semi- to indicate a politics that is also a poetics and vice versa. In 'To give Place: Semi-Approaches to Hélène Cixous', she starts referring to the French writer's expression *écrire l'efface-ment* ('in order to write delicately, one would have to be able not-to-write; there are no words so light as not to crush the lightness of writing': p. 70), and observes that Cixous's writing can easily be stifled by the weight of critical thought, as happens with Sandra Gilbert's introduction to the English translation of *La Jeune Née*.[68] Her critique moves on to Toril Moi who, in her *Sexual/Textual Politics*, had used the disparaging term 'semi-theory' for Cixous, referring to her incapacity to choose between the poetical and the political register. Kamuf appropriates the term, defining Cixous as 'one of our age's greatest semi-theoreticians' and denies the distinction poetical/political: 'once again as regards such distinctions, are we not obliged to have recourse to the notion of the semi- in order to account for a politics that must also be a poetics? . . . this possible politics is that of semi-reference, or of reference without referent, which names the impossible "thing which is not"' (pp. 75–6).

The fictional essays contained in the issue – Maryse Condé's tale, Assia Djebar's 'fantasia' on the female resistance to fundamentalism in Algeria, Brossard's 'The Textured Angle of Desire' – are examples of the collapse of further distinctions, between essays and fiction, utopian visions and material oppressions, as Brossard's concluding words best illustrate:

> Feminist consciousness links us creatively to the essential *(l'es-sentielle)* as in writing (her) consciousness commits us without respite to face the inner necessity that urges us to exorcize nightmares, to trace dream and utopia, to put color and sense into the most preposterous angles of desire, to braid language with ties so strong and slender that at times we will no longer dare to move for fear and joy. (p. 114)

Once more, the confrontation with the ethnic other undermines all simple dichotomies.

These and other essays appearing in the issue evade the restrictive confrontation between essentialism and anti-essentialism, but on the other hand show no fear of 'big bad' essentialism. In spite of all the hostility that her defence of 'woman' as a globalising category has attracted, we have found Irigaray once more posing herself on the side of the inalienable difference. In the interview given to Lynn Huffer, Nicole Brossard also speaks of the female look 'filling the gap between women' in idealised tones that recall a utopian sisterhood: 'What women see between them is as important as what they see of each other and in one another. The back and forth of the gaze between women (writer and reader) textures the space between them and to me that creates a social semantico-imaginative environment where meaning can be debated' (p. 119).

This kind of reappraisal of essentialism after so much downright suspicion in the second half of the eighties is not totally new. *the essential difference*, the collection of essays edited by Naomi Schor and Elizabeth Weed in 1994, is a rethinking of the whole issue, on the basis of a careful redefinition of the word 'essentialism' and of the abuses of anti-essentialism. The volume attempts 'to de-hystericize the debate' through the essays of those very scholars who had strenuously fought against a globalising difference, such as Teresa de Lauretis and Gayatri Spivak.

In the introduction Naomi Schor declares that the aim of the essays is not so much to defuse the debate or to promote essentialism. 'Anti-essentialism in its positive form, constructionism, has won the day; and if essentialism is anathema, constructionism is dogma.'[69] She concludes that if the multiplication of subject positions which is at the centre of much recent feminism has de-essentialised feminism, it has also brought about an identity politics 'which in many respects reinscribes essentialism'. The very title of the subsequent essay she includes in the volume, 'This Essentialism Which Is Not One', signals that the re-thinking commences precisely from Irigaray. She defends Irigaray's concept of mimesis, which is not a reversal of misogyny but an emergence of the feminine from beneath femininity, where it is buried. 'The difference within mimesis *is* the difference within difference.'[70]

In the interview with Ellen Rooney, Spivak returns to the problem of essentialism taking a position that is a partial revision: 'The critique of essentialism should not be seen as being critical in the colloquial, Anglo-American sense of being adversely inclined, but as a critique in the very strong European philosophical sense, that is to say, as an acknowledgement of its usefulness.'[71] A deconstruction of essentialism consists in underlining its usefulness alongside its dangers.

The constant movement between the necessity of overcoming globalising differences, and the contrasting need for separatedness, reaffirms the richness that can come from the coexistence (far from pacific) of such positions. It is useful not to forget that between the one and the other there is a rich and varied range of positions, of nuances to use Schor's words, that is part of a complex and shifting itinerary with which feminist theory must, and wants to, come to terms.

The rethinking of French feminism which is the object of this issue of *Yale French Studies* leaves the encounter and the conversation among feminisms open: the process of approaching the other (the other woman, another thought, another feminism) will be the object of new rewritings, of a text that is partly yet to be written. There will be new encounters, and, rather than re-translations and re-readings, a new 'rejoicing' as Mary Lydon's title suggests: Re-joicings, new joys.

What is real and what is not

'Look, love,' I says to him, eventually, because I'm not in the mood for literary criticism. 'If I hadn't bust a wing in the train wreck, I could *fly* us all to Vladivostok in two shakes, so I'm not the right one to ask question of when it comes to what is real and what is not, because, like the duck-billed platypus, half the people who clap eyes on me don't believe what they see and the other half thinks they're seeing things.' (Angela Carter)

Jacqueline Rose has reminded us of the challenge to binary oppositions – such as feminine and masculine, inside and outside, reality and fantasy, history and stories – that feminism poses. In recasting these terms into more extensive narratives, both historical and imaginary, fabulation as the mark of the 'female' becomes central. Though fabulation has been contrasted with the concrete lives of women and men, a new interest in the issues of pleasure, fantasy and the body has encouraged a focus on fiction, art and creativity, and has weakened the barrier between what is fiction and what is not.

I wish to argue, with some of the novelists I refer to in the following essays, that fact and fiction are different but crucial aspects of the same reality. The debate within history studies suggests that there is more than one history, and that official histories exist in parallel with hidden ones. Michel Foucault's *Moi Pierre Rivière* is at one and the same time the documentation of a criminal case, the study of the power relations between psychiatry and law at the beginning of the nineteenth century and a personal

memoir, where the historical and the novelistic meet. Fantasy
becomes another way to connect with reality and history.

In 'Grandma's Story', the last chapter in *Woman Native Other,*
Trinh Minh-ha fights against the equation of truth with fact, of
imagination with falsification:

> since fictional and factual have come to a point where they
> mutually exclude each other, fiction, not infrequently, means lies,
> and fact, truth. DID IT REALLY HAPPEN? IS IT A TRUE
> STORY? . . . Which truth? the question unavoidably arises . . .
> Truth. Not one but two: truth and fact, just like in old times when
> queens were born and kings were made in Egypt . . . No wonder
> that in old tales storytellers are very often women, witches, and
> prophets. The African griot and griotte are well known for being
> poet, storyteller, historian, musician, and magician – all at once.
> But why truth at all? Why this battle for truth and on behalf of
> truth? I do not remember having asked grand mother once
> whether the story she was telling me was true or not.[72]

The novels of Native American writers forcefully pose the impossibility of the equation between stories and lies. In Leslie
Marmon Silko's *Ceremony,* the ceremony itself which is at the
centre of the novel stands between past and present, fact and fiction.
The medicine-woman who has an important role in it belongs both
to the 'inside' of the ceremony, and to the outside plot; it is a figment
of Tayo's imagination, while he undergoes the process of healing,
and at the same time – through their physical love – his one grip on
reality. The same is true of Louise Erdrich's *The Bingo Palace,*
where the dénouement of the story is tied to the appearance of a
ghost – once more as in *Ceremony,* and differently from *Hamlet,* the
ghost of a mother – who will solve the impossible riddle of the story.
The ending unfolds in a blurring snow storm recalling the uncertain
zone between life and death, imagination and reality; we have left
Lipsha Morrissey preparing to die in the storm, after his father has
gone with his mother's ghost, but Shawnee Ray is making a ribbon
shirt for him.

> As she worked out the design for Lipsha's shirt in her head, she
> found her thoughts drifting. A deeper part of her was listening.
> From time to time, the wind picked up outside, whirling a scythe,

sifting snow down the shingles, sending clouds skittering into the frozen night . . .

In her dream, Lipsha had kissed her with matter-of-fact joy, deep and long. The kiss still seemed so real that she could smell the smoke on his jacket. She closed her eyes – again his lips brushed hers once, twice, then carved a dark blossom.[73]

Most of the motifs I have discussed in this introductory chapter lead to the analyses that follow. Fiction translates the overcoming of dichotomies – theory and politics, art and life, surface and depth, substance and appearance – into hybrid shapes and languages; its characters (sometimes monsters, sometimes shadows, sometimes ghosts) inhabit borders, intermediate spaces, and move in an indistinct zone at the intersection between the human and the animal, the natural and the supernatural, the beautiful and the horrid, the self and many other selves.

The stories and the bodies that have been the object of this work might at times recall the 'mere box of spatio-temporal tricks' of which Baudrillard complains, but female fabulation often uses 'pure illusionism' in a way that subverts the location of illusion.

Chapter 2

'D' for Difference: Gender, Genre, Writing

In the following discourse I wish to deal with the relation between gender and genre as an important aspect of experimental contemporary fiction. I shall refer briefly to the literary debate on genres, that from classical times onwards has known an alternation of reassertions and denials, making and unmaking criteria and laws, from Aristotle to Shakespeare, Todorov and Genette to Derrida. In recent narrative, the blurring and transgression of boundaries, the conscious play with these and other formal constraints has found a focus in the break-up of a fixed notion of genre, in connection with the changes in the notions of gender difference that I have discussed in Chapter 1 and to which I shall return.

The novel in general from its inception has constituted a challenge to classical notions, and women's novels in particular have proposed interrogations or travesties of genres. This trend is accentuated in recent female narratives, finding a correspondence in postmodern aesthetics and in the feminist habit of putting in question the alphabet of accepted meanings and laws. It has a resonance in what has been happening in television serial fiction, and this will be developed later.

The analysis in this chapter looks at generic transgression in recent novels by authors who are usually placed on either side of the divide between high and popular art, from Angela Carter, Christine Brooke-Rose and Antonia Byatt to Joanna Russ, Fay Weldon, Patricia Highsmith and P. D. James, constituting an artistic continuum that is the first symptom of the de-generation of genre.

An imperfect closure

The *story* is coming to its end. Turning and returning, in a closed space, an *enclosure* that is not to be violated . . . We are not going to cross a certain boundary line, we are not going above a certain peak . . . We would have needed, *at least, two* genres. And more. To bring them into articulation. Into conjunction. But at what moment? In *what place*? And won't this second one be just the other side of the first? (Luce Irigaray)

It follows from this emphasis on sexual difference as nomadic attachment to the project of making a difference through feminist bonding with other women, that feminism, for me, is also a 'genre' – with its own specific textual and methodological requirements. (Rosi Braidotti)

Genre as narrative category, gender as sexual determination. Between genre and gender there is only the difference of a 'd'. According to the *Shorter Oxford English Dictionary (SOED)*, the 'd' is excrescent, the two words having the same origin (from Greek through Latin to Old French), and one root: *gen* = to produce. The original word had multiple meanings, each of them referring to the common traits, to the constants, and at the same time to the distinctions between one category and another (as its limits and barriers). We know that the definition of genre refers to the common features of a whole, but the whole is also defined in relation to *other* genres, to the difference: 'genres are instances of repetition and difference'.[1] While gender refers to 'each of the 3 (or 2) grammatical kinds of sex corresponding more or less to distinctions of sex (or absences of sex)' (*SOED*), it first recalls the difference, and only within the difference does it then recognise wholes.

The 'd' is the difference between the two words, the intractable difference within a thinking of totalities. Genre is the study of a systemic totality; gender is the split in the totality, meaning reversal, upturning, rupture. 'D' is always there in presence/absence, indicating the imperfect closure between genre and gender, and within each of the two: the boundaries between genres constantly redefined through the endless play of repetition and difference, the boundary masculine/feminine forever open and constantly deferred. The reader/viewer is the essential final link for the constitution both of genre and of gender in the narrative discourse.[2]

Sex in society, gender in language, genre in narrative: the notion of genre is already a part of the whole; it is a fragment in itself. Genre: the definition goes with readership rather than with inherited expressive forms, with language rather than content. This in turn leads to the emergence of new forms. Genre and gender are reified, exhibited, drawing attention to themselves, there is no danger of neutrality. On the other hand reification also leads to an aestheticisation of masculine and feminine that interrupts 'social' and 'emancipative' discourses.

An English definition gives gender as 'the cultural differentiation of male from female'.[3] Genre, on the other hand, is seen as existing only in the realm of the formal. There is never anything natural about it. It is a signifying paradigm. If the natural aspects of gender are denied – 'its sources in nature are neither here nor there' as the above definition continues – we are again in front of a signifying paradigm, occurring only in language, in culture. Thus the quarrel between essentialist and anti-essentialist feminism could here be displaced by observing that the difference between nature and culture is yet a further essentialist argument: who can say where the one ends and the other begins, and how can we assume that the boundaries between the two are the same from one culture to another?[4]

In his essay on 'The Law of Genre', Derrida reminds the Anglo-American reader that in French the semantic area of genre is more expansive than in English (and also in Italian): 'And this can be said of genre in all genres, be it a question of a generic or a general determination of what one calls "nature" or *physis* (for example, a biological *genre*, a genre of all that is in general), or be it a question of a typology designated as non-natural . . . (for example, an artistic, poetic, or literary genre).'[5]

While noticing that the same word is used both for biological and natural categories, and for literary, artistic and cultural typologies, he discards the opposition between these two worlds. He is also protesting against the dogmatism imposed by the law of *genres*, and denies both prefixed literary categories and a simplistic gender dichotomy: 'What about a neutral genre/gender? Or one whose neutrality would not be *negative* (neither . . . nor), nor dialectical, but affirmative, and doubly affirmative (or . . . or)?' (p. 70).

Genre has been seen as a vehicle of intrinsic charges of meaning, as a sign system, and consequently marked by a precise iconography, in cinema for instance. Christian Metz gives the example of good and bad cowboys in white and black shirts respectively as typical of genre cinema. Neale opposes this reductionism and speaks of filmic genres as aesthetic systems that can be referred to different subjectivities.[6] He proposes a model of genre as a neutral container and not as carrier of an intrinsic charge of meaning. Genres function as communication and guiding codes, a guide in competence and expectations, a way to choose. As Todorov says, 'they function as "horizons of expectation" for readers and as "models of writing" for authors'.[7]

The law of genre, the law of the father

Polonius. The best actors in the world, either for tragedy, comedy, history, pastoral, pastoral-comical, historical-pastoral, tragical-historical, tragical-comical-historical-pastoral, scene individable, or poem unlimited. (*Hamlet*, 2.401–5)

As soon as the word 'genre' is sounded, as soon as it is heard, as soon as one attempts to conceive it, a limit is drawn. And when a limit is established, norms and interdictions are not far behind: 'Do', 'Do not' says 'genre', the word 'genre', the figure, the voice, or the law of genre. (Jacques Derrida)

Polonius' sarcastic comment in *Hamlet* puts in question the law of genre: genres start as wholes, then transgress their boundaries and become ambivalent signs suspended in a liminal zone, a border in which each term irresistibly winds up, going beyond the other side of any 'limit' or 'division' towards an infinite. Derrida lays down the imperatives of such a law – 'as soon as genre announces itself, one must respect a norm, one must not cross a line of demarcation, one must not risk impurity, anomaly or monstrosity' – only to suggest later that any law contains the *a priori* of a counter law, that the imperative might simply underline its impossibility (p. 53). The very same essence of genre, repetition, engenders variation, deformation, proliferation and decomposition. The passage is from genre through engendering, generation and genealogy, on to degenerescence. These two moments constitute a particular epiphany of the evanescence of genres.

The reaction to fixed generic criteria has a long history. At the end of the last century positivism, though partly accepting the classical principles and referring them to a 'scientific' norm, considered genres as supple transformative structures, establishing a sort of theory of the evolution of genres.[8] In opposition to this, Benedetto Croce, in his *Estetica* (1908), condemned all scientific classifications and other intellectual mistakes as an offence to the uniqueness and ineffable quality of the work of art: genres for him were *vuote fantasime*, empty phantasms of artistic expression.[9]

With formalism and structuralism, genres were seen as the bearers of the dynamics between normalisation and estrangement, and referred to the synchronic breaks in a linguistic system rather than to the genealogies of natural history. Every new example changes the whole, and this change is the condition for a text to appear in the history of literature or science. Todorov opposed the distinction between generic works, with their mechanistic application of the rules, and the unique handicraft text because the latter, even the most individual one, is linked to the works of the past. No text is the simple product of a pre-existing combination but is always the transformation of that combination. According to him there is a double movement, from work to literature (or genre) and from literature to work.

Both Genette and Todorov distinguish between historical and theoretical criteria in genre definitions. Genette defines genres as literary and aesthetic categories, differentiating them from linguistic or enunciation modes. In 'Genres, "types", modes', he gives a sustained overview of the theory and the history of genre theory. In his critique of the deformations to which Plato and Aristotle's theories have been subjected, he stresses that many are the dislocations, the substitutions, and the re-interpretations of the Aristotelian triad, in spite of the declarations of conformity and obedience to genre orthodoxy, even during classicism. The acceptance of mixed genres, hyphenated genres as he calls them, becomes noticeable at the beginning of this century but had already been anticipated by Goethe and others.[10]

Derrida, writing after Genette's essay and moving away from it, defines the law of genre as something posed between itself and its own transgression, a liminal zone: the definition of a genre, as it emerges from his fascinating analysis of Maurice Blanchot's short story, is the mark of a border, a signal outside the text. The word *récit* (account) in the title acts as a guardian at the door of that text, like Cerberus who is always on the threshold. The essay, ostensibly a discussion of this term, is actually a way to put in question (and, as we shall see, 'feminise') the law of genre. He shows that Blanchot's story, whose title is sometimes *La Folie du Jour* and sometimes simply *Un Récit* (with or without a question mark), makes 'the récit and the impossibility of the récit its theme, its impossible theme or content at once inaccessible, indeterminable, interminable, and inexhaustible; and it makes the word "récit" . . . its titleless title, the mentionless mention of its genre' (p. 59). He had already specified that he has no difficulty in accepting Genette's statement that *récit* is a mode and not a genre, though he is sceptical about such distinctions, starting from the one between nature and history.

There is a link between the Derridean questioning of the law of genre and a more straightforward ethical view. In *The Political Unconscious,* Fredric Jameson stresses the ideological aspects of genre: 'in its emergent, strong form a genre is essentially a socio-symbolic message, or in other terms, that form is immanently and intrinsically an ideology in its own right'.[11]

Feminism has taken position on the conservative ideology of genres, considering them a terrain of contestation and resistance for feminist literary practice and theory. Anne Cranny-Francis observes that genre is a form of social practice and not only a formal category: 'Feminist genre fiction is an intervention in this configuration, an attempt to subvert the dominance of patriarchal discourse by challenging its control of one semiotic system, and specifically genre writing.'[12] She insists on its ideological character:

> The gender ideology most often detected in generic fiction is extremely conservative, stereotyping women into the role of virgin or whore, and as the object of a quest or adventure, not the subject. With this ideology sedimented into the text, feminist writers are forced to develop innovative strategies for dealing with what appears at first a no-win situation.[13]

The sexualisation of genres has become prominent with the diffusion of women's studies. Feminist theory, in proposing a new geography of knowledge, has challenged pre-existing boundaries and demarcations in writing modes and voices. The thinking of difference has first of all evoked the right to a re-reading that pays attention to how women and gender relations are represented.[14] The critical debate on separatedness has followed an evolution not too dissimilar from the one on narrative genres. The stress on the dangers of a rigid binary dichotomy, as leading to a simple over-turning of former position, seems to be connected to the denial of the 'law of genre'; displacement, transfer, ambiguity and plurality in women's contemporary writings include the contamination and transgression of genre.

*   *   *

The historical development of genres had already widely contra-dicted the uniqueness of forms. The novel from its start had proved to be a flexible, comprehensive, changeable form, with its internal fragmentation into genres and subgenres, its increasing specialisa-tion and the blending of former categories (epic and poetry, tragedy and comedy, diegetic and dramatic codes). Its multiple registers can be descriptive or dialogic, direct or indirect, in presence or absence of a narrator, with a unique or multiple point of view, and variable tone or mode.

These features have become even more distinctive in the twenti-eth-century novel with its contamination of discursive levels and its diversity of 'modes, subjects and tones'. According to Walter Benjamin, in the novel the close-shot on individual narratives tends to prevail over the diffused, fragmented perspective of the story-teller: 'The birthplace of the novel is the solitary individual who is unable to express himself . . . is uncounselled and cannot counsel others. Writing a novel means to bring the incommensurable to the extremes in the representation of human life.'[15] The duality between interior and external events can be overcome only through the understanding of the meaning of life. 'The meaning of life is really the centre about which the novel moves . . . Here "meaning of life" – there "moral of the story": with these slogans novel and story confront each other' (p. 99).

He is making a distinction between story-telling, which is closer to the oral tradition, and the novel or information, bound to the book and to print; the former linked to collective experience, the latter to the isolated individual; the one escaping all explanations, the other intent on psychological analysis.

Memory creates the chain of tradition which passes a happening on from generation to generation. It starts the web which all stories together form in the end. One ties on to the next, as the great storytellers, particularly the Oriental ones, have already readily shown. In each of them there is a Scheherazade who thinks of a fresh story whenever her tale comes to a stop. (p. 98)

There might be an identification of the female with story-telling, the 'story with a moral', the memory and re-memory of collective history, in line with Native American or African myths and folklore, while the individual psychological narrative is left to the male. Benjamin does not mention gender differences (one wonders whether Scheherazade was not after all a man: 'The storyteller is the figure in which the righteous man encounters himself', is the conclusion of Benjamin's essay), but there is a hint of it in the distinction between male interiority and female collective memory. It is a distinction that seems to contradict the customary one assigning the outside and the inside, history and domesticity, respectively to male and female. But only apparently so, since male interiority is still directed to the search for the 'meaning of life'.

It is a division that goes back and beyond high and popular, modernity and postmodernity, production and reception, subjects and modes. From the *Odyssey* to *Moby Dick* and beyond, a duality is delineated between, on the one hand, the search for knowledge and the philosophical meaning of life, and on the other the conservation of life and of the species, located in the fixity of time and the repetition of the everyday; the staticity of Penelope as opposed to the journeying Ulysses. The dilemma of many modernist heroes, from Captain Ahab to the asexual human form immersed in mud in Beckett's *How it is*, is the essential expression of male metaphysics.

From the juxtaposition of the inside and the outside to the presence of different registers and languages in the prose narration, the step is not too long. The intrusion of poetry and drama, or the interruption of the plot by speculative and reflexive writing, brings about an explosion, or implosion, of the form in late modernity, pushing forward the modernist fragmentation of the homogeneous narrative: Thomas Pynchon and Raymond Carver, Kathy Acker and Don DeLillo, Toni Morrison and Alice Walker, Italo Calvino and Garcia Marquez, Anna Maria Ortese, Marguerite Duras,

Clarice Lispector, and in Britain Jeanette Winterson, Alasdair Gray or Salman Rushdie.

In postcolonial literature, particularly in Asiatic, African or Native American forms, the novel moves between journalism and literature, history and fantasy, the anthropological narrative and the search for new languages, a mixture of modes, genres and forms, and even among discrete disciplines. To Rushdie and the others mentioned above, we can add V. S. Naipaul and Amitav Gosh, or Leslie Marmon Silko. There is a conscious play on genres making them into self-referential forms; transparency gives way to parody, irony and pastiche in a search for new languages, a rupture of old barriers; for subaltern voices there is the urgency to recount their culture through story telling. As Leslie Silko says: 'You don't have anything/if you don't have the stories'.[16] There is also the necessary conscious reference to the great Western canon while, at the same time, transgressing and upturning it.

Amitav Gosh speaks of his need not to be read for contents alone, of his aspiration to new languages along the lines of writers like Woolf and Proust.[17] The innovation in his works is represented precisely by the coexistence of different genres and fields: history and story, journalistic enquiry and poetical vision are present both in his 'reportage' *Dancing in Cambodia,* and in his 'novel' *In an Antique Land,* subtitled *History in the Guise of a Traveller's Tale.* Such contamination is frequent in female writing. In the case of Luce Irigaray and Hélène Cixous, the critical voice is poised between the poetical and the argumentative code, essay writing and psycho-analysis, anthropology and art.

*   *   *

The relationship between genre and gender is a difficult one to establish and not only because today all categorisations are slipping and are in crisis. In all the numerous studies on the typology of genres, from the formalists to the structuralists, gender determinations occupy a marginal space. Derrida has made reference to the double valence of genre, from nature to culture, repeatedly returning in his essay to the history of the relationship of 'this strange couple'.

The link has been more pronounced in popular literature and culture since the middle of the last century, when women's social presence contributed to the increasing commercialisation of fiction, while making control and instrumentalisation more urgent. The increase in literacy, and the subsequent widening of the reading public, determined the creation of a new female reading public and a wider circulation of narrative literature. Janet Batsleer, in the wake of F. R. Leavis, speaks of the birth of female narratives as coinciding with the diffusion of the love tale with a moral purpose and of circulating libraries.[18] The only gender specialisation mentioned was female; what was left was by subtraction male, tacitly defined as universal. Soon after, with the beginnings of the cultural industry and the diffusion of paperbacks and bestsellers, gender labels appeared, starting from children's literature, in the same way as genre coding became essential in mass and industrial culture, connected as it was and is to specialised modes of production.

Production requirements and the organisation of cultural consumption, editorial or authorial strategies necessarily led to a more rigid gender coding of genres, sometimes associated with gendered colours such as pink and blue. Popular narratives, from crime to gothic and fantasy, from adventure to domestic melodrama, respected overall gender distinctions, in spite of exceptions and contradictions. In the media this has become even more evident. Institutional constraints both in cinema and television have from the start created quite distinct genre containers, and alongside them gender specificities. It is the language of cinema that has frequently associated genre and gender, sometimes defining the former through the latter in the label 'woman's film'; film noir and domestic melodrama have found a definition in the female heroine, from the dark lady to the self-sacrificing mother and bride.

Television has devoted research and study to viewing differentiations by age, gender, class and ethnicity. Genre studies gave particular attention to the question of gender, both as a textual determinant and as a feature of the audience, usually by women writing on the so-called 'gynocentric genres'. This was particularly true of television serial fiction which tried to create a quite distinctive male or female discourse, differentiating genre, format, subject matter, and the other elements of verbal and visual languages.

Yet even when the distinction between pink and blue (or noir) genres was highly coded at the level of marketing and the allegiance to the genre emphasised by the external packaging, covers, advertising and editorial blurbs, there were constant exceptions, or at least further internal subdvisions: the detective story, originally connoted

as male, became increasingly femininized;[19] science fiction, partly
originating from male genres such as adventure and travel narrative,
found female and feminist voices, often bringing into it another male
genre, the political novel. As to serial fiction, gender distinctions,
not too neat or easy even at the beginning, soon became the basis for
exceptions, inversions and trespassing, as we shall see.

The same happens to genres in popular literature: the excess turns
into proliferation and play, the play links author to viewer or reader,
the latter is interpellated and then eluded and baffled, or more often
it is she or he who becomes expert at playing between respect for and
elusion of the model. Genre constraints become a metatextual and
intertextual discourse for an expert fruition (one of the ways to play
with surfaces, as Deleuze says). The spreading of genre usage has
generated its own transgression. Derrida, in his essay, presents us
with the hypothesis that in the imperious law of genre, in its very
heart, a law of impurity or a principle of contamination is embedded. We are again far from a notion of genre as a neutral
container, as a transparent bearer of meanings, but now moving in a
different direction. Genres become quotations, frames, thresholds
and, at the same time, parody, contamination and play with forms.
In this function or absence of function, they remain essential
elements of the aesthetic game.

On the other hand the contaminations between the gothic and the
sentimental novel, or travel and adventure tales, had long been
established within the official canon as well. In Radcliffe and
Austen, Melville and Stevenson or Conrad, the intimate subjective
mode is inextricably mixed to the objective detached tone of a
narrating voice. Today the distinction between one and the other
mode is even less pronounced; the play with genres and modes and
voices touches both narrative and levels of reality. This kind of
pastiche can be found in the novels of more recent decades (what is
normally termed postmodern fiction), and both Patricia Waugh and
Linda Hutcheon have discussed this aspect in relation to women's
creativity.

Intertextual palimpsests, or, exterminate the text

The contamination of genres is most evident in the practice of re-
writing, which seem characteristically to mark the literary scene of

the end of the twentieth century. Are we moving perhaps towards a re-making of the canon and a re-writing of all the great works of the past? Or is all this simply a last nostalgic look at something that will soon be irretrievable?

Most so-called postmodern stylistic devices and aesthetical features are involved in this practice: parody, pastiche, citationism, juxtaposition of original and copy, the creation of complex authorial webs, temporal leaps and a vision of the present as a vestige of the past. In women's fictions the re-writing is motivated above all by an estranged look and can rather be defined as re-visitations from another side. Very often they are critical revisions, mostly effected through the practice of associating critical and narrative registers, of characters or literary environments observed from another point of view, whether real or fictional. The gender point of view passes through the denial and the reversal of the original and, at the same time, the bravura of moving between the most disparate modes and genres.

The re-elaborations of famous classics constitute a genre on its own. *Robinson Crusoe* is rewritten in Muriel Spark's *Robinson* and Jane Gardam's *Crusoe's Daughter*, among others; William Golding's *Lord of the Flies* – a second-degree novel within the same palimpsest – in Marianne Higgins's *John Dollar*; Stevenson's *Dr Jekyll and Mr Hyde*, another important prototype, in Emma Tennant's *Two Women of London*.

In this last example, the double Mrs Hyde/Miss Eliza Jekyll, while re-proposing the coexistence of good and evil, expresses the frustrations and difficulties, both material and psychological, of a single mother in the London of the eighties; the ending of this burlesque version of the Victorian novel sees the criminal Mrs Hyde happily escape justice, leaving the only clue of a shopping list, in which after 'Ajax', 'fish fingers', and before 'ketchup' and 'sliced bread', appears the reminder 'KILL', all in capitals to indicate a greater urgency, and hopefully a different scale of values.[20] In this case Hyde is a kind of avenger, as the object of her crime is a rapist persecuting the women at Ladbroke Grove (an area of London famous for the Caribbean festival at the centre of the novel, among other things).

Alongside John Fowles's much discussed and well-known *The French Lieutenant's Woman*, there are quite a few fake re-writings and pseudo-archeological reconstructions: Antonia Byatt's *Possession* (1990) or Rose Tremain's *Restoration* (1989) are interesting examples of this practice, a mixture of pseudo-literary 'fantasy' and of carefully researched critical practice, respectively on Romantic poetry and on the court of Charles II.[21] Tremain looks at seventeenth-century society from the point of view of Robert Merivel, a man without qualities and owing his presence at court to his French name alone.

A similar 'take' on Victorian mores is performed in Margaret Forster's *The Lady's Maid* (1990). Her novel is a perspective from below on Elizabeth Barrett Browning's artistic and private life, and moves on the border between fictional and documentary writing, at the edge of the research that Forster had done for her biography of the English poetess.[22] It is the story of her personal maid, named Elizabeth as well but called by her surname, Wilson, of her unhappy, deprived life and of her dependence on a repressed and elusive relationship. It is above all the harrowing recognition of the difficulty – nearly an impossibility – of the relation between women, implied in the one between servant and mistress.

Antonia S. Byatt offers the most sophisticated example of the contamination between the fantastic and the critical code in the pseudo-archaeological, second-degree writing of *Possession*, recalling the eighteenth-century fabrications of antiquity and the mixture of imitation and originality produced by Chatterton or MacPherson. The novel gives a historical reconstruction of the biography of the Victorian poet Randolph Henry Ash and of his contemporary Christabel LaMotte, two imaginary (?) characters, also providing the reproduction of their prolific writings, from short and long poems to diaries and letters. As far as we know they might be real people in disguise, and it is up to us to start the guessing or even do the research to find out. But they might also be totally invented characters, in which case it would be original writing. But even so, one would have to wonder how original: maybe simply *a la manière de* . . . At this point it is evident, even from the reader's own 'writerly' reactions, that the book is also a parody of biographic writing, and of academic research in general.

The novel starts in the British Library's famous and much fictionalised reading room, as is befitting an academic novel. We wonder at this point whether after all it is a parody of this genre, to which *Possession* belongs by right. The Victorian scholar Roland Michell, while browsing among Ash's personal books, jealously kept by the library, happens to find an incomplete letter by him in his personal copy of Vico's *Principi della scienza nuova*. The reference to Vico is of course not casual in this novel of courses and recourses.

The happy finding (we know already that it will acquire him an academic future) puts in motion that mechanism of successive Chinese boxes that is one of the main stylistic devices of postmodern fiction. It will push Roland and his girlfriend Maud Bailey to investigate a possible secret liaison between the great and famous Victorian poet and the less known but much admired Christabel, author of *La bella Melusina*, who has a cult following among feminists and lesbians. The past romance mingles with the one blossoming between Ronald and Maud; the parallel between the two couples is reinforced by the discovery that Maud is a descendant of the first union, which after all and in spite of all careful reconstructions – and of Christabel's lesbian preferences – had not been exclusively spiritual.

The novel has also the structure of a thriller: the enigmas and subsequent clues – ranging widely from the unusual categories of poetry and aesthetics to the more common genealogical and love plots – slowly unravel through a series of gradual twists building up to hundreds and hundreds of pages. The stylistic blend – from the epic and mythical to the epistolary and diaristic – responds to a deliberate plan but does not allude to multiple personalities or subject splits so much as to a diegetic practice of displacement, a technical exercise of great bravura, an extraordinary *tour de force* proceeding from one narrative slippage to another, in an infinite chain of simulations. It is certainly the proof of that 'aesthethical courage' that the author admires so much in Iris Murdoch.[23] This clever set of devices unexpectedly finds emotions and feelings in the representation of the real/false figure of the poetess Christabel that becomes also a reflection (never told, always implied) on the nuances of femininity and feminism.

In the end, when after many *coup-de-scènes* the two lovers find themselves again in the present, Maud confesses to Roland her fear of possession: 'I feel as she did. I keep my defences up because I must go on *doing my work*. I know how she felt about her unbroken egg. Her self-possession, her autonomy' (p. 506). This is the moment that unites the two women, in an open acceptance – unusual in the novel – of feelings and of a feminist allegiance. But soon after the discourse slips into rhetoric again (it is not difficult to detect the author's self mocking reference to her own aesthetics). Maud goes on:

'You understand?'
'Oh yes.'
'I write about liminality. Thresholds. Bastions. Fortresses.'
'Invasion. Irruption.'
'Of course.'
'It's not my scene. I have my own solitude.'
'I know. You – you would never – blur the edges messily –'
'Superimpose –'
'No, that's why I –'
'Feel safe with me –'

In the end he promises that he will let her be, and they decide to accept all the things they grew up not believing in: 'Total obsession night and day' (ibid.).

This novel has exhibited a *mélange* of genres that has found in romance a unifying instance, as Byatt tells the reader in the epigraph from Nathaniel Hawthorne's *The House of the Seven Gables* (the other epigraph is from a poem by Robert Browning on the poet's privilege of seeing 'the real world through the false'). But not unlike Blanchot's *récit*, the label romance asserts and denies genre at the same time, being a polyhedric multifarious form. The definitions given by Hawthorne – the freedom to present the truth 'under circumstances of the writer's own choosing or creation' and the capacity to connect the past to the present – can certainly be used for this book, but in the end there is the triumph (however ironic) of a more contemporary, popular version of romance, dealing with the hindrances and triumphs of love and feelings.

Browning's 'Mr Sludge, "The Medium"' provides another important insight into the genres and the lies of this novel, and at the same time a wider commentary on this and other contemporary fictions:

There's plenty of 'How did you contrive to grasp
The thread which led you through this labyrinth?
How build such solid fabric out of air?
How on so slight foundation found this tale,
Biography, narrative?' or, in other words,
'How many lies did it require to make
The portly truth you here present us with?'

Though all these forms can be attributed to the metanarrative and parodic mode dominant in the novel during the last half of this century, the more specific element of re-vision, the look from the other side, is specific in these female authors. A female way of being is expressed not only in the tragicomic inclusion of Mrs Hyde's practice of pure evil in a shopping list, but more generally in the presence of a real subgenre, a hybrid between the utopian (or distopian) novel and the feminist *pamphlet*, between fantastic and socio-realistic genres. The intertextual or transtextual relations of which Genette speaks in *Palimpsestes* (1982), whether they are referred to historical or fictional models, are here part of that chain of revisions, of backwards looks, of re-readings from which every woman writer finds it necessary to start. The difference from other examples of modernist art is realised here in constant deferments that end up in undecidability.

The hybridity of languages and genres can be brought to an even more self-conscious degree of artificial sophistication. In *Texterminations* (1991), Christine Brooke-Rose accomplishes a real extermination of the text, as the play among the various parts of the one-word title illustrates: apart from the ambiguity between termination and extermination, the concepts of ending ('ex') and mystery are suggested by the graphical emphasis on the 'x', in bold in the title and iterated in the cover design.[24] She presents a heterogeneous group of characters originating in different narratives from various genres and modes and levels, and puts them in an extradiegetic context, moving them out of fiction into contemporary historical realities.

The metaphor of the journey, so central to most of her narratives, is the trans-temporal and trans-spatial device. Jane Austen's Emma has Goethe as a fellow-traveller in place of her Mr Elton; Flaubert's other famous Emma passes from Léon's *fiacre* to the criminal Vautrin's, moving from high to low literature; one of the two Emmas, but who knows which one, or maybe it is George Eliot's Dorothea, receives the compliments of Philip II of Spain at Atlanta airport. Though not knowing German, she discovers herself speaking it (German is the most frequent among the many languages constantly intruding and prevailing over English) and wonders whether this can happen without her becoming another character; the possible loss of control on their narrative identities is the nagging worry of all these characters, as they exist under the threat of wrong readings.

The transversal juxtaposition of events belonging to different genres and *media* is constant in the novel: the Atlanta fire on the set of *Gone with the Wind* is at one with the fires of Thornfield Hall in *Jane Eyre* and of Moscow in *War and Peace*, and, going on backwards into the past, reaches the destruction of Troy in the *Aeneid*. The mixing of characters of such disparate origins gives rise to problems of class relation and etiquette:

> And Lady Audley – who on earth was she? . . . And a Lady Brett Ashley, oh yes, out of Hemingway, she did remember that one. Now how could Brett, a kind of nympho, get on with all those people simply because she has a title by marriage? Does Emma Woodhouse feel more at ease with Dorothea Brooke or Mrs Dalloway than with Emma Bovary, a mere doctor's wife? And who can Jude talk to, bookish but poor? And Mr Verloc, can he only talk to anarchists out of *The Possessed*. (p. 86)

The combination of genres is meant to demonstrate that the reader is passively ready to be introduced in any kind of narrative, with perhaps a mocking reference to structuralist theory: the conference in which they take part (yes, one more parody of academia) is interrupted by Arab terrorists who are then beheaded by Calvino's invisible knight (the signalling here is to postmodern fiction); the detective, called to investigate, is Columbo emerging from one of the many television series, from *soap* to crime, whose characters threatens the invasion of the conference. One of the witnesses (we have now moved to court drama) falls in love with Christa Wolf's Kassandra.

The parody of literary conferences emerges from the clashes and conflicts of genres, but also of academic factions and fractions, while the hostilities and verbal attacks typical of conferences in this case end up in terrorist acts and violent intercontinental plots. The play on the word 'plot' easily operates the move between the political and the literary. The novel, not unlike *Possession*, could belong to the campus novel genre, while parodying and denying it at the same time.

The conference takes place in San Francisco, at an annual event called Prayer for Existing, where they have gathered; it is still Emma speaking, 'To pray together for our continuance of being, but also for all our brethren, far more numerous than even we who are here, who remain dead in never-opened books . . .' (p. 17). The participants are gripped by the fear of being forgotten by the reader, a kind of death considered more fatal than textual death. The prayer is addressed to this fearful Divinity haunting the conference (that is, the reader): 'Our Implied Reader, Our Super Reader, Our Ideal Reader, who gathers unto Himself all Readers, and to His Interpreter, who gathers unto Himself all interpreters, of all interpretive communities' (p. 26). The final invocation closing the rite is obviously 'The Reader be with you.'

One of the main motifs of this novel is the parody of literary criticism and of its priests, the critics or interpreters who attend the event in the role of organisers and surveillants and also as spies of Extrapol (from extrapolation). Brooke-Rose gives a sarcastic analysis of the main critical trends and fashions of recent years, from structuralism to psychoanalysis, from reception theory to poststructuralism ('But the text is all . . . It has the ambiguities on which survival depends. It's in illogics that the interpreter takes his pleasure': p. 36).

Feminist studies are not spared either, firstly through a precise reference to Cixous and to her study of Clarice Lispector's works ('feminists who find complex structures in flux and fragmentation . . . and in menstrual rhythms and body language': p. 41), and successively through a more general attack on 'minority groups, who are now so numerous as to constitute a majority, those who ask to alter the canon, you know, dig up forgotten works ignored by what they call white male warmongers – a lousy pun on canon-makers – in favour, I guess, of black female warmongers' (p. 102). Through her language ruses, Brooke-Rose presents an immense tapestry, a palimpsest of narrative culture in the modern era, that becomes a sort of epitaph, an ironic look putting into question all narratives including her own. Through the satire of postmodern feminism, this parodic meganarrative involves her own practice, providing a self-mocking distancing.[25]

The erasures of the boundaries between different styles and modes can also be found in female novels which are not revisitations of the past. In Joanna Russ's *The Female Man* the passage from prose to poetry, dialogue to narration, novel to drama is stressed typographically as well. This novel, alongside Margaret Atwood's *The*

Handmaid's Tale and other feminist science fiction novels, proposes a *mélange* of genres, as it colours utopian (or distopian) narrative and science fiction with feminist militant tones. The contamination between the fantastic and the political mode had been anticipated by Doris Lessing, who in much of her writing has transgressed traditional boundaries: her *Memoirs of a Survivor* is an excellent example, and *The Golden Notebook* with its pluricoded forms precedes them all.

The pastiche of genres can be found in Toni Morrison as in Jeanette Winterson, in Angela Carter as in Fay Weldon. The ambiguity between story and stories is described in Jeanette Winterson's *Oranges Are Not The Only Fruit*. This novel of adolescence, mostly autobiographical, presents the contamination between fiction and fact, creative and argumentative voice, novel and criticism, history and fable. In *Sexing the Cherry*, another of her novels, the historical setting goes with mythology and fantasy, the introspective with the grotesque satirical mode, in the absolute anarchy of genres. Toni Morrison's *Beloved* has a historical and political theme structured like a *thriller*, with many of the paradigms of a terror or ghost story, and to this I shall come back as ghosts will be cropping up again in my discourse.

Angela Carter's *The Passion of New Eve* mixes gothic tale, metropolitan phantasy, science fiction and mythology, oneiric representation and feminist pamphlet, all played against sexual ambiguity. The transgression of gender boundaries finds its correspondence in genre contamination: the features of the Great Mother and the description of the subterranean city of Beulah couple one of the basic topoi of science fiction with those of mythological tales; both genres are traversed by motifs of contemporary horror and consistently informed by the political feminist intent. The farcical mode is an important element in the distortion of genres.

Carter oscillated between realism and fantasy from the start: her first novel, *Shadow Dance* (1965), founded on the observation of her metropolitan milieu, was soon followed by *The Magic Toyshop*, close to a fable. She felt a strong attraction for 'the material truth of our world' that is at the centre of most of her journalistic and critical prose, while at the same time writing novels peopled by hybrid beings suspended between the animal and the human, female and male, monstrosity and normality. Her novels have been assigned to *fantasy*, a hybrid genre itself at the border of science fiction, utopia and metropolitan novel.

Popular genres and avant-garde freedom

What may seem a contrivance of avant-garde (or post-avant-garde) writing has come first of all from popular literature; from the hybridity of the bestselling genres of the last decades, and the extraordinary transformations and metamorphoses of classical genres in the cultural industry. It is here, in this *mélange* of generic forms, that the frontier between high and low becomes fluid and more difficult to ascertain, and the two modes become part of a continuum. Brooke-Rose has given an histrionic (and dismayed) description of this state of things in her clever parody of the intricate juxtaposition of the great novels of the past with television serial narrative of recent years.

However, it is above all Angela Carter who has consciously adopted a curious farrago of folklore and literary traditions, of popular images and myth, flamboyant melodrama and sophisticated symbolic patterns. She has presented popular spectacles and brassy heroines with an eye on Virginia Woolf and Djuna Barnes in *Nights at the Circus*, and mixed Shakespeare with music hall in *Wise Children*, in neither case forgetting the complex theoretical questions that arise for feminist writing in its relationship with these mothers and fathers. In an interview with me in Naples in 1990, she spoke of the possibility of uniting popular genre literature and experimental writing, giving the example of J. G. Ballard, a writer she admired very much: 'if I use genre, it is in a way to help me answer questions that I am asking myself about the nature of certain styles of writing'.[26]

Female crime stories are great examples of the slide between high and low, often presenting a complex knot between metaphysics and criminal violence, refinement and murder. This is true of Patricia Highsmith and Ruth Rendell, P. D. James and Sara Paretsky, among others.

Highsmith's *Ripley's Game* constantly proposes genre as border or limit. A series of contradictory signals is given from the beginning. The first sentence 'There's no such thing as a perfect murder', is an ironic signpost or label for 'thriller'. Soon afterwards, the murderer and art forger Tom Ripley, a recurrent hero in her novels, mentions a possible involvement in a spy story. Another ambiguous feature is offered by his refined taste and character, further reminding the reader of neighbouring genres, such as the sophisticated comedy-thriller in the tradition of *The Thin Man*. On the other hand, a link is established between the aestheticism of this world and the more matter-of-fact brutality of the other one, bringing us back to the major genre: 'The light in her hair was gold, however, which made Tom think of money.'[27]

The subjective point of view, unusual in the traditional crime story before Chandler, not only displaces the mode of scientific objectivity that is properly of the genre, but also breaks the rule of suspense as it is the subjectivity of the criminal, and not of the detective, that is involved. More importantly, it impinges the genre ethos as Tom Ripley – a hero *manqué*, the master of re-playing, of plagiarising, of jarring repetition – is a subversive super-ego. Jonathan is his alter ego, a sort of sacrificial victim, marked by death from the beginning. Even in bonding with him, Tom's role is ambiguous: it is between executioner and witness, his actions casual and detached.

The novel is recounted in his thoughts and words but cannot be really narrated: there is no 'crime and detection', no classic suspense, no confrontation between good/evil as it is not clear where order or disorder stand. There is no ultimate meaning, not even in Jonathan's death, except maybe in Tom as Jonathan's deathly destiny.

> Tom was driving the car, Jonathan thought, like God himself. This was death now, which he had tried to face before and yet had not faced, tried to prepare and yet hadn't been able to. There was no preparation possible, it was merely a surrender, after all. And what he had done, misdone, accomplished, striven for – all seemed absurdity. (p. 246)

In the end only secondary details and objects seem to matter, mostly tied to Tom's and Heloise's consumerism. Objects have a symbolic charge, like the toothbrush that Jonathan has used in Tom's house or the harpsichord, but their sense is obscure.

The reader may find a partial consolation in the possibility that Jonathan has meant to save Tom's life but even this is left uncertain. The only thing that subtracts the novel from this unclear border zone is male bonding: the creation of male alter egos, frequent in most popular genres, the western in particular, is central here. Wim Wenders's beautiful film, based on the novel and called *The American Friend*, underlines this motif; it also deals with the death of genre by playing on genres, in the ironic (and sometime hilarious, as in the train scene) quotations from Hollywood genres, from the western to the gangster or Mafia movie.

The temptation to read echoes of a Dostoevskian unmotivated murder is strong, but there is no itinerary of punishment and purgation. Jonathan's wife's extreme act of spite for Tom seems to assign the role of putting the moral seal on the story to a woman, as many other times before: 'as Tom almost came to a stop also, thinking at least to say "*Bonjour*, madame," she spat at him. She missed his face, missed him entirely, and plunged on towards the Rue St Merry' (p. 257). But her contempt for Tom, rather than consigning him to the hell without redemption of a Beckettian character, includes her in the motionless, static, nearly frozen, horizon of the novel: like Tom's exquisite wife Heloise, Simone, however involuntarily, becomes an accomplice too. Tom's cynical reflection on this closes the novel:

> In fact, the spit was a kind of guarantee, whether it hit or not. But if Simone hadn't decided to hang on to the money in Switzerland, she wouldn't have bothered spitting and he himself would be in prison. Simone was just a trifle ashamed of herself, Tom thought. In that she joined much of the rest of the world.

Genre is transformed and deviated to the point of negation; the novel is constantly and simultaneously inside and outside the thriller, recalls it in its structure, events, characters and quotations and challenges it continuously. Here Highsmith achieves the difficult task of combining genre with experimentation, as Angela Carter says of Ballard. She speaks of the freedom that a talented writer can get from working within genre, and I believe that Highsmith is a writer who uses genre to elaborate symbols and ideas, thus succeeding in illuminating a bleak post-Dostoevskian world.

P. D. James's *Innocent Blood* is also closely knit with symbolic and detective plots. 'Philippa Rose Palfrey is what I am called. I'm here to find out who I am' is the beginning of the novel. The heroine places herself in the role of detective required by the genre: to uncover guilt, and at the same time her own identity (an equation to be found both in the thriller and above all in the spy story). At the end guilt is detected but not her identity, unless you count the anagraphical one.

Beside the thriller, the writer unfolds the picture of an unfeeling, heartless society with its cruel game of making fun of the weak and the inferior through a chain of snobbish dismissive attitudes, of cold claustrophobic power games. At the centre there is Maurice's cynical attitude to his adoptive daughter and his abuse of her, and, as an indirect revenge, Philippa's supreme trick on her mother, a poor ex-convict (what she was before remains a mystery as she never becomes a speaking subject), once she finds her.

The crime plot, which is unusually confined to the subplot, is the story of a father's vengeance for the rape and death of his daughter, committed by Philippa's father with the complicity of his wife. In parallel, the heroine pursues her revenge on her mother for her refusal of motherhood, more than for her crime (her father is dead and out of reach). The object of the two detections is one and the thriller slowly unravels this truth in a gripping murder scene that brings the narration back to a classical twist of the genre and at the same time eludes it: its ambiguity is underlined by the fact that the avenger strikes a dead woman, as Philippa has got there before him. In the end who killed whom does not matter: 'His child was dead. Her mother was dead. Words, explanations, excuses were an irrelevance. About that final negation there was nothing new to be thought, nothing new to be said, nothing that could be put right.'[28]

Here too there is no easy 'progression' from crime to punishment, though there is an explanatory epilogue giving at least the vision of change and purgation through love. 'Surely this need to see her again, to be comforted by her, was the beginning of love; and how could she have expected that there could be love without pain?' (p. 291). Philippa Rose has not reached purgation but is aware that by killing her mother she has killed her hope to love and be loved: 'I'm not sure that I really knew her . . . She didn't say very much. But when she was there·she was more there than anyone I've ever known. And I was there too' (p. 311). Her heart of stone gives some sign of life, which is the only foundation for a weak hope, 'a small accession to grace': 'Just before she fell asleep she remembered that there was someone for whom she needed to weep. But she had no tears left, and she had never found it easy to cry. And that didn't matter either. She had a lifetime ahead of her in which to learn how' (p. 304).

The thriller is traversed by other genres, such as sensational melodrama (the circumstances of Mary Ducton's death, and the claustrophobic dark staging and atmosphere) or the metropolitan Victorian novel, for its insistant descriptions of the urban landscape, particularly the slums of popular London in the seventies. Here as well, there are signals and labels for the genre and its transgressions and there are also self-referential hints as when the amateur detective is described thus: 'He ought to be writing thrillers. He had the mind of a thriller writer, obsessive, guilt-ridden, preoccupied with trivia' (p. 296). These conscious narcissistic looks are not infrequent in popular literature, as Austen Meredith recalls: 'like the woman *in* an Elinor Glyn novel who describes another by saying: "She is like a figure in an Elinor Glyn novel".'[29]

Against the economy of the same

The element of re-vision, of the look from the other side, is dominant in what might seem indistinguishable from postmodern fiction in general; as Adrienne Rich says, it is above all an act of survival. The female monster, in Emma Tennant's revision of Stevenson's novel, escapes the police and survives, unlike her male model who does not make it. But the revision is primarily in the reconstruction of an important moment in the feminist history of recent decades. Genre is traversed by the discourse of sexual difference as if the vicinity of the two English words – genre and gender, divided by 'd' (for difference?) – recalled coincidence and dislocation, obedience and transgression at one and the same time.

The critical voice that speaks of displacement and ambiguity for sexual difference denies the rigidity of the law of genre. Repetition and change, loyalty and betrayal, reassurance and elusion, movement between the heart of the narrative and its borders; all these are at the centre of contemporary fiction and its use of genres. Genres become borders to cross over and over again, simulacra of a past to be resurrected and erased, palimpsests that are continually rewritten; for female writing, one of the ways to avoid the assimilation to the same. As Luce Irigaray says 'the domain of the logos in philosophy derives from its power to *reduce every other to the economy of the same*'.[30]

Chapter 3

The Lure of the Image: Fe/male Serial Narratives

Has Trisha got married?

As I was going up the many stairs to my flat, a little girl was frantically ringing a bell on one of the first floor doors. A woman came to open, an aunt or a friend, or mother herself; the girl impatiently pushed her aside and started running while asking at the top of her shrill anxious voice: 'Has Trisha got married? Has Trisha got married?'.

'Once I got home, I switched on the soap they were watching (I had never watched it before), just to get that simple reply. And I discovered – obviously not at once – that it was not so simple, that hardly anybody could answer that question (except her wicked fiancé and he never would), and last of all Trisha herself, that she was under drugs and in terrible confusion, and probably had fainted at the crucial moment . . .

What to my surprise I then realised was that my little neighbour's voice was not expressing the romantic expectation of a long-dreamt event (marriage is normally that, in romance) but the dread of it happening. That Trisha was in love with somebody else and was being forced into this marriage with the villain by all sorts of circumstances was less important than the total subversion of one of the pillars of romance . . . And I remembered the time when, as a child, I went to the wedding of a very young aunt of mine, Annamaria, to whom I was very close. To the horror of the guests and of the extended family, I unaccountably and desperately wept the whole day as one would at a funeral, not a celebration. As things went, Annamaria's marriage . . .

In this chapter I will be considering the link between reality and narrative in terms of the genre (and technology) of soap opera, first reviewing the negative aura that still surrounds what is called 'women's television', and then analysing its features and narrative codes along certain paths: bodies, rooms, claustrophobic spaces, romance and paranoia, couples and pairs. To these paradigms can be added metaphorical and structural dimensions orbiting around questions of opening and closure, space and place. It will be impossible to do this without referring to film aesthetics, and particularly to previous feminist discussions on cinema and women: from one point of view, television melodrama can be considered as the 're-memory' of some filmic genres.

The 'melodramatic mode' is filled with invention rather than information, fantasy rather than facts, tales rather than events. Its form is one of suspension, both because it is serial and because it moves from one interrogation to another, one enigma to another. It is as if soap operas reproduced the structure of narrative itself, an endless flow crossing the screen in parallel lines or in succession. The analyses may lead to the outline of a female aesthetic mode but they also show how this is not an unchanged and unchangeable enclave but a shifting discourse moving across gender and genres boundaries, and sometimes overflowing its own confines. This is best seen in crime or cop series, where an original male paradigm gave way first to a femininisation of its features, and then to new forms in which gender divides are confused and transgressed, and genre itself transformed.

A word on the examples I use in this chapter. Among the many existing series and serials, the choice of a few specific ones may seem particularly arbitrary (but is this not so mainly because they are considered so ephemeral and expendable?). Most of the day-time soaps may be unknown to my reader (even among those who watch soaps, to each his or her own); my choice has sometimes been dictated by their success in Italy (as with *Capitol* and *The Bold and the Beautiful*), a success that has singled them out for me in the myriad of American shows. Some of them go some way back, as my research on the subject started in the mid-eighties. Among them, *Dallas* and *Dynasty* have achieved the status of 'classics' (the inverted commas allow the shelter of ironic distance, and the defence against those who would deny the possibility that a canon might exist in this field) and I can trust that even those who never watched them know what they are about.

The Female Eye, the female 'I'

Everything leaves me cold that is not the affirmation of my self.
(Carla Lonzi)

Female narratives pose the problem of proving the existence of women's subjectivity on the small screen; to analyse the dialectic between woman as subject and object of a multiple gaze both as spectator and as character. It would be easier just watching and liking it. But liking soap opera – and what I would more generally call women's telefilm, recalling a similar cinematic term – is still quite a suspicious activity, precisely because it is not considered to provide sufficient proof of a subjective space for woman.

Romance and love are still under accusation, though it may be more fashionable for women to find pleasure in them. This moralist attitude is reflected in the analysis of women as object of the look in the audiovisual spectacle; the existence of the woman's gaze has at times been forgotten, in the assumption that our guilty pleasures derived from watching other women or ourselves through men's eyes.

The advantages offered by the use of psychoanalytical theory in the analysis of the conscious and unconscious pleasure of the viewer are partially offset by a limited view of woman as subject who, if she exists at all, is seen largely as sharer and accomplice of the voyeuristic and fetishist look. In the strict 'division of labour' that was established within a heterosexual economy, the space left for the woman viewer was minimal. This is one reason why closer attention is now paid to the complex and contradictory patterns to be found in women's 'ways of looking', most notably in feminist criticism. The intention is to avoid the limitations of a binary structure that leaves little space for the pleasure of the female look and for the representation of women's desire towards other women. Jackie Stacey, in 'Desperately Seeking Difference', poses the following question: 'if these pleasures have been organized in accordance with the needs, desires and fears of heterosexual masculinity, then what is place of women's desire towards women within this analysis of narrative cinema?'[1] And Julia Lesage, in her detailed analysis of Griffiths' *Broken Blossoms*, says:

> The critical question that remains unresolved as a feminist viewer is this: where does Lucy's pathos, which affects me so strongly, derive from? Are my eyes constantly on Lucy in the way that a male viewer's would be, insofar as traditional feature films constantly have us look at women as objects in stories told through men's eyes?[2]

Stacey, speaking of 'difference and desire among women', points out that the relation between identification and desire is one of complex interplay rather than reciprocal elision. The look of women at other women is not mechanically divided between identification or (by analogy with male looking) objectification.

In the most banal of these female narratives women are present in multiple roles: viewers, actresses, characters, writers or producers. This diffused subject works against an assumed singular universality. The passage from a centred subject to a dispersed one seems to be a feature of women's space on the small screen: not the singular subject or the displacement into the third person, but the multiple points of a voyage of the 'I' along the narrative path.

A double 'double standard'

A double standard applies not only to the question of 'value', but also to the ways in which feminine narrative is discussed: that is, mainly with an eye to contents alone. And, even if such narrative is not forgotten or despised or discussed for 'what it is about', it is usually labelled, whether it falls within high culture or popular culture; in the latter case it easily acquires the dismissive tag of 'women's matters' or 'sentimental rubbish'.

The positions vary from contempt for 'silly novels by lady novelists' and the 'sentimental rubbish' that is produced for women to the scientifically argued thesis that women 'seek to escape from reality'. Tania Modleski has noted that negative judgements, starting from George Eliot, have more markedly come from female critics and has observed that the dismissive, mocking tones assumed by women internalise 'the masculine contempt for sentimental (feminine) drivel'.[3] A century later, Germaine Greer sees in love a 'cheap ideology'.[4] Elisabetta Rasy, in *La lingua della nutrice* (1978), has spoken of the devaluation and the censorship to which romantic novels have been submitted and of the refusal to acknowledge their symbolic value. More recently, romance is judged by Teresa Stratford as decreasing women's power, though in a context offering a positive open attitude towards it.[5] The discrimination has many fronts, and one of them passes precisely through popular culture where the role of women was long forgotten (in the study of subcultures, for instance).[6]

This is particularly true if we look at the attitude of the press towards popular television narratives. In the quality press the programmes that attract the majority of viewers are never previewed by the critics and hardly ever reviewed except in dismissive terms, while the popular press in England gives constant attention to their stars' supposedly scandalous lives. This perspective extends to all kinds of serial dramas, but those usually associated with women, and to soap opera, take up a substantial space. 'Soap is a term used by British critics as synonymous with junk . . . These programmes are the most-lamented programmes on British television, criticised as the staple diet of the unintelligent, and dangerously sapping the literacy of British youth.'[7] It is not by chance that the apocalyptic view of popular culture collapses together the popular and the feminine, from George Eliot to Jean Baudrillard. Both lend themselves rather easily and (why not?) willingly to the mocking comments of most television critics.[8]

On the other hand the invisibility of women's criticism on popular culture, noted above, may be due to the deep mistrust that feminists have long held towards the exploitative character of commercial and mass culture in relation to women. This anxiety has sometimes fed into a continuation of the old attitude of contempt or neglect. Very interesting studies of the seventies and the eighties have been dominated by a sometimes necessary caution or even by a moralistic outlook. Words like 'pleasure', 'desire', and 'needs' have found their way into the critical vocabulary, but not always to the point of redeeming such frivolous narratives.

Dorothy Hobson, writing about the English soap opera *Cross-roads*, notes the contradiction between the disparaging judgements given on it and its wide popularity among women viewers.[9] Charlotte Brunsdon, on the other hand, shows how important the analyses of 'heroine television' have been in feminist criticism, especially in the eighties. She notices that the feminist interest denotes a positive commitment to mass media femininities except for a negative view linked to the opposition between real women and the images of women.[10]

The suspicion is widespread. In an interview with Jacques Le Goff, Eco has stressed the biological function of narrative that came before writing and will survive in the post-writing era, making the link between an originary moment and the recent flow of fictional television. He does not fail to express his contempt: 'The novel as a genre may disappear, not narrative, as it has a biological function. During this century the narrative need has been in charge of cinema and television. Unfortunately narrative has been debased in television series of very bad quality.'[11] In less apocalyptic tones, Stephen Heath describes this fictional continuum as essential and omnipresent in our lives.[12]

Bodies, stories, identities

There is a lot to be said on the use and abuse of stereotypes in television narratives, which can sometimes achieve an uncanny effect. Everything is stated and counterstated, everything can be read in a different way. We can refer this to the Gramscian difference between common sense and good sense: in spite of it all, television narratives often offer a demystification of the very commonsensical situations they are presenting. Any story can be inscribed in the text through contradictions, reversals and constant erasings; the infinite variations come also from the decoding, from the possibility of reading stereotypes against the grain, of playing between sense and senses. Cultural ambiguities in the reception and in the textual construction have an influence on how the charm of the heroine works in different contexts, how the clichés of masculinity and femininity function and how they can be deflated by kitsch or irony.

Character, this solid structural whole of much great literature, loses all coherence and undergoes a deconstructive process usually found only in experimental narrative. The search for the self is reflected in the play on identities that is at the centre of these narratives: splits and changes, loss of memory (this one is the most insistent one, and its variations are infinite), the reduplication of characters and actors. The change of actors often intersects in this complex play, further destabilising reality and fantasy. Identity becomes a shifting concept and moves from one body to another; bodies oscillate between one individuation and another. Only a surface naming is maintained.

Whatever the reasons, it all amounts to the construction of an aesthetics of flux and fragmentation. As in all melodrama, the play between the loss and the finding of identity (and/or memory) is a recurrent motif. It is a device used to complicate and enrich the narrative, to make adventurous and surprising what would otherwise be predictable and linear, to lengthen what would be too short. In serial narrative, and especially in soap opera, all this seems particularly necessary since the economy of narration is one of lingering, delaying, pausing, as an end in itself rather than as an instrument for suspense.[13]

The play on identity, one of the most ancient narrative devices of all ages, finds a further twist in the requirements of a production process that, due to the length of series and serials, can span several years. The characters are unavoidably influenced by the changes undergone by the actors, and change face and voice as the actors go away or die; for the same extradiegetic reasons, they disappear and sometime reappear as 'other'. Well-known examples of a glorious past have been Miss Ellie, Jock and Pamela in *Dallas*, Fallon and Stephen in *Dynasty*; in all these cases there was a conscious interplay between the character and the actor, between fact and fiction, a device constantly taken up by the popular press, and not only in Britain.[14] More recently, this device has been used in day-time soaps of the nineties: Caroline, one of the heroines of *The Bold and the Beautiful*, disappeared from the soap in its early stages (due to her melodramatic death from leukaemia, reminiscent of *Love Story*), and reappeared later as her own twin sister.

The reduplication of a character is more complex and usually occasioned by diegetic reasons. The use of a double has been widespread in great novels (Dostoevsky and Conrad have created great 'doubles') and also in Hollywood cinema, from the classic of its kind, *The Dark Mirror*, with a superb Olivia de Havilland, to David Cronenberg's *Dead Ringers*. In television narrative the double is a recurrent motif in contexts and languages otherwise confined to naturalism.

The 'case' of Crystal Carrington occupied a whole series of *Dynasty*, with the real Crystal imprisoned down in the dungeon, without ever losing her shoulder pads, while the double was upstairs in Crystal's place beside her husband Blake. In the bedroom, the false Crystal put up the excuse of constant headaches in order to avoid paying her conjugal duties; was it the usual malicious skirting with sexual matters that is typical of mainstream soap opera? Or would Blake's incapacity to realise there was another in his bed have been too much even for the large suspension of credibility of the viewer? Freudian theory and its echoing in literature and cinema, where the evil double is usually hidden in the depths, was here perversely upturned.

The use of the same actress for two characters is yet another variation, mostly inexplicable as there is hardly any diegetic motivation. The parallel agonies of Julie Clegg and Jenny Diamond, both played by Catherine Hickland, have been an important part of *Capitol*, one of the few day-time American soaps that chose to come to an end.[15] The need to make better use of a good and popular actress, once her first role has been fully exploited, is a possible motive. But the physical juxtaposition of an open and simple character such as Julie with the complex, dark personality of Jenny, troubled by amnesia and a dangerous instability, had an uncanny effect in this soap. Greta Colmenares in *Manuela* has interpreted the two roles of rich and spoiled Isabel and of humble and modest Manuela, both brought by the chances of life to love the same man. More surprisingly, Veronica Castro in *My Little Solitude* has interpreted both mother and daughter, subverting a few theoretical debates in a single blow.

In spite of any practical explanations, this movement between actor and character, mind and body, involves a wavering over the diegetic edge, and has the effect of blurring the divisory line between the inside and the outside of narrative, fact and fiction, subject and object. It becomes an important component of a metanarrative that is not infrequent in popular fiction, though it is usually encountered in avant-garde art. When the game is pushed too far, effects of excess and parody are reached: as is well-known, excess is a recurrent feature of melodramatic aesthetics. There is rarely a resolution to these cases of lost or split identity, and that creates an area of uncertainty and suspense around the individual character. Women are the most frequent cases: the movement between the two

Female Stories, Female Bodies

Krystles and the two Fallons (here a second actress replaced the
original, though playing the same role), or between Jenny and Julie,
becomes a passage between one woman and another, between one
and the same.

This passage can take place within one (un-split) character who
then becomes a palimpsest of female attitudes. There are many
characters in soaps who drastically change attitudes and behaviour
during their long serial lives, but it is usually the figure of the
matriarch, director of all intrigues, that displays varied and contrasting features: a ruthless opponent to the 'other' family (there is
always another family), a bad and tyrannical mother, a competitive
business woman, an envious plotting friend, she can be at the very
same time a protective wife and mother, and an affectionate friend,
from Myrna Clegg in *Capitol* to Gwyneth in *Loving*, and above all
Stephanie in *The Bold and the Beautiful*. In all these contradictory
aspects, they are always excessive.

Gore Vidal has given an elitist ironic vision of popular culture and
its fictions in *Duluth*, a metanarrative saga crowded with characters
moving freely from one plot to another, among different media, in a
void deprived of temporal, spatial or syntactical limits. He makes
one of them declare: 'We are simply formulations of words. We do
not live. We are interchangeable. We go on, and we go on, from
narrative to narrative, whether in serial form or in those abstract
verbal constructions so admired by the French and boolaboola
Yale! It is all the same.'[16] Though not belonging to either of these
two categories (but undoubtedly influenced by them), I must say
that this differing of the I, this moving back and forward of
identities, bodies and stories is one of the elements of the seduction
– for me – of such disparaged tales.

A place within the self

In an essay on Gertrude Stein, Catherine Stimpson quotes 'Attacks',
a fragment from her *Bee Time Vine*:

She is.
She is the best way.
She is the best way from here to there.

These lines are arrayed so as to suggest a female expansion into space; they are certainly a 'tribute to women's being, and being in space'.[17] As Jessica Benjamin puts it, 'what is experientially female is the associations of desire with a space, a place within the self'.[18] She states that from this comes the strength to own one's own desire, the only one that allows 'being oneself, being alone' in the presence of the other.

I wish here to give some attention to the screen space materially occupied by women. Those who fall into the temptation of thinking of such a space as a space *for* women have been accused of falling into 'the seductive trap of the image', of taking its sheer presence as triumph or at least as the mark of presence, of a subjective position, of the independence of desire. This has been widely argued for cinema. Julia Lesage wonders about the fascination she feels for the heroine in *Broken Blossoms*, and for Lillian Gish, the actress performing the role: 'as a woman I must ask how the media can so seduce me that I enjoy, either as entertainment or as art, works that take as one of their essential ingredients the victimization of women'.[19] She further notes that identification with the heroine places the viewer in a passive role.

Identification is seen as the real problem: Mary Ann Doane, in a fascinating analysis of *Rebecca* and *Caught*, and of the scenes focusing on women's relation to the image, speaks of the lack of a gap between the female gaze and the image, and of how this effects a confusion between subjectivity and objectivity, between the internal and the external: 'the most disturbing images of the two films are those which evoke the absence of the woman. In both films these images follow projection scenes which delineate the impossibility of female spectatorship.'[20]

In television it is easy to be fascinated by the crowd of women moving from one plot to another in the uninterrupted flow of day-time soap operas. It is nearly impossible to avoid being seduced by 'presence' when two women, invariably representing rival families, occupy the scene. These dramatic confrontations, even when caused by financial or economic matters, frequently hide a personal rivalry over the same man. It is true that this female power in the last instance lies in men's love (the limit of romance?), but how can one resist the fascination of the triumph of such 'limit', of feeling, female desire, the body?

It could occur in the female collective scenes in *Gabriela*, the tele-novela based on Jorge Amado's novel, often rigidly structured in a symmetrical view of sexual and class differences in the village that provides the choral background of the tale. One of the episodes opened with a series of alternate shots of the notables' wives rebelling against their husbands and of dressmakers in revolt against the boss. In both scenes, female bodies, first seen together in medium shot and then individually in successive close shots, were a strong statement of an alternative strength. In another episode, the sequence of Gabriela herself (the beautiful Sonia Braga) dominating with her phallus-like body the men around – who are literally on their knees – was dangerously inducive to the lure of the image.

The dangers of women's reification in the image have often been underlined. Popular narrative has been blamed for its uncritical emphasis on the female icon, in contrast to the 'resistance to the image' that can be found in avant-garde cinema, or in any language that refuses obvious readings and prevents easy identifications. Some film critics have claimed feminist experimental cinema as the only discourse for women, as against the traps and pitfalls of the 'classic realist text', mostly identified with Hollywood cinema.[21]

As to television, the danger would be confirmed by the dominance of the image over other languages, the pretence of being a 'window' open on the world, the subsequent absence of distancing elements, and, finally, the lack of a dividing line between avant-garde and popular. Even in such a desperate case, I believe that there are elements that work against the closure of the predominant realistic convention. The blending of avant-garde and popular languages, quite frequent in certain genres, especially in satirical shows, seems to me one of its advantages.

A claustrophobic space

> As for woman, she is place . . . She is able to move within place as place. Within the availability of place. Given that her issue is how to trace the limits of place herself so as to be able to situate herself therein and welcome the other there. (Luce Irigaray)

Mary Ann Doane has spoken of the filmic visual space as 'con-tinually being outlined, territorialized, divided along sexual lines'.[22]

In television narratives the split is between open spaces, mainly the metropolitan scene, specific to male narratives, whereas the closed claustrophobic places are allotted to women, mainly in soap operas or in those femininisations of male genres, such as the female police series.

The room is the one dominating space in most day-time soap operas and tele-novelas. It is important even when the main space is public, used as a meeting point and a common background. Hospitals, courts, police headquarters, squares and a housing estate (corresponding to a smaller *palazzo* in Italy) are some of these choral spots, but they all end up among four walls. In more expensive soaps, whose stories often move between the American province and imaginary exotic places, the room is still there, unmoved and unmoving. This is usually the site of romantic love, where the 'I' faces a 'you'; the natural space for the heterosexual couple, speaking, flirting, scheming, confronting one another but mostly making love. The female spectator's gaze is split in a double fascination: she is looking at a woman looking at love, and at a man as fetishistic object.[23] The heterosexual couple is a recurrent icon, a sort of linguistic constant of sentimental and domestic narrative, from novel to film and television.

There is also another space, however: that of the woman alone, the space of lack and desire. Often represented as a prison, it is a topos of melodrama, from cinema to television. Thank to a succession of metonymic passages, we go from the home to the room, from the room to parts of it, but mainly to the markers of its boundaries such as doors and windows, arches and angles, as Julia Lesage had already observed in *Broken Blossoms*. Melodrama is the favourite arena for the many links between film and television languages, and in fact this discourse follows the seams of a coincidence that is not casual. Traditions, languages, production sites, teams and technical skills are not too dissimilar, and create common guidelines for the two aesthetics.

The motif of the woman at home lonely and desperate was taken up in the recurrent image of Kelly Harper in *Capitol*; she was anxious and distressed, looking for comfort in alcohol and drugs. Kelly was the mistress, the eternal third party, with dark hair and a dark past. She was frequently seen in the large downstairs room in her flat, a space exhibiting the elements of her paranoia: the staircase leading up to her son's room (she was a single parent and all her problems – mainly the loss of love – were tied to this maternity); the tools of her work as a painter; the drugs to which she became slowly addicted, hidden in drawers, pots, bags; the door as object of her obsessive gaze, torn between fear and need of the other, the outside, freedom; and finally the famous window, a fundamental icon of melodrama, with its obvious reference to prison, closure, victimisation.

The comparison with the woman's film is obvious but the elements are blurred, repeated, parodied, in a jarring reworking of those themes. There is the conscious memory of classical topoi of Hollywood cinema, but these images come *after*. They are quotes, overlappings, memories; they unite past and present, underline and deny the similarity.

The 're-memory' is particularly evident in the epilogue to one of the serial's last episodes. As Trey goes out of the door, Kelly rushes to the window, and the camera from outside frames her crying behind the window panes looking at him leaving for ever. The recurring image of the heroine in *Madame X*, looking at the rain from behind the window of the mansion in which she is sadly alone, comes to mind; or the final scene of the much analysed *Stella Dallas*. This famous window scene, in King Vidor's version (1937), is shot from behind Stella's shoulders, with Stella (Barbara Stanwyck) outside the room and not a prisoner in it. In spite of this, the window is again a screen, a barrier, through which she observes her beloved daughter's marriage. Stella's final position is identifiable with the spectator's look.

Madame X, played by Lana Turner, was instead the passive object of the camera, and her desperate gaze was the foreboding of her subsequent downfall. Not by chance, like many heroines in contemporary melodramatic novels, she does not have a name, and after the parenthesis of her brilliant marriage, she will re-enter anonymity. Kelly, like her, is a prisoner behind the window panes, and her situation is not too different. In this case the objective shot is tied to the neutral language of television 'realism' and to the instrumental diegetic hook; the sentimental leading tune of the serial brings the emotions to a climax at command and stops them to defer the closure to the next programme. The still of Kelly's face in tears freezes the viewer's feelings in a metanarrative twist that ensures that the emotions can continue while at the same time breaking 'realistic' rules. It suggests a gallery of similar images built on the long memory of this icon: the tragedy of the loss of love in the life of a woman.

Towards the end of *Dynasty*, there was a long sequence intended to recall Fallon's memory of a distant dramatic episode in her childhood. The allusion to a similar sequence in Hitchcock's film *Marnie* cannot be mistaken, with the dramatic use of the flashback to reach the same hidden truth: the mother's lover has been killed by the child herself rather than by her mother, as was suspected. A close comparison between these two texts, apart from signalling the change in genre towards the end of this soap and paying homage to one of its forerunners, is extremely helpful when studying similarities and differences between the two languages. The same motif is taken up in the search for the roots of Kimberley's mental illness in a 1995 episode of *Melrose Place*, but it seemed to me to have been done in a much less conscious way.

There have been similar icons in British soaps. In its early stages, *Eastenders* found a leitmotif in Angie Watts' despair over her failed marriage, and the failure coursed through many programmes and quite a few narrative twists. The numerous close shots of Angie in the upstairs room above the pub, crying with a glass in her hand or hoarding pills for her planned suicide, were a contrast with the pub full of people and animation, where Angie appeared smiling and controlled.[24] In the same serial Michelle, a young unmarried mother, after agonising (with the whole of the British audience) over whether she should make a marriage of convenience with Lofty, decides not to do it (not this time, anyway) in a memorable scene at the church. Even more memorable is the scene in which, having to meet him to explain her behaviour, she arranges the empty room carefully and maniacally for the site of rejection.

The paranoid state in soap is nearly always linked either to the loss of love or to the impossibility of accepting it, and its subsequent displacement in alcohol or drugs. Single parenthood, belonging to the wrong family (in the interminable familiar feuds) or to the wrong social group are possible variations. These are some of the conditions for which the enclosed room becomes the space of paranoia, the non-place for the self, the space for the other: the other (invariably a he) is not there, so the room is the setting for his absence.

In *The Bold and the Beautiful,* paranoid Sheila has a room upstairs for her mad soliloquies, and one in the basement, a space for torture, where she keeps her enemies (usually men threatening and at the same time attracting her) in chains and develops her plots. It is not a simple return to the stereotyped vision of women's loneliness, but rather its dark side.

Luce Irigaray asks: 'What is place? Shape? Matter? Interval between the two?', a matter and a form, in which to wed the other 'to infinity', but the reply is:

> This would be so for both masculine and feminine if the split between them (in the division of both work and nature) were bridged. But it can be bridged only by passing back through the definition of place and of the singular situation of the sexes in relation to place.[25]

Further on, she links it to the impossibility of a woman placing herself as an object for herself, and therefore for the love of self. She cannot see herself in a place, but only from inside, 'a place of passage, and its movement'.[26]

The other woman

As important, and interesting, in this discourse is the space of two women together. The recurrence of the image of two women – mothers and daughters, sisters, friends, colleagues or assistants, enemies and rivals – is a specific motif of television domestic drama, more so than of other kinds of popular fiction. If we were trying to trace the woman's gaze in the televisual text and its pleasure, we could examine the space between women on the screen as the narrative inscription of this gaze. The movement between sameness and difference is particularly explored in the pair of confronting females, in all its nuances, from solidarity to tenderness and protection, and from tension and rebellion to hostility and hatred.

The privileged liaison is mother and daughter, or anyway women belonging to two generations. In a crucial scene in *Eastenders*, the chain extended to three and even four, with Michelle discussing with her grandmother and mother her right to choose the way to give birth to her child. Here women's presence was expressed in a relatedness that varied from tenderness to tension, and sometime opposition, or simply to their bodies and voices held together by the camera. Scenes of mutual solidarity between mothers and daughters have been frequent in both *Brookside* and *Eastenders*, underlining the crises in the heroines' lives. This mostly positive picture does not find a correspondence in American soaps, where a varied spectrum between tenderness and antagonism in the mother–daughter relationship can be found.

The relation between women in the same age group can also be marked by rivalry, opposition and hostility. The traditional motif of the opposition between the good and the bad woman reappears here. This trait, present in mythical narration and fables, has become the mark of the variegated genre literature that is behind soap opera, from melodrama and sentimental novels to the gothic and noir, right up to the popular women's romance of recent years.

Enmity is mostly expressed through the gaze; the gaze was certainly female in *Dynasty* due to the recurrent 'duels' in gazing between Alexis and Krystle, Alexis and Dominique, Alexis and every other woman in the serial, including her own daughter and rival Amanda; *Dallas* was only a modest follower. Love and ambition are invariably the most frequent motives of the hostility in today's soaps as well. Day-time soaps have not been far behind; often, as with the relationship between Nina and her mother in *All My Children*, the hostility between two women is not necessarily tied to the opposition good–bad.

In *The Bold and the Beautiful*, the confrontation is always and only between two women; the male figures who are at the centre of their hostility or rivalry are mere pawns. The motif of incest runs through the series, and the men in the Forrester family seem always to be involved with one another's women, but they never engage in a male confrontation; they are rather the object of a female competition. The rivalry between the brothers, Ridge and Thorn, over Caroline was always secondary to the one between her and Brooke. The female duality, even more than in other cases, is inhabited here by different women constantly shifting, though Stephanie confronting Brooke is a fixed icon of the serial.[27] The matriarch Stephanie Forrester was first the rival of Brooke's mother, and then of all the wives and lovers of her sons and of her ex-husband. Finally, there has been the opposition of every woman in the serial to Sheila, the dark lady of the series, an exceedingly evil character always involved in murderous plots. In the spring of 1995 she disappeared from the series as her wickedness had come to a dead end but not for long.

Once a series starts spinning towards crime and noir there is no limit to it.

Tele-novelas occupy a remarkable place with their strong, fierce women expressing their strength above all when confronted with the other woman. Veronica Castro has played many roles as the great opposer of the wicked woman, in a line transcending the barriers of this or that novela. Sometimes it is a sort of necessary syntactical twist defying the narrative logic, as for instance in the case of *The Rich Also Cry,* where the fierce enmity between two women in the first part of the novela melts into friendship.

Cherríe Moraga speaks of the sense of betrayal between women and again relates it to the mother–daughter relationship. She speaks of her desperate and impossible need for the exclusive love of her mother, who always put her husband and brother first. Any Chicano woman is a betrayer to her race if she does not put the man first of all; and in doing so, she betrays her own daughter, the other woman. It is a sort of perverse chain that is present even in mythical history. '*Traitor begets traitor.* Malinche betrayed her own race by aiding Cortez as she had been betrayed by her own mother.'[28] It is this myth of the inherent unreliability of women, our natural propensity for treachery, which has been carved into the very bones of Mexican/Chicano collective psychology.

In 'Love of Same, Love of Other', Irigaray analyses the reason why love among women is a matter of rivalry, going back to Freud:

> Does this mean that love of the mother among women can and may be practiced through substitution? By a taking the place of? Which is unconsciously colored by hate? . . . The competition equally paralyzes love among sister-women. Because they strive to achieve the post of the *unique one: the mother of mothers*, one might say.[29]

The most perfect shape love can take for Freud is the one of mother for son and vice-versa, the prototype of the relation of the god incarnate in the feminine. This is why the configuration of love among women is mute, in latency, in abeyance. According to Irigaray, women prove to be the worst enemies of themselves when they accept the indifferentiated state, the magma, 'a sameness that is not their own', out of which only the competition emerges to occupy a place or space: 'It is still not another woman who is loved but merely the place she occupies, that she creates, and that must be taken away from her, rather than respected.' She stresses the necessity for women to establish a love that is both maternal and filial, in a female whole that is never closed-off, 'a path into infinity that is always open, in-finite'.[30]

The movement between sameness and difference is essential also in the solidarity among women. Female bonding recurs in another genre, the female police series. The best example came from *Cagney and Lacey*, in which the two police women were constantly expressing reciprocal support through looks and words at the most unlikely moments, but also through bodily touch. Other instances in the genre were to be found in *Cassie and Company* and even in the much maligned *Charlie's Angels*, where the solidarity among the 'angels' was no less important than their subordination to Charlie, the absent male.[31]

This confrontation and closeness between women – whether it is hostility or solidarity – shows the complexity of a relationship that in an earlier moment had seemed clear and 'natural'. The complexity is there, inside and outside fiction. It also involves the relation of the woman spectator to the woman on the screen through a series of mirror images: the gaze recreates the difficult relationship to the other woman, in the recurrence of the images of mothers and daughters, sisters and friends, enemies and rivals. The relation to the other becomes relation to the self, while autobiography becomes vision and fantasy. The same as other is known and familiar, yet at the same time hidden, mysterious, unknown, 'uncanny'.

Serial narratives: female or male?

At this point I wish to return to the odd couple, gender and genre, in serial fiction. There has always been the assumption that soap opera, and all that goes with it (melodramatic, sentimental or domestic fiction) is a female genre, just as thrillers, adventure and action stories are predominantly associated with male identities. As Charlotte Brunsdon says, 'women have been targeted by the makers of soap opera, women have been investigated as the viewers of soap opera, and the genre is widely and popularly believed to be feminine, despite stubborn evidence that it is not only women who watch'.[32]

More than the audience, it is the soap opera consistent aesthetics, variously defined as the melodramatic mode (Christine Gledhill) or the melodramatic imagination (Ien Ang), that contributes to its female specificity. The elements I have examined previously in this chapter characterise a definite aesthetic mode. The horizontal, repetitive pace of the plot, the circularity of the structure, marked by the open format and the lack of closure, the absence of a preferred point of view and of authorial markers (such as the voice over, for instance), are some of its distinctive traits.[33] The characters do not make a claim for continuity, whether temporal, psychological, or even physiognomical; space and time hardly have any reference to our industrialised notion of regular, logical progression. The cuts between one shot and another, especially in tele-novelas, are not syntactically marked by any sort of stop; they are sudden and unexpected, within a temporal rhythm that is normally dilated and diluted to an unbelievable degree.

The formal and structural coherence regulating these representations of love and hate, of victory and defeat, is striking. It seems all unified and glossed in the same soft pink that touches the unblemished peachy cheeks of the beautiful heroine, whether it is Nola in *The Guiding Light,* or Taylor and Brooke in *The Bold and the Beautiful,* occasionally interrupted by a shade of dark amber in the case of the tele-novela stars.

In spite of this apparent uniformity, there have always been differences within the format.[34] British soap opera, from the start, occupied a peculiar position. Its heroines and heroes displayed much less glamorous and impeccable looks; its 'structure of feeling' was tied to a documentary style of representation, owing much to an iconography of the urban working class, either Northern or Cockney, with its alternation of houses, pubs, launderettes, cafés and shops. The fragmentary structure, typical of the genre, was characterised in Britain by a combination of high and popular techniques, increasingly becoming a characteristic of editing right across the genre. This less glamorous, more down-to-earth universe, dominated by everyday events, by gossip, by the ties of family, friends and neighbourhood, was inspired by a realist literary and filmic British tradition.

This peculiarity was accentuated by successive developments. *Brookside* and *Eastenders* soon gave more space to men and young people, and to independent, strong female characters. Gay characters moved in and became outstanding in a mode rarely to be found in American soaps or television movies. Important issues such as Aids, homosexuality and rape slowly made their way into soaps and television movies, but had a more problematic, less sensational character in the British versions (in the mid-nineties, even *Eastenders* and *Brookside* have respectively introduced hired killers and incest). Race has always been the main difference between the productions in the two countries: practically absent from the American productions (at least as an issue) it was a very prominent feature in the British productions and from early on.[35]

In the nineties the shifts in genres and gender definitions have stretched much further. Soap opera, as such, in spite of its apparent immobility through the decades, has overflown its own confines, and in its pure form has become more peripheral within women's fiction. Day-time soaps still go on, but prime time is invaded by the television movie, which has appropriated many soap opera devices and languages while responding to the increasing demand for hybrid real-life fictions: works of fantasy interpreted by actors and using all the technologies of fiction are at the same time based on real events. This indeed is the main advertising caption to attract viewers – 'a story based on true facts' – and the narrative is punctuated by intermittent titles dramatically anchoring it to specific times and places. Soap opera's viewing is declining probably because it cannot compete without this added spice: the fictionalisation of reality. In the meantime *ER*, the excellent NBC series based on the hyper-realistic frenzied routine of the emergency ward in Chicago main hospital, shows that a romantic view of hyper reality is reentering the scene. One of its episodes, broadcast in Spring 1995 and directed by Donna Deitch, shows one glorious evening in which all the women in the hospital, from nurses to doctors, dominate the accelerated and anguished rhythms of the emergency ward in a triumph of harmony and rewards that is almost like a dance – if I remember rightly it ends with a dance.

Otherwise, prime time is occupied by serial fiction that is a contamination of various genres but still keeps some of the features of soap opera. For shows like *Moonlighting* (actually begun in the mid-eighties, in competition with *Remington Steele*), *Law and Order*, *ER*, and particularly *Twin Peaks* and *The X Files*, it would be difficult to name a genre, or a gender, or even consider them a variation of one. The pastiche soap/crime (and crime/romantic comedy, or fantasy/horror/thriller . . . like Polonius, we could go on and on) has become more and more frequent as soap operas develop and decline. The ambiguity extends to gender, and a good example is *Melrose Place*, one of the few prime time soaps left; it is lurid and sensational, but is it male or female?

Ien Ang and Jon Stratton make a strong case for a transformation in soap opera that they relate to the transition from modernity to postmodernity, and from a realist to a post-realist aesthetics. They argue this extensively, analysing the Australian soap *Chances*: 'what makes *Chances* different is that it opens itself up to what in the fictional worlds of *Neighbours* and *A Country Practice* is constructed as radically excessive, and therefore either excluded or contained'.[36] The category of radical excess has been considered fundamental to the aesthetics of melodrama by Peter Brooks and others, and soap opera from the start has given expression and space to this element. The passage from *Dallas* to *Dynasty* was a first move in the direction indicated by Ang and Stratton.

The BBC situation comedy of the early nineties, *Absolutely Fabulous*, is a very interesting example of a shift in female narrative. The variation is on a genre that in the USA has always found space for women-oriented shows, from *I Love Lucy* and *The Mary Tyler Moore Show* to *Cybill, Murphy Brown, Roseanne* and *Grace Under Fire*. In *Absolutely Fabulous*, the two friends who are at its centre, Edina (Jennifer Saunders, who is also the writer) and Patsy (Joanna Lumley), offer a strong counterstatement to female stereotyping. They are always excessive in their dedication to drinking and smoking, in their flouting of all conventions, in their posture and appearance: they are ludicrous but at the same time fabulously independent.

More noticeable transformations have found their way into the crime series, where the distinctive features are very different from those of soap. Here things are prevalently tied to a documentary style, to the very precise contemporaneity of an urban context, with constant references to the cinematic tradition, and to dominant male iconography. The emphasis is more on action, on the outside, on the relationships between men and the external world, although there has been some attention given to interpersonal relationships, especially male comradeship, as far back as *Starsky and Hutch*.

Within this convention, the introduction of women detectives was a significant break. It began with dependent women still protected by the boss or by the male colleague (whether in the office or by phone, as happened respectively for Pepper Anderson and the Angels), and arrived at autonomous women, often critical of the surrounding male milieu and very suspicious of authority (in most cases there is still a male boss), or preoccupied with the difficulties of being 'in charge' in a man's world.[37] Though the systemic structure of the genre was substantially unchanged – the symmetrical oppositions between legality and criminality, social order and chaos, conservative and subversive forces – there was nevertheless a slight shift in perspectives, caused by ambiguities, uncertainties and disorientating conflicts of loyalties that sometimes came close to subverting the rationale of the genre. The manichean atmosphere of classical Hollywood gave way to a chiaroscuro, and the final triumph of justice was often accompanied by an acid smile due to the unavoidable frustration of being a woman.

The tension between the public and the private, always present in police stories, became predominant; but it was on the conflict with the male-dominated environment that the emphasis was placed. This was accompanied by an accentuation of seriousness, moralism, and dedication to work, conferring on women the function of being super-egos for their male colleagues. The iconography of the series was altered: there was a stress on the inside shot, on dialogue, on close-ups, and less insistence on action and violence, although this was far from absent. Cagney's and Lacey's lives often got entangled with the cases they were handling as detectives, whether it was Lacey's maternal instinct or Cagney's inability to trust men. The camera observed the private and the public with a parallel close attention.[38] A step up in this direction has been Lynda La Plante's British series of the early nineties, *Prime Suspect*, with Helen Mirren as a police inspector investigating serial killings of women and getting personally and dangerously caught in the hunt.

The 'straight' police series was not left unchanged. *Hill Street Blues*, the American series of the mid-eighties, is a good example. While being a predominantly male series, it had moments when the emergence of female characters (Joyce with her resistance to marriage, Fay in her 'feminist' phase, and Lucy with her maternal instinct on the one hand and the problems of suddenly acquiring leadership in a male environment on the other) altered the quite powerful all-male paradigm of the series. More interesting than this, however, was the particular male pathos that dominated the series, as if the female aesthetics had spilled over and invaded other zones. This pathos came out in the multi-faceted relations among the men working in the district (sometimes reverberating on men in the outside world, as in the case of Mick and his youthful admirers), all summarised in the relation of each of them to the father-boss, Captain Furillo. The fundamental icon of the series is his seriously concerned face opposing that of one or two of his men, in alternate shots: a recurring close-up in a crowd of long shots encompassing different plots and events through quick, sharp camera moves.

It is not surprising that what has been defined as the first progressive police series (and since then Stephen Bochco has moved to bolder expressions and styles) is also the one that works most seriously and determinedly on the construction of a male ethos while questioning the stereotypes of masculinity. Its careful delineation of atmosphere produces a subtle 'feeling', and not only alongside the bursts of activity and subsequent violence that are the trade mark of most crime series. If I were to define its 'structure of feeling' as Ien Ang did for *Dallas* and Terry Lovell did for *Coronation Street*,[39] I would term it 'sentimental maleness'. While reaffirming the police series as a male genre, it involved a distinctly softer edge and gestured towards the femininisation of a male paradigm.

NYPD Blue, its successor, follows on this line only partly, as the all-male look is more dominant in this cop story of the nineties. But it does confirm the male pathos (at times nearly 'sick') and moves even closer to the Chandleresque prototype of the defeated, clumsy detective. Its real novelty is in the exhibition of male nudity rather than female, in particular of Andy Sipovicz who cannot be described as thin and glamorous. The role is interpreted by Dennis Frantz, more marginally present in the first series, and his clumsy body with its illnesses and shortcomings gets full relief. The female cops are more peripheral than in *Hill Street Blues* and impersonate women with problems, either alcoholism or drugs, or embarassing family secrets, all preventing them from being fully efficient police officers.

Genre and gender conventions have been shifting, and audience specificities are not so neat either. Even when the male style is unfaltering, the viewing figures inform us that a 'male' series can be watched by nearly as many women as men, and sometimes more. This also applies the other way round to soap opera, or at least up to a point. In this female enclave, which seemed to be such a clear-cut case for the gender-specificity of its audience, it has been discovered that, though women usually represented the majority of viewers, men were not too far behind. In the second episode of his film *Caro diario,* Nanni Moretti effectively shows that men do watch soap opera (at least in Italy). This happens against the dramatic background of the volcano Stromboli, with his male friend pushing him to ask – actually to shout to, because of the distance – some American tourists for the latest in *The Bold and the Beautiful.*

The fall of genre boundaries was eased and suggested by more active viewing conditions, by the collage and the causal superimposition resulting from zapping. Videotape recording and other technologies have offered new modes of viewing and widened the spectrum, leading to the creation of a new type of seriality, to the construction of different kinds of flow, to a personal collage based on an aesthetics of fragmentation and excess. In these new modes the suspended circular narrativity of soap opera invades the thriller, and enigma enters the claustrophobic rooms of soaps.

The female visual continuum

Women's narratives on the screen have created a sort of continuum and constituted a space that has been occupied by a crowd of wives (from those of Hollywood to the less glamorous ones of northern working-class England or of the American Midwest), of single or married barmaids, of scheming or innocent mistresses, of 'spinsters', of powerful, independent business women (who can also be black, like Dominique in *Dynasty*). This space was further supplemented by a range of homely or ruthless women detectives, single or married, working alone or in pairs. They have inhabited the imaginary of women, as dream and fiction, but also as part of reality (in comparison, confrontation, identification, or therapy): a bodily extension on the domestic screen of needs and desires; everyday life as the site of the textual performance; a narrative linking reality and fiction, inside and outside, conscious and subconscious.

In the mid-nineties most of these images have gone sour. Cagney and Lacey appear now occasionally in evening movies: they are middle-aged and not any thinner (yes, glamorous Cagney as well), and their running after criminals, pistol in hand, requires a stronger suspension of disbelief. They are harsh and loud, and smile less:

Cagney, still single and in search of a partner, suffers from the prejudice inherent in her situation; Lacey goes on battling with (by now weary) family problems. Promotions (entailing a personal room, a better car) are short lived or fail to materialise. They fight with their colleagues in a much tougher way and sometime use macho insults. Even their reciprocal support and friendship is thorny and difficult, and often on the verge of vanishing.

However, the television movie in which all this happens (*Internal Affairs*) opens with a disquieting close shot of a female androgynous face recalling one of Kathryn Bigelow's female cops, only less glamorous, more disquieting: an airy shot of a being not quite of this world. Once the narrative starts, we realise that she was the coroner performing the autopsy of a murdered man, an autopsy shown in close, shocking detail during the titles. We never see this asexual thin, tall creature again; instead the narrative moves to Cagney's and Lacey's two unwieldy bodies in baggy clothes or loud colours: a sharp voluntary contrast that is probably a historical, and quite pitiless, look by television at itself, from one format to another, from one generation of women to another, from a language grounded in reality to a technological computerised language in which women like Agent Dana Scully in *The X Files* are the sure link between the sensible world of science and technology (she is both a doctor and extremely competent in electronic languages) and an extra-psychic, or extra-terrestrial, universe. Where are the routines and rhythms of everyday life? Where now are the kitchens that have been a fixed point of many soap operas, especially the British versions (though they were not absent in the North American ones)?

Once more, film provides a model. The obvious one is Maggie Turner, the police cop interpreted by Jamie Lee Curtis, in Bigelow's *Blue Steel* (1989). She is pitched between male and female in her marvellously androgynous look and in her ambivalent relationship with the phallus-like symbolic gun, always present in her sexual encounters. Maggie is sometimes threatened by a gun, but more often is holding one. She chose to be a cop because she likes shooting but like the maniac assassin who is her counterpart does not dislike to be on the passive end; he is the only one, though, who reaches the *jouissance* of being shot by her. In its sometimes naive insistence on this allegorical structure and on its sado-masochistic innuendos (her name is carved on the bullets the assassin uses; the colour of violence – blue steel – invades her face and uniform), the film pointedly goes beyond masculine and feminine roles and challenges one of the main conventions of the genre. There is a prolonged frame, reminiscent of the titles of an old television female cop series (in this case the model is television, and the circle is closed), in which she slowly puts on her uniform, piece by piece; but whereas the series (*Juliet Bravo*) described the gradual superimposition of one role on to another in well-ordered shots, this dressing-up leads to no resolution whatsoever: this female cop, faced by the internal 'blues' of violence, will be unable to unravel the enigma, right up to a disconsolate ending.

The X Files itself is a crossing between a surreal series of the seventies and a cop story, though here the cops are not police or private detectives, but FBI agents, mostly antagonistic to the force. Fantasy, horror, thriller and detection intermingle here, producing a result that is not a simple addition of *Twilight Zone* and *The Untouchables*, but a cult programme of the nineties. It is seen by many as a follower of the 'genre' that *Twin Peaks* inaugurated (and of its cult popularity), and in many ways is a continuation of its disquieting capacity of moving on borders.

The show proves that the distinction between a male and a female series is difficult to establish. The blurring of the frontier has gone even further in this futuristic series: the two agents here are male and female. Like Cagney and Lacey their bond is strong and isolates them from the other FBI agents, but unlike them (and in spite of the gender difference) their roles are interchangeable. At first they seem to occupy contrasting spaces: Scully the rational, tough, level-headed one; Fox Mulder a dreamy, pensive, sad man, more inclined to accept the existence of other forces and worlds. In the end we realise that weaknesses, uncertainties and defeatism belong to both, and so does their capacity to connect to other worlds.

Popular television has gone some way – though not too far – from the time in which 'she' would invariably be saved by 'him' in the nick of time. Undecidability has further engulfed the gender distinction while at the same time self-consciously repeating and quoting the difference.

Chapter 4

Hybrid Fictions . . .

This chapter focuses on feminist literary theory and practices in their junction with other strands in the thought of modernity. I have looked at the encounter of feminism with postmodernism and psychoanalysis, referring to a range of issues, common to the three areas, and yet different in the specific reverberation they have in contemporary works of fiction by women. Re-reading as a practice of re-appropriation, the notion of deferral, the overcoming of a binary logic, the decline of the metaphysics of presence and of a stable subjectivity: these are some of the features common to such critical modes.

The debate on difference and sexual identities is here referred to that on the separatedness of the canon and to the uncertain passage between modernism and postmodernism crossing women's writing from the mid-century onwards. Finally I analyse the dialectics of story and history, past and present, mothers and fathers, and the juxtaposition of reality with worlds of the second and third degree in some contemporary novels by Toni Morrison, Jeanette Winterson, Angela Carter and others.

Feminism, postmodernism and psychoanalysis: an itinerary

[T]here are currently three kinds of thinking that best present (and represent) our own time 'apprehended in thought': psychoanalysis, feminist theory and postmodern philosophy. (Jane Flax)

In the controversial relation between feminism and postmodernism, lately it has been the *and* dividing, or uniting, them that has been put in question, for it might indicate a complicity, an addition, a simple juxtaposition. It would be more accurate to substitute it with 'intertwining', 'crossing', 'antagonising', 'including' or 'excluding': all of this has been true at one point. Jennifer Wicke and Margaret Ferguson, in their introduction to *Feminism and Postmodernism*, say that 'the neutrality of the *and* covers a multitude of critical questions and fierce debates' and argue at length that the relationship between the two terms goes beyond a binary relation.[1] If they were turned into characters, we could write a novel of manners or, more likely, a post-stream-of-consciousness novel, with Chinese boxes opening up on to a vista of variables and shifts, and on to many debates. It would be a superb novel and very suited to the end of the century and the millennium. Mary Russo imaginatively captures this in what she calls the carnival of feminist theory: 'This has included all manner of textual travesty, "mimetic rivalry," semiotic delinquency, parody, teasing, posing, flirting, masquerade, seduction, counter-seduction, tightrope walking, and verbal aerialism of all kinds.'[2] The genre here moves from novel to spectacle, with the staging of the 'play' between the poetics of feminism and postmodernism. It is a sort of dance, and dance by no chance is a recurrent topos in the present feminist imaginary, in the same way as – to go back to Russo's 'aerialists' – flying and flight, wings and angels are. Or else it is a conversation.

Of such a conversation speaks Jane Flax in her book *Thinking Fragments*, a conversation within and among psychoanalysis, feminist theory and postmodern philosophy, joined together in the confrontation with issues of self, gender, knowledge and power. These three strands of thought can best present (and represent) the climate of 'change, uncertainty, ambivalence' of our own time but none of them, taken singularly, responds adequately to all of these issues: 'Any theory that is blind to or erases one or more of these issues is less and less satisfactory. Unfortunately, I have also become increasingly convinced that psychoanalysis, feminist theories, and postmodernism are each partially constituted by and through precisely such blindnesses and erasures.'[3] These three modes are 'fragments in a fragmenting culture' (p. 6): the conversation among them can – through 'blindnesses' and 'erasures' – provide the subjective and intersubjective space that (according to Jane Flax) each of them on their own lacks. She interrogates postmodernism and psychoanalysis from the standpoint of feminist theory, and devotes a substantial space to her reservations in the conclusion to the book, though remaining attentive to the positive and fruitful aspects of the confrontation.

The importance of the reciprocal links has been variously stressed in feminist theory, and I have discussed this elsewhere in this book, but always with the caution that postmodern philosophies and theories hardly ever take women into account, except for appropriation. The sense of crisis pervading them is still the crisis of Western man: 'Postmodernists too often ignore or obscure the nonlinguistic aspects of humans – hence the many important ways that gender and other social relations and internal psychic life structure speakers and narrative-linguistic forms are rendered invisible by and within postmodernist stories.'[4]

The contradictory relations between these two fields are further complicated by the confrontation of each of these modes of thought with literature, creating hybrid modes founded on an impossibility. The contested field is mainly literary criticism. I have already pointed out that Gayatri Spivak, who defines herself as 'feminist and deconstructionist', creates a parallel between woman and literary analysis: the latter is not a progression towards a final truth but rather an itinerary indicating the impossibility of finding it.[5]

Jerry Aline Flieger speaks of another troublesome trio involved in a complex web of love-hate relationships. She remarks on the natural alliance that seem to unite a humanist philosophy (or ideology as she says) like feminism to psychoanalysis and to literature and the arts, in spite of much suspicion and subsequent attempts at ghettoising it from traditional literary criticism. The relation between literature and psychoanalysis is reciprocal: 'the psychoanalytic master narrative of love and murder has looked to literature for its inspiration, imagery and even its technique. For Freud himself, of course, is an accomplished storyteller, able to involve his reader in the psychoanalytic detective story, the search for the answer to the riddle of the sphinx.'[6]

In a temporary conclusion, I should like to go back to Flax's insistence on blindness and erasure as the substance of this relationship *à trois*: the hidden and the repressed have been crucial in modernist thought and philosophy, from Freud and Lacan to Heidegger and Derrida, but it is important to underline that feminist theory has appriopriated these elements and made them the basis of their analyses. Lack, absence, emptiness become constitutive of the female essence (or rather, non-essence): while they say this word, they erase it. In *Speculum*, Luce Irigaray defines it as 'lack, fault or mime', an inversion of the subject, from which an excess, an upturning of that logic can come: *'how can a girl be conceived? Except by a chromosomal anomaly?* In any case she couldn't lay claim to any substance. Merely added to – or taken away from – essence, fortuitous, troublesome, "accidental", she can be modified or eliminated without changing anything in "nature".'[7]

La lectrice, or the re-reading of difference

Where is she? Activity/Passivity Sun/Moon Culture/Nature Day/Night
Mother/Father Head/Heart Intelligible/Palpable Logos/Pathos
Form, convex, step, advancing, seed, progress.
Matter, concave, ground – where steps are taken, ground of harvest and debris.

Man
Woman

(Hélène Cixous)

The antithesis stands.
I am
the sun and the moon and forever hungry
the sharpened edge
where day and night shall meet and not be
one.

(Audre Lorde)

Feminist critical theory has moved from a renewed attention to women's literature, and from the vast area that had been ignored or neglected within that, to the encounter with other critical modes, and to a new look at old objects through the practice of reading and re-reading. Adrienne Rich, in a much quoted passage from 'When We Dead Awaken', has spoken of the necessity of revision for women, of understanding the assumptions they are framed by in order to know themselves: 'Revision – the act of looking back, of seeing with fresh eyes, of entering an old text from a new critical direction – is for women more than a chapter in new cultural history; it is an act of survival.'[8]

Women's fresh vision turns to listening in the opening line of *An Atlas of the Difficult World*, a sort of dedication framing the poems in the eponymous collection:

> A dark woman, head bent, listening for something
> – a woman's voice, a man's voice or
> voice of the freeway, night after night, metal streaming downcoast
> past eucalyptus, cypress, agribusiness empires

Perhaps the same woman is at the centre of the trans-historical memory flowing through the sections of *Eastern War Time*, 'a woman wired in memory . . . forbidden to forget', an iterative presence in the many locations of sorrow and destruction of our age.

> I am a woman standing in line for gasmasks
> I stand on a road in Ramallah   with naked face   listening
> I am standing here in your poem   unsatisfied
> lifting my smoky mirror[9]

Barbara Christian, thinking of Foucault's 'Fantasia of the Library', imagines substituting the male reader of that essay with a female reader who will occupy a different space: 'her reading would be seen as time away from her main work. Interruptions would be normal and she would likely be reinterpreting the book she is reading without even being aware of it, reinventing herself in the midst of patriarchal discourse, as to who she is supposed to be.'[10]

Catherine Belsey and Jane Moore, in their introduction to *The Feminist Reader*, see in the practice of reading a privileged site of feminist struggle: 'For the feminist reader there is no innocent or neutral approach to literature: all interpretation is political. Specific ways of reading inevitably militate for or against the process of change.'[11] Literature becomes the object of a new look observing how women and gender relations are represented, how sex difference is defined. Re-reading means re-qualifying, making specific and idiosyncratic the obvious, the taken for granted, the neutral.

Jane Miller, in *Seductions*, proposes a feminine and feminist re-reading of other readings: 'Reading and rereading are method and substance here . . . Feminist readings do not displace other readings, or settle once and for all the meaning and value of texts. As they challenge readings which suppress women, they must also coexist and contend with such readings, even borrow from them.'[12] The title of the book refers to the seduction that these readings operate on women, 'the daughter's seductions' by such fathers as Raymond Williams, Mikhail Bakhtin, Frantz Fanon and others.

Beyond the deconstruction of an intellectual itinerary, which frequently is not only individual but of a specific group, such readings have led to radical re-interpretations and re-elaboration. The contribution made by women's critical studies to psychoanalysis, postmodernism and new historicism, and by women's recent re-reading of such thinkers as Jacques Derrida, Michel Foucault and Jacques Lacan, is in many ways a feminist reply and a re-appropriation of the major critical strands of recent years. Revision is a crucial constituent of a female critical voice and anticipates analogous movements of 'deferring' in postmodernism.

At the beginning of the seventies a group of works offered a feminist re-reading of famous literary authors and texts, Shakespeare and Lawrence among them. Germaine Greer, Eva Figes and Kate Millett observed male writing with a polemical eye, displacing it from its secure 'un-differentiated' niche; as Olga Kenyon says, their vision was considered 'a sort of anomaly, a proper mutation'.[13] It was the first attempt at an organised critique of a literary canon that had long been considered untouchable, and at the same time the expression of an angry mood.

Ten years later, moving from Mill's famous sentence in *The Subjection of Women,* Elaine Showalter started her search for a specifically feminine tradition of writing, a line made of continuity and innovation, heredity and breaks, of minor and unacknowledged writers beside those that had already entered 'the great tradition'. She saw English female writers from the Brontës onwards as part of a literary subculture, with its own values and conventions, experiences and attitudes, in spite of the lack of a conscious historical continuity and of the self-isolation of the individual writers. She was not alone in her task: Sandra Gilbert and Susan Gubar worked in the same direction, specifically on a revision of the nineteenth-century canon, which had either excluded women or considered them artists whose aesthetics had to be placed above gender identity. In partial contrast with Showalter's continuity, they put their emphasis on the necessity for women to rebel against the preceding tradition in order to build their literary 'subculture': 'women writers, longing to attempt the pen, have longed to escape from the many-faceted glass coffins of the patriarchal texts.'[14]

This put an end to a falsely neutral canon, that either ignored women or assimilated them into men, but opened an interminable debate on the dangers of separateness and its complexity. In underlining the male nature of the canon and women's exclusion from it, the work of these critics poses the question of whether it is possible, or even desirable, simply to include the feminine. Women's estrangement – women as an adjunct body, a monstrous resistant addition – might be preferable. Whether an autonomous space is claimed, or whether women are strong enough to exist as part of a whole, the canon will never be the same; from inside or outside, the 'difference' will mutate its values and features.

The question becomes more complex for black feminist critics, for whom canon formation has been a troubling dilemma as they had to fight against a double bias, as Beverly Guy-Shetfall says: 'Women's studies courses . . . focused almost exclusively upon the lives of white women. Black studies, which was much too often male-dominated, also ignored Black women.'[15] Barbara Christian echoes this perplexity and others in her accumulation of adjectives: 'What is a literary critic, a black woman critic, a black feminist literary critic, a black feminist social literary critic?'[16]

In the meantime, the debate on the canon was dividing white feminism as well. In *Sexual/Textual Politics*, Toril Moi takes up her position against essentialist theories, directing her critique to the feminist critics who claim a separate literature and tradition, and to their defence of a realist language. In Julia Kristeva's wake, she operates a deconstruction of rigid binary oppositions. She criticises Sandra Gilbert and Susan Gubar for confusing female, feminine and feminist literature in *The Madwoman in the Attic*, and Elaine Showalter for her notion of a unitary identity, and for her opposition to modernism and the avant-garde. The traditional humanism of that first position within feminist literary theories, which she extends to Patricia Stubbs and Marcia Holly, seems to her part of patriarchal ideology with its notion of an integrated subject, without conflicts, contradictions or ambiguities. 'In this humanist ideology the self is the *sole author* of history and of the literary text: the humanist creator is potent, phallic and male – God in relation to his world, the author in relation to his text.'[17]

Moi refers to Showalter's criticism of the use of a mobile, pluralist point of view in Virginia Woolf's and Doris Lessing's novels, particularly the presence of a subjectivity dispersed in androgyny in the former or in a wide collective conscience in the latter. Woolf's great merit for Moi is precisely what she calls her 'deconstructive' writing, her free play of signifiers, the refusal of a unified and final meaning. Ultimately, she accuses Showalter of re-affirming that distinction between experimentalism and tradition that has been at the centre of a long feminist debate.

The distinction between formal innovation and revolutionary aims is advocated in some of the essays in *Women's Writing in Exile*. In their introduction, the two editors propose a re-revision of the canon, polemicising white liberal feminism for adopting new forms while accepting old contents, and for failing to confront racism, ethnocentrism, elitism and heterosexism.[18] The collection is a very interesting attempt to look at female modernism, but it runs the risk of echoing an old debate of the twenties on social realism and the avant-garde, artificially separating form and content, politics and arts. One of the specific contributions of feminism is precisely the overcoming of such dichotomies. On the other hand, moralism and conservativism are the dangers of 'political correctness' too.

Virginia Woolf has been at the centre of feminist debates in other ways as well. Her novel *Orlando* gave literary substance to the theory of coexistence of masculine and feminine in human beings, and has been widely used as a pivot in the debate. This famous androgynous figure traces an emblematic itinerary of the movement back and forward from modernism to postmodernism. It is sufficient to look at two cinematic re-visitations of her novel, Sally Potter's *Orlando* (1992) and Ulrike Ottinger's *Freak Orlando* (1984). Potter's film, more directly inspired by Woolf's novel, already proposes a new nuance of difference in the image of the asexual angel singing at the beginning and the end of the film.

In *Migrancy, Culture, Identity*, Iain Chambers connects Benjamin's angel of history to the black and white angels that inhabit the fragmentary, dream-like cinema of Isaac Julien, and to Potter's angel, in a line leading to disquieting vistas, to a break-up of linear time and space:

The angels condense past, present and future. Under their gaze we find ourselves caught between the apparent ineluctability of time and its continual crisis . . . For the angels announce history as a perpetual becoming, an inexhaustible emerging, an eternal provocation, a desire that defies and trangresses the linear flow of historicist reason with the insistent now, the *Jetz*, of the permanent time of the possible.[19]

With Ottinger, the transcendence of the traditional gender boundaries moves to new vistas and new forms of representation. In her book *The Female Grotesque* Mary Russo comments:

> *Freak Orlando* is a far less conventional film than Potter's. It is much less centered on the main character . . . and on cross-gender identification as such, than on the ensembles of male, female, and male/female freaks who come together and disperse as couples, troupes, families, employees, workers, patients, fanatics, male flagellants, skinheads, heretics, vagrants, 'ugly' contestants, irate consumers, and carnival performers.[20]

This bizarre, heavily baroque picture does not speak of heavenly harmonies but moves towards an exploration of grotesque, hellish forms that are close to the monstrous shapes peopling some of the female fictional worlds.

The hybrid bird-woman who is the heroine of Angela Carter's *Nights at the Circus* is a kind of Orlando of the end of the century, journeying through countries and identities like her but differently from her traversing many diverse realms. She is both a freak and a strong independent being, but might at times recall an angel, pitched as she is between the natural and the supernatural, the human, the divine and the animal, the female and the male. To all these ambiguities she adds one more, being always on the verge of the angelical and the diabolical.

The itinerary traversing these images seems to follow the lines of the feminist debate on difference. An insistent, and sometimes intentionally paradoxical, enforcing of the notion of difference has been followed by the emphasis on margins, borders, thresholds; on de-centring and displacement. The female subject is defined by the shift between inside and outside, centre and margin. In this movement towards marginality it is possible to recognise the assonance with some postmodern positions, that can be summarised through linguistic markers: margins, borders, rhizome, nomadism, third space, living-in-between, hymens. The explosion of the margins and the implosion of the centre are due to the impact of other stories, of other voices, of off-centre presences. Crucial to this are the decentred and multiple ethnic identities characterising postcoloniality, and the fall of the boundary between organic and inorganic, human and artificial in cyberfeminism. In *La Jeune Née*, Cixous speaks of 'a bunch of new differences'.

> What today appears to be 'feminine' or 'masculine' would no longer amount to the same thing. No longer would the common logic of difference be organized with the opposition that remains dominant. Difference would be a bunch of new differences . . . But we are still floundering – with few exceptions – in Ancient History.[21]

This complex range of differences, though only in a utopian perspective, gestures towards an overcoming of any binary divide that in Woolf's novel was overturned but not erased.

A delicate passage

British diffidence towards experimentalism, linked to a sort of national antipathy for theory, delayed the incidence of postmodernism in feminist writing.[22] The seventies and the eighties on one hand saw the continuation of the great tradition of realistic or symbolic-naturalistic fiction, and on the other the beginning of writings linked to the first phase of the women's movement. In these works the themes of emancipation and liberation blend documentary with fiction, autobiography with fantasy, the denunciation of collective marginalisation with the search for individual identity.

Tales I Tell My Mother (1978), a collection of short stories and discussions, was produced by a feminist collective formed by the novelists Zoe Fairbarns, Michele Roberts, Sara Maitland and Valerie Miner, and by the poet and playwright Micheline Wandor. Both the fiction and the essays deal with sexual identities and writing, the new relations among women, the difficulty of continuing with old conceptions of love.[23] Love and its new geographies were the arguments of *Sex and Love* (1983), a collection of essays edited by Sue Cartledge and Joanna Ryan, and a sign of a diverse moment in which different individualities emerge. In other autobiographies, the history of the women's movement is joined to personal histories; for instance, in the track of Doris Lessing's *The Golden Notebook* (1962), a novel that has preceded and announced the movement.

In *Contemporary Women's Fiction*, Paulina Palmer notes that feminist criticism has mostly dealt with the male avant-garde or with female popular literature, neglecting novels historicising the women's movement like Elizabeth Wilson's *Hidden Agendas*.[24] The latter is a good example of a hybrid mode of writing. After some prose and critical writing, Wilson starts her creative writing with an autobiography, *Mirror Writing* (1982), where the picture of feminism in 1968 London is traversed by the search for her lesbian identity. Her subsequent novels, among which is *Prisons of Glass* (1990), still move in the space between fact and fiction.

In *Talking Back* (1989), bell hooks speaks of her attempt to write an autobiography as a way to reconcile fiction and her own past:

> I was compelled to face the fiction that is a part of all retelling, remembering. I began to think the work I was doing was both fiction and autobiography. It seemed to fall in the category of writing that Audre Lorde, in her autobiographically-based work *Zami*, calls bio-mythography . . . Autobiographical writing was a way for me to evoke the particular experience of growing up southern and black in segregated communities. It was a way to recapture the richness of southern black culture.[25]

This was so much more important for her as, in growing up, she lived in predominantly white communities.

Years before, Doris Lessing's *Memoirs of a Survivor* (1974) had adopted a surreal and allegorical mode, though being, in the author's words, 'an attempt at autobiography'.[26] The novel describes a dystopian future in which all known forms of civilisation crumble and collapse around the narrator shut in her room, suspended between the violent events seen out of the window on one side, and what happens beyond the wall (the world of memory) on the other. The window opens up on the barbaric world of outlaw youth bands which are the outsiders of that society and, at the same time, its only hope. Beyond the wall, instead, there is memory, the past, childhood, the oedipal triangle, the double; but there is also the making of history and in the end, in spite of all, the world of utopia.

The narrator, who at times is at one with the writer, observes and remembers the formation and the progress of an alternate ego, little Emily, in a complex web of past and future; Emily's life is told in a *continuum* with the kingdom of shadows behind the wall and the narrator is the mediating gaze: 'There she was enclosed in her age, but in a continuum with those scenes behind the wall, a hinterland which had formed her . . . From that shadowy region behind her came the dictate: You are this, and this and this' (p. 85). The gaze behind the window observes the various stages of a development that are both cultural and personal. The dog-cat Hugo, a pre-historical relic of the old humanitarian values of solidarity, tenderness and unselfish love, is the link between Emily and the narrator, a hybrid creature between worlds, both animal and human.

This dark and visionary novel seems very far from any feminist account but the feminist movement does re-appear in the all-girls' band that kidnaps Emily for a while; they are no different from the other youth bands except for their critique of male authority. The narrator describes them as efficient, tender and generous, but her tone is detached, impartial and unenthusiastic; in the same tone she speaks of the probable lesbian relationship between their leader, June, and Emily. This coldness may be directed towards the developments in the feminist movement, or simply be due to the caution that a violent transition requires. When she wonders why Emily, though possessing all the necessary qualities, has failed to become the commune leader, the reply is that she prefers to be the leader's woman, an old and discouraging reply for a woman of the future.

There was nothing to stop her. No law, written or unwritten, said she should not, and her capacities and talents were every bit as varied as Gerald's or anybody else's . . . The trouble was, she did love Gerald; and this longing for him, for his attention and notice, the need to be the one who sustained and comforted him, who connected him with the earth, who held him steady in her common sense and her warmth – this need drained her of the initiative she would need to be a leader of a commune. (pp. 98–9)

Soon after, non-committally she adds: 'This is a history, after all, and I hope a truthful one' (p. 99). It is difficult to understand from her tone what the narrator really hopes for: perhaps for her interpretation to be replaced by one speaking of female autonomy and ambitions.

By posing this open question on the immutability of women's condition, Lessing anticipates that blurring of the frontier between fiction and other modes of speech that is to be found in successive generations of novelists. *The Golden Notebook,* though containing reflections common to many feminist collectives of the sixties, had already made recourse to experimental devices such as metanarrative strategies, multiple personalities and a mixture of the critical and the fictional voice. Through the parody of feminine writing itself, she was expressing an implicit critique of the realistic novel, though being still enmeshed in it. *Memoirs of a Survivor* goes even farther in the presentation of these two parallel worlds, one sadly real and split into two zones, the other belonging to an oneiric, utopian world. They are at first in sharp opposition but soon become indistinguishable, in a dimension in which past, present and future are all one.

The use of experimental forms had already been present in novelists of earlier generations, like Zora Neale Hurston, Rosamond Lehmann, Jean Rhys, Djuna Barnes, Carson McCullers, and above all Jane Bowles (to whom I shall return). In novelists of later decades, it is possible to find the adoption of hybrid forms and languages, a delicate passage from the language of satirical realism (which has characterised much British narrative of the mid-century) to fantasy and surrealism. The jarring, morbid, horrific detail insinuates itself in the formal mode of the conversation novel, in the same way as metanarration enters the realistic novel, attracting attention to the creative process which later will become dominant.

In Iris Murdoch's fiction, for instance, subterranean spaces have the function of creating a parallel world undermining the one on the surface: in *The Nice and The Good* (1968), one is underneath the Ministry (where an otherwise impeccable clerk executes his rites of black magic), and another is the underwater cave of the final dénouement. Similar is the role of the threatening house and of the magic woods in *The Sea, the Sea* (1978). In Muriel Spark's writing, the minute descriptions of everyday life or the satirical picture of a specific social group are often interrupted by a disquieting detail: in *The Bachelors* (1960), it is Ronald's epilepsy, that 'animal frenzy' possessing him and singling him out as a fury and at the same time as the observer-witness. In *The Comforters* (1957), she had presented characters who could hear the voice of their masters and, after strenuous resistance, accepted the proof of their virtual existence, as later would happen in *Lanark* (1981) by Alasdair Gray.[27] A later novel of hers, *The Hothouse by the East River* (1973), describes a group of people who have been killed during the war in one of the London bombings, and who have lived on, ignoring the event. Their comfortable and pleasant upper-middle-class life slowly moves from inexplicable failings to complete deterioration. The awareness of being dead – coinciding with that of being narrated – will bring about the erasure of this totally projectual life.

Writing is always projectual and is unavoidably followed by the act of cancellation.[28] In the conclusion to Beckett's *Malone Dies*, the end of writing coincides with the extinction of the last of Malone's alter egos.[29] But it is not necessary to wait for novels occupying the ambiguous position between high modernity and postmodernism to find the emphasis on the act of creation in fiction. The ending of Virginia Woolf's *To the Lighthouse* coincides with the last brush stroke that Lili Briscoe puts on the picture she started at the beginning of the novel. In this case the final note is one of completion and achievement: the look of the woman painter has finally captured the elusive essence of Mrs Ramsay, now that she is not there, 'on the steps', any longer. It is the triumph of the vision of one woman by another.

> There it was – her picture. Yes, with all its green and blues, its lines running up and across, its attempt at something . . . She looked at the steps; they were empty; she looked at the canvas; it was blurred. With a sudden intensity, as if she saw it clear for a second, she drew a line there, in the centre. It was done; it was finished. Yes, she thought, laying down her brush, in extreme fatigue. I have had my vision.[30]

Such narrative devices become dominant in later fiction. Self-erasure is achieved through the coexistence of different endings, of unrelated worlds, of characters extinguishing themselves in Borges and Beckett, and later in Fowles. Descriptions can be changed, erased and then re-written as in Christine Brooke-Rose's *Thru* (1975). Angela Carter reminds us that 'the end of all stories, even if the writer forebears to mention it, is death, which is where our time stops short. Scheherazade knew this.'[31] Contemporary writers do not usually avoid the mention.

Speaking of such devices and authors – mostly male – Brian McHale makes a distinction between experimental epistemology and postmodern ontology in high modernist authors like Beckett and Burroughs, though stating that the one flows back into the other and vice versa. The temptation to attribute to the 'post' a linear temporal value is strong – and McHale sometimes succumbs to it – but the distinction is extremely subtle and not easy to ascertain, and sometimes traverses the same text. As far as female writing goes, the transition is marked by forms of experimentation that are more distinctly tied to a gendered voice, to a female inflection and specificity, though it is not easy to say what it is without falling into a kind of stylistic essentialism. The same indistinct line divides modernism from postmodernism in different generations. Between Muriel Spark and Christine Brooke-Rose, Doris Lessing and Angela Carter, Iris Murdoch and Jeanette Winterson, there is a slippage, a passage across modernity, marking an uncertain and blurred frontier that does not bear definitions.

Ellen Friedman and Miriam Fuchs notice a substantial continuity between three generations of female writers of experimental fiction.[32] In Brooke-Rose and Acker, Young and Quin, as in Sarraute, Duras and Wittig, they see the closeness to their female predecessors – Virginia Woolf, Dorothy Richardson and Gertrude Stein, and successively Jean Rhys, Jane Bowles and Djuna Barnes – rather than to their male contemporaries, following Showalter's, and Gilbert and Gubar's critical line. On the contrary, Rosalind Coward detects a break in the conventions of the novel, tied to the deconstruction of the notion of identity:

> Writers like Doris Lessing or Fay Weldon both occasionally disrupt the conventions of a central narrative voice or character, and their writing becomes a myriad of historical, social and sexual concerns which do not belong to any individual subjectivity. And both Doris Lessing and Angela Carter explore the fantastic and the erotic in ways that do not appeal to any realistic identification with a self-discovering heroine on the way to her personhood.[33]

We shall see soon how the search for identity – according to Jacqueline Rose, a 'resistance to identity' – can be expressed through bodily transmutation, a stubbornly researched metamorphosis of the beautiful into the monstrous, and vice versa. A transformed, altered body develops out of the fragmentary subject of modernity. Hybrid and polymorphous bodies circulate more freely, though not less mysteriously, in women's writings today; polymorphous is the word Freud uses for hysteria.

Between ananas and bananas: sons and mothers

History is always real *as such*. (Angela Carter)

I am telling you stories. Trust me.
(Jeanette Winterson, *The Passion*)

Before moving on to such monsters, I should like to stop at other hybrids coming out of female fabulation: history and criticism are invaded by narrativity and fantasy, while not renouncing their status as document. The opposition between the imaginary and the concrete becomes unclear and mirrors other oppositions. As Jeanette Winterson says:

People like to separate storytelling which is not fact from history which is fact. They do this so that they know what to believe and what not to believe . . . Knowing what to believe had its advantages. It built an empire and kept people where they belonged, in the bright realm of the wallet.[34]

McHale observes that the world of fiction is neither false nor true, suspended as it is between belief and scepticism; in this ethero-cosm, fiction not only relates to the real but to other fictitious worlds as well, and finds its place among the unreal – or nearly real – ontologies in a given culture. He speaks of 'an anarchic landscape of plural worlds'.[35]

This leads us to Winterson's novels. In *Sexing the Cherry*, the political and social upheavals of seventeenth-century England are traversed by the fantasy world of Dog-Woman and her son Jordan. In *Oranges Are Not The Only Fruit* and *Boating for Beginners* (the title is an ironic reference to Noah's Ark), Biblical history provides the narrative structure but it intersects with fantasy and autobiography. She stresses the importance of not distinguishing between history and stories, both in the plots of her novels – which move between invention and historical reconstruction, autobiography and myth – and in the discussions interspersed in the narrative. 'Deuteronomy – The last book of the law', one of the chapters in *Oranges*, is a reflection on history as story and story as history:

> Of course that is not the whole story, but that is the way with stories; we make them what we will. It's a way of explaining the universe while leaving the universe unexplained, it's a way of keeping it all alive, not boxing it into time . . . Some people say there are true things to be found, some people say all kind of things can be proved. I don't believe them. The only thing for certain is how complicated it all is, like a string full of knots . . . It's an all-purpose rainy day pursuit, this reducing of stories called history. (p. 91)

The image of the string full of knots had already been used to describe the heroine of a novel written by Jeanette for the dead, during her work at the funeral parlour; Jeanette is both the author and the narrator in *Oranges*, and the narrator is also the author of this other novel contained at the heart of this series of Chinese boxes:

> I went round making sure that the dead had everything they wanted . . . We did photograph albums, best dresses, favourite novels, and once someone's own novel. It was about a week in a telephone box with a pair of pyjamas called Adolph Hitler. The heroine was a piece of string with a knot in it. (p. 57)

The critical and argumentative voice speaks as a first person, deliberately crossing the frontier with fiction and sometime moving from one novel to another. The sentence 'Time is a great deadener' opening 'Deuteronomy' will be taken up again in *The Passion* and in *Sexing the Cherry*. Time, this great deadener, that flattens and extinguishes everything, is tied to history, which 'very often is only a way to deny the past'.[36]

The denial of the past appears in a great novel of this century, Toni Morrison's *Beloved*, where once more history and fiction meet. The little ghost, whose presence haunts both the house and the narrative from its very first lines, is also the spirit of history, a spirit full of hate and contempt. She occupies the space between love and hate, as is hinted in the epigraph from *Romans* 9, 25: 'I will call . . . her beloved, which was not beloved.' Beloved has been forgotten like a bad dream and has even lost her name:

> Everybody knew what she was called but nobody anywhere knew her name. Disremembered and unaccounted for, she cannot be lost because no one is looking for her, and even if they were, how can they call her if they don't know her name? . . . It was not a story to pass on.[37]

Between Beloved and her mother Sethe, between her and her sister Denver, there is the love–hate one has towards a past that is at once both unacceptable and deeply rooted within the self; the reference here is also to the problematic relationship of black women with their history. In the stream of consciousness uniting them (sometimes expressed in a flux of indistinct voices, typographically marked out amidst the prose), each of them thinks of the other 'she is mine'. Here is a dialogue between mother and daughter:

> Tell me the truth. Didn't you come from the other side?
> Yes. I was on the other side.
> You came back because of me?
> Yes
> You re-memory me?
> Yes. I remember you
> You never forgot me?
> Your face is mine.
> Do you forgive me. Will you stay? You safe here now.
> Where are the men without skin?/Out there. Way off . . .
> They can't hurt us no more. (p. 265)

The ghost of the little girl – who once in the past has been deprived of life by her mother thus 'becoming' a sepulchral inscription, the marker for what has been buried – stands for historical memory, the reminder of slavery, a cataclysmic event remembered and forgotten at the same time, a trace joining the individual and the collective consciousness, stories and histories. She stands for a savage time in which murder, self-mutilation and infanticide were a form of resistance to slavery. Infanticide, as an attack against the master's property and a way of reclaiming the child as her own, was an essential part 'of the slave woman's self definition', according to Elizabeth Fox-Genovese. Homi Bhabha thus comments on her words, at the same time clarifying the complex intertwining of the three women's identities in this work:

> Through the death and the return of Beloved, precisely such a reclamation takes place: the slave mother regaining through the presence of the child, the property of her own person. This knowledge comes as a kind of self-love that is also the love of the 'other': Eros and Agape together.[38]

To the question 'Who is Beloved', he gives three replies, one for Sethe, one for Denver and one for herself: 'she is the daughter made of murderous love who returns to love and hate and frees herself. Her words are broken, like the lynched people with broken necks; disembodied, like the dead children who lost their ribbons' (ibid.).

'Re-memory', as Toni Morrison calls it, is the re-making of history, deconstruction but also reconstruction of a particular cohesion to be found in the modes of everyday life, in the minute rites marking it, in the magic-ritual perspective through which to look at great events, from within a complex network of female ties tying one generation to another. Re-memory gives freedom and produces havoc at the same time, and its contradictions speak of the problematic link between black women and history. This re-writing of history is the interrogation of its epistemological value as the discourse of truth; questioned by the excess of the unconscious, this discourse loses its teleological certainty and its statute of document coming before all 'fiction'. In the repetition of history, other spaces and voices are expressed, fact and fiction dissolve into narrative, and become metaphors without losing their historical value.

Moving back to Jeanette Winterson, the opposition between history and fantasy is echoed and multiplied in the juxtapositions of the historical and the fictional, the mythological and the Biblical, which constantly intersect in all her novels. In *Boating for Beginners* the critical and metanarrative register prevails, not without hints of playful and ironic parody: Gloria, the young heroine, does nothing else but pontificate, with her bizarre women friends or even by herself, on diegetic interruption, on subject and object, narrator and narratee, on the spatial-temporal continuum and, repeatedly, on Northrop Frye. In the novel there is a metanarrative voice proper, that of an orange demon (other variously coloured demons have different functions). Its first lesson to Gloria is on the plurality of reality and its apparitions shape language and forms of the narrative.[39]

Sometime the stress is on the plurality of fictions: in *Oranges*, one of the most important discoveries in Jeanette's young life is that her mother has lied to her about *Jane Eyre*'s ending (the novel keeps on coming up in these fictions), a discovery comparable for her only to the finding out of her adoption papers.

> *Jane Eyre* was her favourite non-Bible book, and she read it to me over and over again . . . Later, literate and curious, I had decided to read it for myself. A sort of nostalgic pilgrimage. I found out, that dreadful day in a back corner of the library, that Jane doesn't marry St John at all, that she goes back to Mr Rochester. (p. 74)

She is horrified by the lie: she would not want to marry Rochester (at that time she has just sensed men are beasts) but she would certainly not marry a missionary either, or become one as her mother desires. In any case, not long after the discovery that Jane is finally reunited to her true love, she falls in love with Melanie and starts on the course of 'unnatural passion'.

Sexing the Cherry is structured in three parts: the past, the present (a short contemporary intermission presenting the doubles of the seventeenth-century characters) and the fable. The fable is the story of the twelve dancing princesses who have become eleven as one has gone missing and is dispersed here and there in the book. Each of the narrative sections intersects with the others, and this fragmentary structure floats over time, like in Woolf's *Orlando* but without the cohesion that allowed the heroine's identity in that novel to survive changes of gender, epoch and atmosphere. In *Sexing*, time moves backwards and forwards without control, and the multiplicity of genres (history, mythical tale, philosophical meditation, didactic sermons, numbered aphorisms and numbered paintings) further break narrative and temporal unity.

The tale of the past is the frame and substance of the novel, and is centred on Dog-Woman, her adoptive son Jordan (whose name comes from the river as he was found on a river) and the naturalist John Tradescant. They live in seventeenth-century London and witness the main events of that troubled time: faithful servants of the king and fervent monarchists who hate the pleasure-denying puritans, they witness his trial and execution; successively they get involved in the civil war, in the great plague and the fire of London. They are victims but also begetters of violence, especially Dog-Woman in her merciless and bloody extermination of many Puritans.

Even within the main narrative there are disparate motifs and polarities: identity and writing, the large and the small, female and male, violence and sweetness, wandering and staying, bananas and pineapples, all undistinguishable the one from the other. The banana is the marvel the mother gives to the child, but also marks the first vision he has of the tropical island; the pineapple is what Jordan brings back from Barbados, a reminder of colonial plunder and at the same time the marvel grown in the elsewhere, in another time and another space outside the colonial.

The pineapple arrived today.
    Jordan carried it in his arms as though it were a yellow baby; with the wisdom of Solomon he prepared to slice it in two.[40]

The story is alternatively told from two internal points of view, two participating narrators, announced at the beginning of each section by the symbol of a banana for the mother and a pineapple for the son. In correspondence with the contemporary scenes they appear cut into two halves, a mark of the temporal slippage. Pineapples and bananas, like cherries and peaches, are important metaphors, 'both real and imaginary', beyond being the only marks of identity for the two narrating voices. The female voice tells the historical events and the details of their concrete everyday life together, and is mostly associated with the comic register or with self-mocking tones. The male voice has a dreamy, more poetic quality and speaks of interiority, the search for identity, and the theme of writing. 'I discovered that my own life was written invisibly, was squashed between the facts, was flying without me' (p. 10). The former describes the real city, the latter the utopian one. A sort of reversal of sexual identities is present here, as between Henri and Villanelle in *The Passion*.

Dog-Woman is a liar, a fantasist, a murderer and a parricide, enacting the oneiric phantasy of male dismemberment and castration; here *le corps morcelé*, in an ironical reversal, becomes male:

Scroggs reached up to ring the bell, but I chopped the cord and one of his thumbs as he did so. I have never seen so much bobbing and screaming over a minor injury . . . Then, without more ado, because I am not a torturer, I took his head off in one clean blow and kicked him off the block.

By this time Firebrace was whimpering in a corner and had soiled his toga with excrements . . . I fetched his leg from by the window and offered it to him, but he only lamented more and begged me to spare him. (p. 88)

She does not, and relentlessly goes on, in gruesome detail. Her irony is exercised over everything: sexual – or rather genital – minutiae; masculine power; popular genres and their heroes.

In the short contemporary intermission, Nicolas Jordan joins the Navy, a correlative to Jordan's many journeys; the woman, a chemist doing pollution research, has problems similar to those of Jeanette in *Oranges*, divided between bulimia and anorexia, a thin identity and a fat one: in her hallucinations she imagines herself to be Dog-Woman. Like her, she is very disappointed and angry after the one sexual encounter and has fantasies of cannibalism. This part begins with the description of an unknown artist, probably Dutch, representing Mr Rose, the Royal Gardener, offering the pineapple to Charles II, that very same fruit that the seventeenth-century Jordan had offered to the new king after coming back from Barbados. After many transversal looks at the past – the present of the novel – through the history books that Nicholas Jordan keeps under his bed, the contemporary world flows back into the past without any other warning but the reappearance of the fruit symbols, now whole again.

The book is interspersed with Fortunata's story, the twelfth princess and follower of Artemis; she is a dance teacher and teaches her pupils to become points of light, a theme announced in one of the epigraphs of the novel ('Matter, that thing the most solid and the well-known, which you are holding in your hands and which makes up your body, is now known to be mostly empty space. Empty space and points of light. What does this say about the reality of the world?') and taken up in a metanarrative meditation on the nature of time, space and light, connected to painting and dance. Dance is one of the essential metaphors of this novel and refers to its importance in Native American ritual and stories. To 'the dancing life of light', constantly in movement like Fortunata's feet, the book returns at the end, together with the theme of the other epigraph inspired by the Hopi language where there are no tenses for past, present and future as time is only an invention of our minds.

Fortunata is the woman Jordan has been looking for in all his journeys, the double he will be reunited with in the last scene under his mother's eyes: 'I looked at Jordan standing at the prow, his silhouette black and sharp-edged. I thought I saw someone standing beside him, a woman, slight and strong. I tried to call out but I had no voice. Then she vanished and there was nothing next to Jordan but empty space' (p. 144). Jordan leaves the city for ever on his ship, like the river flowing incessantly from one country to another, towards the mirage of other cities and other futures existing only in his mind: 'And even the most solid of things and the most real, the best-loved and the well-known, are only hand-shadows on the wall. Empty space and points of light' (ibid.).

Finally the multiple elusive identities of Artemis and Fortunata – who are one and twelve at the same time, one and many dancers, one and the other – overlap. The end of the novel is its beginning. At the start of the novel Jordan walks in the fog: 'I began to walk with my hands stretched out in front of me, as do those troubled in sleep, and in this way, for the first time, I traced the lineaments of my own face opposite me' (p. 9). At the end, after the Great Fire of 1666, the fog comes again, and, his arms outstretched, Jordan touches her face (another's face). 'For a second the fog cleared, and he saw that the stranger was himself' (p. 143).

The metanarrative reflections are here uttered by Jordan, rather than by the extra-diegetic voice of Winterson's other novels, though he echoes many of those motifs: 'time is a great deadener', 'passion and love', the parable of destruction. But the narrative ego is fragmented in the two Jordans, that of yesterday and today and in his many identities (Tradescant, Fortunata, Dog-Woman). Dog-Woman herself, though more strongly structured and with a unified narrating voice, is many other women: the prostitutes, a witch living in the kennel, other degraded urban dwellers, and finally Artemis.

The Passion brings us back to the link between history and fiction. There are again two narrative voices, two alternate subjectivities: he is Henri, Napoleon's cook, idolising him in spite of all his slaughters; she is Villanelle, the Venetian with webbed feet, pursuing an impossible love for another woman. The novel develops between

France (Paris and Boulogne) and Venice, the labyrinthine town between two worlds, two dimensions, land and water, the real and the magical. The historical reconstruction is the framework for unrequited passion: Villanelle's, who in Venice has materially lost her heart to a beautiful woman, and Henri's for her. In order to win her heart back, he will kill and end up in a prison on an arid rock, like his former idol. The 'passion' is a metaphor of art, as Henri says throughout the novel, and confirms at the end:

> I say I am in love with her, what does that mean?
>
> It means I review my future and my past in the light of this feeling. It is as though I wrote in a foreign language that I am suddenly unable to read. Wordlessly she explains me to myself; like genius she is ignorant of what she does.
>
> I go on writing so that I will always have something to read. (p. 159)

Daughters and fathers

'Father' is a hypothesis but 'mother' is fact. (Angela Carter)

In *Wise Children* (1991), Angela Carter addresses a father for the first time, no less than Shakespeare, the father of English literature. She does it through a series of temporal and spatial juxtapositions, mixing genres in another of her multiple palimpsests, inspired this time by the *real* metamorphosis to which this symbolic father has been subjected by a whole genealogy of interpreters: first of all, the great Victorian actor Ranulph Hazard and his wife Estella; successively their son Sir Melchior Hazard, followed by the numerous pairs of twins he has (but more probably has not) generated. The fictional characters give glimpses of famous actors and directors, starting with Ellen Terry and moving on to Henry Irving, Lawrence Olivier, Max Reinhardt and John Gielgud, or to a mixture of all these and others.

She goes back to the world of the circus and the music hall, outlining them as the shadows of the official Shakespearean theatre represented here. The novel is founded on the accurate study and observation of a concrete world, made of people, actors and audiences, theatres, tours and performances, stage scenery and props, critical reviews; a world, however, which (not unlike the circus) is parallel to reality. Among her novels this one is the farthest from fantasy, founded as it is on accurate research into Shakespearean criticism and performance over a hundred years, and on the study of a particular artistic milieu. But if it is reality, it is a reality of the second degree, where the displacements multiply *ad infinitum*. The Shakespearean world is constantly crossed by others, London music hall or Hollywood cinema, and the representation shows other representations. Its plot again draws a female *bildungsroman* (here the growth and formation of a feminine double, the twins Nora and Dora, the latter being the narrator), with roots in two Shakespearean dramas, *A Midsummer Night's Dream* and *Hamlet*. The performance of the former occupies great part of the plot, while *Hamlet* is a phantasmatic understood presence. But through Sir Melchior's paper crown, left to him by his father and by some miracle escaping the many fires and cataclysms, other links are created with *King Lear* and *Richard III*.

The language of the novel is ornate and sumptuous, attentive to the description of costumes and ornaments (theatrical and not) changing from one epoch to another, in the zigzagging path followed by Dora Chance's erratic memory and diary. The dynasty of the Hazards and of the Chances constantly mixes and overlaps as happens with 'risks' and 'chances' both in human destiny and in play and games – and reproduces itself through successive double births, mostly female, and in reversals of legitimacy and illegitimacy. Dora and Nora are Sir Melchior's illegitimate daughters (officially known as his brother's, and adopted by him), and for this reason rejected by the great 'Shakespearean' family moving between theatre, cinema and television. They are at the margins of that world also as stars of an inferior form of spectacle. Music hall and variety, recalled in the first epigraph from Cole Porter, 'Brush up your Shakespeare', re-emerges in their final act of singing and dancing in Bard Road and in the final sentence: 'What a joy it is to dance and sing!'[41]

The two worlds will meet in the moment in which their father gives them the role of the fairies PeaseBlossom and MustardSeed in the Hollywood version of *A Midsummer Night's Dream,* defined as 'a kitsch work of art', and directed by Sir Melchior, remindful here of Max Reinhardt. Their first work with their father had been a musical comedy called *What You Will*, a miscellany from 'Will'

Shakespeare, in which they danced and sang a sketch from *Hamlet*, a Scottish piece on the 'weird sisters' from *Macbeth*, a 'Roman Scandal', and so on; while Melchior Hazard played the part of the Bard, and Peregrine (his brother and twin) that of writer and 'producer', a word announcing successive *coups de théâtre*.

Melchior's alleged legitimate children will be discovered not to be his after all, their biological father being Peregrine who must have repeatedly taken his brother's place in his wives' beds. Nora and Dora, though not recognised by him and adopted instead by Peregrine, are his only real progeny and, as another epigraph says, 'it's a wise child that knows its own father' (but do they really know, or did Peregrine even on that occasion . . .?). They have never met their mother, except through the words of 'grandmother' Chance; when she dies, she takes with her 'the last living memory of that ghost without a face' that their mother has been, having died in giving birth to them (p. 164).

Wise Children is the story of a 'hypothetical, disputed, absent father' (p. 227) but also (and ultimately) of many displaced mothers: Estella Hazard, the grandmother, probably the greatest among the great actors of the novel; grandmother Chance, who might be the twins' real mother; the Lady A., a mother rejected by the Hazards and picked up by the Chances; and finally Nora/Dora who, at seventy-five, become mothers of the last pair of twins, who magically materialise out of one of the pockets of Peregrine who, faithful to his name, has wandered away and miraculously reappeared, 'such a material ghost' (p. 207). The new twins are a boy and a girl, a break in the long sequence of same-sex twins.

Differently from Shakespeare, Angela Carter may have told a story of mothers and daughters after all; in English the title keeps its ambiguity and the children can be both sons and daughters, whereas Romance language must make a choice (the title of the Italian translation chose the daughters). Genders mixing in the last pair of twins may gesture towards the utopian future in which the difference between sons and daughters will not really matter so much. This is Nora's comment in rejoicing over their newly-found children: ' "We're both of us mothers and both of us fathers", she said. "They'll be wise children, all right" ' (p. 230).

*   *   *

'Hard to swallow, huh?', is the narrator's sarcastic comment addressed to her readers, after 227 pages:

> Well, you might have known what you were about to let yourself
> in for when you let Dora Chance in her ratty old fur and poster
> paint, her orange (Persian Melon) toenails sticking out of her
> snakeskin peep-toes, reeking of liquor, accost you in the Coach
> and Horses and let her tell you a tale. (p. 227)

In her colourful language, she takes a last irreverent metanarrative
sneer at Dora, and at herself as the narrator, using the language of
soliciting and prostitution for narration. She has not spared anybody, Father Shakespeare or Father God either.

This gigantic pastiche – going in and out of a Shakespearean
world of the second degree, in which the fluctuation of subjectivities
is coded in the double structure of every character, placing Shakespeare in the *music hall* and the *music hall* in Shakespeare – ends on
the ambiguity of fiction, at the border between a tale that is 'real' as
such and a truth that is more unreal than any story. The comment I
have just quoted grows out of Dora's refusal to disclose the whole
truth about the new twins to the readers (they are not 'family'), who
are addressed directly and therefore placed outside the fiction. This
gives the author a last occasion to stress the thin boundary between
fiction and reality: '. . . these glorious pauses do, sometimes, occur
in the discordant but complementary narratives of our lives and if
you choose to stop the story there, at such a pause, and refuse to
take it any further, then you can call it a happy ending' (ibid.). After
all, even the play between mother and fathers refers to that:
' "Father" is a hypothesis but "mother" is fact' (p. 223).

Jeanette Winterson had insisted on an analogous motif. At the
end of *The Passion*, Henri is found looking at the laguna from the
garden of San Servelo jail, in dialogue with himself, or perhaps with
his readers' scepticism:

> I shall grow red roses next year. A forest of red roses.
> On this rock? In this climate?
> I am telling you stories. Trust me. (p. 160)

Both novels end on the importance of trusting fabulation, fiction,
tales; to give them that same kind of faith that is normally assigned
to undeniable reality.

Chapter 5

... and Monstrous Bodies in Contemporary Women's Writing

Strange unfamiliar shapes, freakish bodies, disquieting forms and hybrid creatures have been creeping into women's narratives, putting in question the frontier between foulness and loveliness, the human and the animal, me and you, female and male. In mythology, there have been many such hybrids on the female side – Medusa, the Gorgons, the Sphinx, mermaids, harpies and chimeras – surpassing the rather kindly satyrs, centaurs and such like, in numbers and wickedness. Mary Russo, speaking of the female grotesque, stresses that the word comes from grotto, meaning cave. 'Low, hidden, earthly, dark, material, immanent, visceral. As bodily metaphor, the grotesque cave tends to look like . . . the cavernous anatomical female body.'[1] Freud refers the uncanny to the same image, to the female womb, 'the place where each one of us lived once upon a time and in the beginning'; like the uncanny, these bodies are familiar – as they embody a return to something where each of us has been – and mysterious at the same time, representing that which cannot be known, or even looked at.

The accumulation and overflow of bodies and languages, the elements of proliferation and giantism, seem oneiric fantasies of compensation for the vanishing of stable singular identities, sometimes for the continuation of an oppressive condition. It can be a derisive counterpoint to the stereotypes of the feminine, to the notions of heterosexual love, the expression of that subconscious that first dilates the strong subject in caricature and then erases it, and with it our nostalgia for the recovery of a strong subjectivity.

This leads, as we have already seen, to the anarchy of genres and to the contamination among different narrative modes: critical and creative writing, high and low, popular and avant-garde, real and fantastic, history and fiction. These very same novels containing monsters are monsters from a generic point of view.

In this chapter I shall look at fictional monsters, and at the theories on monsters, bodies and writing that have played such an important part in feminist thought.

The female text as 'hideous progeny'

Every text is implicitly a monstrous, female double self.

(Jane Gallop)

A woman's coming to writing:
Who
Invisible, foreign, secret, hidden, mysterious, black, forbidden
Am I . . .
Is this me, this nobody that is dressed up, wrapped in veils, carefully kept distant, pushed to the side of History and change, nullified, kept out of the way, on the edge of the stage, on the kitchen side, the bedside?
For you?

(Hélène Cixous)

The link between writing and the search for identity has been underlying feminist thought and practice for a long time, and during the sixties and seventies it was seen surfacing in the prevalence of diaries and memoirs, or at least of a diaristic mode, in female writing. As the concept of a unified identity is put in question, writing is more often tied to the impossibility, or even undesirability, of such a goal and becomes the mirror of a split erratic subjectivity. In *Sexuality in the Field of Vision,* Jacqueline Rose describes the unconscious as constantly revealing, through errors and displacements, the failure of identity. She sees the affinity between feminism and psychoanalysis precisely in such a failure: 'the failure is repeated ad infinitum, and relived moment by moment in our individual histories . . . appearing in dreams and in sexual pleasure outside the norm . . . feminism's affinity with psychoanalysis rests above all with the recognition that there is resistance at the very heart of psychic life'.[2] Luce Irigaray sees female writing as the instrument to break the unity of subject and object, on which the definition of what is female is based. For her, women's writing breaks the phallocratic order of writing, in denying its unitary character, its emphasis on oneness: 'what a feminine syntax might be is not simple nor easy to state, because in that "syntax" there would no longer be either object or subject, "oneness" would no longer be privileged, there would no longer be proper meanings, proper names, "proper" attributes'.[3] It is a tactile, simultaneous, fluid 'style', resisting, and exploding 'every firmly established form, figure, idea or concept'.[4]

For Hélène Cixous, the link between the lack of stability in sexual identity and writing passes through the female body. While defending a female separateness in writing,[5] she speaks of 'a subjectivity that splits apart without regret . . . without the ceaseless summoning of the authority called Ego'.[6] This split subjectivity joins the female body to writing: 'there is a link between the economy of femininity – the open, extravagant subjectivity, that relationship to the other in which the gift doesn't calculate its influence – and the possibility of love; and a link today between this "libido of the other" and writing' (pp. 91–2). Both the body and writing are off-centre: they do not know confines, they come and go and come again, they are one and the other and many others:

> Unleashed and raging, she belongs to the race of waves. She arises, she approaches, she lifts up, she reaches, covers over, washes a shore, flows embracing the cliff's least undulation, already she is another, arising again, throwing the fringed vastness of her body up high . . . She has never 'held still'; explosion, diffusion, effervescence, abundance, she takes pleasure in being boundless, outside self, outside same, far from a 'center'. (p. 90)

Such excess connects body to hysteria, writing to monstrosity. As Jane Gallop says in the above epigraph, the female text has often been defined as monstrous. In her essay 'The Monster in the Mirror', a discussion of the 1981 feminist issue of *Yale French Studies*, she states that monstrosity arises from the lack of individuality and that the monstrous comes from the failed separation between mother and daughter. Referring to Marianne Hirsch's article in the issue, she says:

The word *monstrous* here refers to a 'continuous multiple being' . . . a being whose multiple parts are neither totally merged nor totally separate . . . whose boundaries are inadequately differentiated, thus calling into question the fundamental opposition of self and other. Such a being is terrifying because of the stake any self as self has in its own autonomy, in its individuation, in its integrity.[7]

She refers to Chodorow's theories, and above all to Irigaray's comment on this lack of separation – 'the one does not move without the other' – and wonders who the monster is: the mother or the self. Theorists always attribute the desire for autonomy to the daughter and the longing for symbiosis to the mother, and therefore identify with the former; this is why theory is thought of as male. 'Female theory, theory that is inadequately distanced from its object, or feminist theory, theory grounded in allegiance to the collective body of women, is then monstrous.'[8] The text and the reader are another possibility for the constitution of this monstrous double.

In her essay on Mary Shelley's *Frankenstein*, Barbara Johnson underlines the equation between women's writing and monstrosity.[9] For the concept of monstrosity, she refers to Dorothy Dinnerstein's *The Mermaid and the Minotaur*, which she considers a modern rewriting of *Frankenstein*, and whose title refers to the awareness 'of our uneasy, ambiguous position in the animal kingdom', and to the permanence of pernicious forms of collaboration between the sexes: 'as long as that exists, both man and woman will remain semi-human, monstrous'.[10]

The experience of writing the novel is referred to as monstrous by Mary Shelley herself in the introduction she added to the 1831 edition (the first edition of the novel was published anonymously in 1818, with a preface written by Mary's husband, the poet Percy Bysshe Shelley). She starts asking herself the question that readers had asked ('How I, then a young girl, came to think of and to dilate upon so very hideous an idea?') and concludes, in spite of all: 'And now once again, I bid my hideous progeny go forth and prosper.'[11] The parallel between Mary's and Frankenstein's creatures is unavoidable, and the author's definition of her novel as hideous echoes Frankenstein's words in the novel when he speaks of the dæmon, the fiend he has created and of his female companion, who must be eliminated as she might give birth to a race of devils. Woman's desire to write and man's desire to procreate can both give rise to monsters.

Writing in this case is autobiographical in two ways, as it reflects both the problems of female authorship and the author's divided feelings towards motherhood, associated for her with unwanted pregnancies and death. Her own mother, Mary Wollstonecraft, had died ten days after her birth, and only one survived of the four chidren she herself gave birth to. On the other hand, Mary Shelley openly associates the pangs of artistic inspiration ('that blank incapacity of invention which is the greatest misery of authorship')[12] with reflections on the nature of the principle of life:

> Every thing must have a beginning, to speak in Sanchean phrase; and that beginning must be linked to something that went before . . . Invention, it must be humbly admitted, does not consist in creating out of void, but out of chaos; the materials must, in the first place, be afforded: it can give form to dark, shapeless substances, but cannot bring into being the substance itself. (p. 8)

She then goes on to discuss the contemporary scientific possibility of making life spring out of the inanimate: 'Perhaps a corpse would be re-animated . . . perhaps the component parts of a creature might be manufactured, brought together, and endued with vital warmth.' At this point she has a dream that solves both problems: the spectre haunting her midnight pillow gives her the inspiration for her book while at the same time showing the frightful stirring of life in an inanimate form. The joy of the artist is accompanied by the terrors of creation and the horror for the creature.

The power of feminine contradictions, according to Barbara Johnson, emerges precisely from the hiddenness of the question of femininity in the novel. Shelley's novel is about the repression of such a contradiction, symbolised by the destruction of the nearly completed female monster performed by the doctor. 'What is being repressed here is that a woman can write anything that would *not* exhibit "the amiableness of domestic affection", the possibility that for women as well as for men the home can be the site of the *unheimlich*'.[13] Johnson is referring here to the words that Percy Shelley put in the author's mouth in the 1818 preface: 'my chief concern in this respect has been limited to avoiding the enervating effects of the novels of the present day, and to the exhibition of the amiableness of domestic affection, and the excellence of universal virtue' (p. 12).

His intrusion in Mary's preface recalls Dinnerstein's 'pernicious forms of collaboration between the sexes', adding yet one more monstrous hybridity to the picture.

Writing and the spectacle of hysteria

> As long as the sorceress is still free, at the sabbat, in the forest, she is a sensitivity that is completely exposed – all open skin, natural, animal, odorous, and deliciously dirty. When she is caught, when the scene of the inquisition is formed around her, in the same way the medical scene later forms around the hysteric, she withdraws into herself, she cries, she has numb spots, she vomits. She has become hysterical. (Catherine Clément)

> Text, my body . . . (Hélène Cixous)

The discourse of hysteria has been central in the definition of woman, both in medical science and in psychoanalysis. It was later appropriated by feminist theory to provide a connection from the female body to monstrosity and writing.

The artist Mary Kelly has given an example of art that focuses on the hysterical body, while spanning different languages and spaces. In her installations, writing appears as a visual and material element in a composite collage. Her work places itself between art and theory, plastic art and writing, figuration and word, suggesting the passage from the argumentative to the creative register. *Post-Partum Document* and *Interim* are displayed in diverse spaces, and are composed of photographs, objects, drawings and sculpture, alternating with (or framed by) screens on which writing displays itself in its double statute, both conceptual and figurative. The work of art becomes body – in both her installations there is a female body, the maternal and the hysterical – and the body becomes writing.

In *Interim*, particularly in its first part *Corpus*, she gives attention to the metaphorical meaning of female hysteria, following its formulations from Charcot to Freud and Lacan.

Thus hysteria, marginalised in one realm, becomes central in another, that is, feminist theory. For Irigaray, the hysteric signifies the exclusion of women from discourse; for Monique Plaza – the revolt against patriarchy; for Michèle Montrelay – the blind spot of psychoanalysis; for Jacqueline Rose – the problem of sexual difference; and for the film collective of Dora – the analyst's symptom and therefore the basis for feminism's critique of Freud.[14]

With her work she intends to fill in the empty spaces in psychoanalysis; in *Corpus*, particularly, she has repeated the hysterical question that a woman asks: 'am I like a man or like a woman?' With her emphasis on the 'corporeality' of writing, placed on a par with figurative languages, she has tried to give a meaning to the absence of the female image as iconic signifier.

The hysterical body has been appropriated in feminist theory as the positive symbolisation allowing the female writing ego to emerge. In 'The Guilty One', her section of *La Jeune Née*, Catherine Clément speaks at length of the witch, the stranger and the hysteric, as embodying an impossible synthesis, occupying the space of anomaly, the interstices in the symbolic order, 'du *côté de la règle et du côté des règles*', an imaginary zone of exclusion that needs to be rescued. She looks at the figure of the tarantolata in Southern Italy and considers her 'tarantella', following the imaginary bite of a tarantula, as the reply from a feminine subject subjugated by patriarchal hierarchies, a subversive and rebellious rite expressing 'tragic happiness' and passionate rage, a demonic dance of madness.

Clément states that both the witch and the hysteric woman have a rebellious and conservative role at the same time. These two figures, though much loved by her, must disappear: the newly born woman may only impersonate them. Like the theory of masquerade formulated by Lacan and Irigaray, it gives women the freedom to put on the mimicry of femininity and to take it off, arousing the envy of male thinkers. In her brilliant analysis of this feminist concept, Mary Russo comments: 'femininity as a mask, for a man, is a take-it-or-leave-it proposition; for a woman, a similar flaunting of the feminine is a take-it-*and*-leave-it possibility. To put on femininity with a vengeance suggests the power of taking it off.'[15]

Hélène Cixous, whose writing is in the suspended space between theory and fiction as Clément observes, performs the dance herself;

Sandra Gilbert calls this the 'theoretical tarantella'.[16] In 'Sorties',
she starts from the metaphor of opposition omnipresent in all the
aspects of knowledge (speaking/writing; parole/écriture; high/low)
to arrive at women's alienation from the 'dark continent' of their
bodily egos. The only escape route will take them into witchery and
hysteria. The way out can only be in the attack moved against
phallocentrism through the exploration of the continent of female
pleasure, which she states is neither dark nor unexplorable. 'We,
coming early to culture, repressed and choked by it, our beautiful
mouths stopped up with gags, pollen, and short breaths; we the
labyrinths, we the ladders, we the trampled spaces; the stolen and
the flights – we are "black" and we are beautiful' (p. 69). In the
'Exchange' with Clément at the end of their joint book, she defines
the hysteric as disturbing arrangements, questioning others, moving
and changing things, as 'she cannot be placed or take place' (p. 156).
She recalls Freud saying that 'what is hysterical yields art'.

In *Coming to Writing*, whose title underlines the relation between
writing and orgasm, she says: 'Writing to touch with letters, with
lips, with breath, to caress with the tongue, to lick with the soul, to
taste the blood of the beloved body, of life in its remoteness.' And
again, 'The texts I ate, sucked, suckled, kissed . . . To write: to love,
inseparable. Writing is a gesture of love . . . Read-me-lick-me, write-
me love.' Further on, the cannibalistic side of writing is made more
explicit by the comparison between eating and reading: 'I was raised
on the milk of words. Languages nourished me. I hated to eat what
was on a plate. Dirty carrots, nasty soups, the aggression of forks
and spoons.'[17] Cixous's writing tries to cross the border between
book and body: 'To write – the act that will "realize" the uncensored
relationship of woman to her sexuality . . . that will return her
goods, her pleasures, her organs, her vast bodily territories kept
under seal . . . Write yourself, your body must make itself heard.'[18]
For her writing is the only place that is not compelled to reproduce
the system, 'an elsewhere that writes itself, that dreams, that invents
new worlds'.

From this reaffirmation of themselves, women can 'come' to
writing, through an erotic aestheticisation founded in bisexuality:
a sort of trance that does not erase differences, but animates them,
pursues them, adds to them. It is not a fantasy of unity but the joy of
difference, of multiplicity, of the awareness of the other within
herself. Writing the body as we have already seen above: *écriture*

féminine is a temporary essentialism as it looks towards a utopian time when it will no longer be possible to speak about man or woman.[19]

In *Artemisia*, a novel on the seventeenth-century Italian painter Artemisia Gentileschi, Anna Banti describes Artemisia's body materially reclining on her writing: 'Artemisia, my companion from three centuries ago who lay breathing gently on the hundred pages I had written'.[20] The book is a marvellous instance of the tie between a woman writing on another woman: 'I will never be able to be free of Artemisia again; she is a creditor, a stubborn, scrupulous conscience to which I grow accustomed as to sleeping on the ground . . . a sort of contract legally drawn . . . and which I must honor' (p. 33). The novel starts on the morning of 1944 when the writer finds herself looking at the ruins of Firenze from the Boboli gardens after the German mines, and at those of her own house under which the manuscript of her first novel is buried. From then on, in the rewriting of the lost manuscript, she finds Artemisia in fragments, dialoguing with fragments of herself at different times and moments; the fragments turn into spinning images, glimpses from different phases of Artemisia's life in a temporal flux: of her dying 'in spasms, like a dog that has been run over'; of the child 'skipping among the artichokes'; of the adolescent, 'holding a handkerchief over her mouth to stifle the sobs', or in anger 'with knitted brows' (p. 10–11). It is as if, after the burning of the book, the only things left were a hundred corporeal poses materialising in front of their eyes and crowding in her memory.[21]

The pages are lost, the body is now in fragments, and she will have to put them together again; the second writing of the book is the description of the material resistance of those fragments, a strenuous link between three women, the author, the artist and the character from the first version, and their many selves.

Trinh T. Minh-ha describes the coming and going of 'me' and 'I' in women's writing:

> When i say 'I see myself seeing myself,' I/i am not alluding to the illusory relation of subject to subject (or object) but to the play of mirrors that defers to infinity the real subject and subverts the notion of an original 'I' . . . writing, like a game that defies its own rules, is an ongoing practice that may be said to be concerned, not with inserting a 'me' into language, but with

creating an opening where the 'me' disappears while 'I' endlessly come and go.[22]

She underlines the difference between Cixous's 'Write yourself? Write your body' and writing about yourself and your body: 'The first refers to a scriptive act – the emergence of a writing self – the second, to a consolidation of writing from the self' (p. 28). In fact her own books are invaded by still from her films, and the films by her writing. In *Surname Viet Given Name Nam*, the faces of the women she is interviewing are written over. Women's writing for her is linguistic flesh, organic matter, 'nurturing writing' (*nourricriture*), and it draws its corporeal fluidity from images of water and other female fluids, 'a flow of life, of words running over or slowly dripping down the pages': 'This keeping-alive and life-giving water exists simultaneously as the writer's ink, the mother's milk, the woman's blood and menstruation' (p. 38).

The juxtaposition of the female body with writing is often rendered through images of fluidity, from Irigaray and Cixous to Trinh, from Angela Carter to Gloria Anzaldúa. We find the use of corporeal fluids in the cruel prison for women who have killed their husbands, the total *panopticon* described by Carter in *Nights at the Circus*. In spite of the total surveillance exercised by the Countess P, desire spreads among the women, and love leads to rebellion and freedom. The liquids here have a Rabelaisian addition:

> Contact was effected, first, by illicit touch and glance, and then by illicit notes, or, if either guard or inmate turned out to be illiterate, by drawings made in and on all manner of substances, . . . in blood, both menstrual and veinous, even in excrement, for none of the juices of their bodies that had been so long denied were alien to them, in their extremity. . .[23]

Gloria Anzaldúa has linked the female body to writing through more terrestrial images, relating it to living in the Borderlands, as Chicana, as lesbian, as writer. Writing is like a cactus needle embedded in the flesh. The more one tries to remove it, the deeper it gets. The act of writing gives birth to the soul through the body: 'When I write it feels like I'm carving bone. It feels like I'm creating my own face, my own heart – a Nahuatl concept.'[24] On the other hand, writing is like a vampire drawing blood from the body in an incessant flow. The final image in the chapter is of her sitting in front of her computer that she calls Amiguita, with an altar on top of it and incense burning:

> The Writing is my whole life, it is my obsession. This vampire which is my talent does not suffer other suitors. Daily I court it, offer my neck to its teeth. This is the sacrifice that the act of creation requires, a blood sacrifice . . . And for images, words, stories to have this transformative power, they must arise from the human body – flesh and bone – and from the Earth's body – stone, sky, liquid, soil.[25]

Double as monster

> When the repressed of their culture and their society come back, it is an explosive return. (Hélène Cixous)

> It was certainly an odd monster that one made up by reading the historians first and the poets afterwards – a worm winged like an eagle; the spirit of life and beauty in a kitchen chopping up suet. (Virginia Woolf)

The monsters that have recently invaded female fiction may be instances of a new freedom, signs of the possibility of bringing them to life, after the times when monsters and doubles, just as witches and freaks, had to be suppressed and repressed. As we have seen, one of the first women monsters in modern literature was killed before coming to life by Victor Frankenstein who thus explained his motives: 'she might become ten thousand times more malignant than her mate, and delight, for its own sake, in murder and wretchedness . . . a race of devils would be propagated upon the earth, who might make the very existence of the species of man a condition precarious and full of terror'.[26] The suppression of the woman monster is recurrent in female literature, as Sandra Gilbert and Susan Gubar state: 'the image of a double is often present, the other half, the woman beyond the mirror, the unconscious, the evil spirit of which to rid the self'.[27] As the title of their book recalls, the most famous of these doubles is kept in the attic in *Jane Eyre*, where she is imagined beyond a closed door, or appears in dreams. This is how it finally materialises:

> What it was, whether beast or human being, one could not at first sight, tell: it grovelled, seemingly, on all fours; it snatched and growled like some strange wild animal, but it was covered with clothing; and a quantity of dark, grizzled hair, wild as a mane, hid its head and face.[28]

She is none other than a Creole from Spanish Town, Jamaica, one of many *mestizas* who, as Cherríe Moraga says, 'live and are gendered between and among the lines', and appears as the unnamed other, the discarded wife, the double of the white Anglo-Saxon heroine of the book. In a much quoted essay, Spivak sees Bertha Mason as 'a figure produced by the axiomatic of imperialism', whose function in the novel 'is to render indeterminate the boundary between human and animal and thereby to weaken her entitlement under the spirit if not the letter of the Law'.[29]

Others will attract attention to her: in *Rebecca* (1938), Daphne du Maurier named her bestselling book after her, always the first wife but with a different name, at the same time denying a name to the heroine who becomes 'the girl'; Alfred Hitchcock two years later followed suit, naming his film *Rebecca, the first wife*; in 1965 Jean Rhys, born in the Caribbean, again put her at the centre of *Wide Sargasso Sea*, her re-visitation of *Jane Eyre* from the other side (in this case, it is Rochester who loses his name). As a child she had read *Jane Eyre* and had decided to give a life to this repressed 'other'. Bertha/Rebecca becomes Antoinette, the beautiful Creole abandoned by her English husband. Antoinette finds a threatening double in her mother Annette, constituting for her the shadow of madness, and alternatively, in her black nurse Christophine, with her wisdom; in this case there is no simple juxtaposition as the doubles are all refractions of the other: Bertha/Annette/Antoinette/Christophine/Tia. Maybe the double is no longer an evil force from which to free the self. Jane Eyre came to a sort of happiness after the evil other burnt in fire; for the post-Jane heroines, difference is complex and intertwined with sameness.

This is the case of Sula and Nel in Toni Morrison's *Sula*. The two girls have been friends since childhood, first in play and games, then joined in an unspeakable secret – the drowning of Chicken Little, a younger child with whom they were playing at the river – and later separated by Sula's betrayal of Nel and her wandering away from the Bottom.[30] They are close but very different, one restless and flouting conventions, promiscuous and faithful to no one, considered a sort of witch at the Bottom and even suspected of sleeping with white men; the other tied to her native place, fearful and shy, a dutiful mother, and a single one since she has lost her husband to Sula. During their last meeting, when Nel goes to visit the dying Sula and is unwillingly driven into a fierce confrontation, another truth comes out:

'How you know?' Sula asked.
'Know what?' Nel still wouldn't look at her.
'About who was good. How you know it was you?'
'What you mean?'
'I mean maybe it wasn't you. Maybe it was me.'[31]

After her death, Nel goes to see Sula's grandmother Eva in the clinic to which this all powerful woman – another disquieting motherly figure beside the one in *Beloved* – is now confined. Eva confuses Nel with Sula and in her ramblings recalls the little child's drowning that has hunted them in guilt. When Nel says that it was Sula who dropped him into the water, Eva replies: 'You. Sula. What is the difference? You was there. You watched, didn't you? . . . Just alike. Both of you. Never was no difference between you' (pp. 149–50). The pivotal scene of the little boy's drowning seems to have tied the two girls to a common guilt: a sort of original sin, as Jane Bowles would have said. A similar scene at the beginning of Bowles's novel *Two Serious Ladies* unites two girls, only this time one is attempting to drown the other. In both cases it is a kind of inverse baptism, with water as the ambivalent symbol of life and death.

Eva's words are followed by the surprising offer of oranges ('Want some oranges? It's better for you than chop suey. Sula? I got oranges': p. 150). This ambiguous offer recalls the wrestling relationship between mother and daughter in Winterson's *Oranges Are Not The Only Fruit*, with this fruit as an ambivalent symbol of the relation – and the hostility – between the two women.

Doubles are everywhere in the novels I am discussing here, and sometimes twice over. The fluctuating fragmentary subject of modernism is metamorphosed into the quadruple body of Russ's 'female

man' and the four clones of Weldon's Joanna May; or the ones
surgically modified of Carter's new Eve and Weldon's she-devil.
Ruth and Mary in symmetrical opposition in one of Weldon's
novels find a refraction in Alice-Jael, the double-shaped being of
Russ's *The Female Man*. Angela Carter's *Wise Children* has a double
structure and is peopled with twins, two of whom are the interchangeable Dora/Nora at the centre of the novel. There is also Eve/
lyn, the ambiguous heroine of another novel of hers, hovering
between female and male identity.[32] In these cases the double is
always hinging on sexual ambiguity and is inspired by their mythological ancestor Hermaphrodytus.

Hideous bodies

How hideous am I?
My nose is flat, my eyebrows are heavy. I have only a few teeth
and those are a poor show, being black and broken. I had small-
pox as a child and the caves in my face are home enough for fleas.
                                                    (Jeanette Winterson)

These female monstrous bodies can be multiple, gigantic, fragmented, sexually ambiguous, the product of artificial grafting and
mechanistic (de)constructions, sometimes even of clumsy, old-fash-
ioned surgery. There are four bodies for one erratic variable subjectivity in Joanna Russ's *The Female Man*, and four plus one in Fay
Weldon's *The Cloning of Joanna May*. But even when there is one
body there is a lot of it. Ruth, the demonic being in Weldon's *The
Life and Loves of a She-Devil*, is tall and huge, the dark counterpart
of her alter-ego, Mary Fisher, the best-selling novelist who has
stolen her husband from her. 'Mary Fisher is small and pretty and
delicately formed, prone to fainting and weeping and sleeping with
men' (p. 6: how can one not think of Meryl Streep in Susan
Seidelman's film adaptation of the novel?), while Ruth is a kind of
mountain, 'a vast, obliging mountain':

I am as dark as Mary Fisher is fair, and have one of those jutting
jaws which tall, dark women often have, and eyes sunk rather
back into my face, and a hooked nose. My shoulders are broad
and bony and my hips broad and fleshy, and the muscles in my
legs are well developed. (p. 9)

She has hairs on her chin and her lip, and when she walks she shakes the whole house and becomes larger and larger as her husband falls in love with her minute rival.

Angela Carter also puts a gigantic being at the centre of *Nights at the Circus*, appropriately named Fevvers as she is the mysterious bird-woman delighting the European spectators at the end of last century with her acrobatic spectacle.[33] The spectacle is provided by her hybrid body, playing on the ambiguity between animal and human, truth and fiction, freak or fake. Though the first hundred pages of the novel are occupied by Fevvers telling the tale of her own transformation in an interview with the Californian journalist Walser, the mystery is far from solved. Intrigued by this and in search of the exotic, of the marvellous, of 'laughter and tears and thrills and all' (p. 90), Walser will follow her, inviting his boss (and the readers) for a few nights at the circus, while travelling around the world.

Fevvers is gigantic in her accumulation of limbs and anatomical additions, baroque and decadent at the same time: 'She was twice as large as life . . . she spread out her superb heavy arms in a backward gesture of benediction and, as she did so, her wings spread, too, a polychromatic unfolding fully six feet across, spread of an eagle, a condor, an albatross fed to excess on the same diet that makes flamingoes pink' (p. 15). In contemplating her body, Walser discovers that it is impossible to know whether she is 'a real or feigned bird-woman, genuine miracle or trick' and, by the end, that it does not really matter.

In 'The Laugh of the Medusa', Cixous describes women's flying and plays on the double meaning of the word *voler* ('fly' and 'steal') in French: 'Flying is woman's gesture – flying in language and making it fly. We have all learned the art of flying and its numerous techniques; for centuries we've been able to possess anything only by flying; we've lived in flight, stealing away, finding, when desired, narrow passageways, hidden crossovers.'[34] It seems a fitting comment both on Angela Carter's writing and on Fevvers' vicissitudes: how she shapes her independent life and her strength by learning the art of flying, how she escapes from harm in the nick of time thanks to her flying away through narrow passageways, and how she runs the risk of losing 'her singularity' alongside her wings, in the process of learning to love another.

The Great Mother in *The Passion of New Eve* is a black goddess, a monstrous being that, in its hybrid genitality, represents self-suffi-

cient fertility. Again she is huge, and her shape is a mixture of
human, animal and vegetable.

> She was fully clothed in obscene nakedness; she was breasted like
> a sow – she possessed two tiers of nipples, the result . . . of a
> strenuous programme of grafting, so that, in theory, she could
> suckle four babies at one time. And how gigantic her limbs were!
> Her ponderous feet were heavy enough to serve as illustrations of
> gravity, her hands, the shape of giant fig leaves, lay at rest on the
> bolsters of her knees. (pp. 60–1)

Dog-Woman, another neo-gothic icon in this gallery of female
horror, describes her own hideousness in Jeanette Winterson's
Sexing the Cherry, as we have seen in the epigraph above.[35] She is
uncertain about her looks and identity and has even forgotten her
name, therefore accepting the one given to her by others. Once more
the absence of a name is the mark of a blurred identity, as in the case
of Beloved in Toni Morrison's novel, with her fluctuations between
life and death. Dog-Woman knows she is fat because people
compare her to a mountain range but has contradictory memories
of herself as a child: she broke both her father's legs when he swung
her on his knees, but could be easily carried by her frail mother for
miles. The hybrid physical shape is linked, here as in other cases, to
the failure of identity. She is heavier than an elephant and has
outweighed one in a circus contest, sending it to the sky: 'but how
am I to know what it weighs? A balloon looks big and weighs
nothing' is her comment. At the sight of her nudity, people faint.
'What is love?' she wonders, 'I am too huge for love. No one, male
or female, has ever dared to approach me. They are afraid to scale
mountains' (p. 34).

On the other hand Jordan is proud to have a mother who can
hold a dozen oranges in her mouth at once and Mr Tradescant
accepts her in his house with her animal entourage (she lives with 30
dogs and many fleas, as we have seen in the epigraph above) and,
after trying to protect her, submits not too unwillingly to her
protection:

> Tradescant said nothing, but tried to take my bundle, which
> immediately flattened him to the ground. Very tenderly, as a
> mother knows how, I scooped him up in my arms, the bundle on

top of him, and with my thirty dogs and Jordan coming behind we
entered the gate of the great house and began our life as servants
of the king. (p. 29)

No wonder that at the end of the description of her own physicality,
she asks again 'How hideous am I'?

In *Nights at the Circus*, Fevvers' nakedness is described in the
same way by Walser: 'without her clothes on, she looked the size of
a house' (p. 292), though in this case it does not stop his love, and
Walser ends up happily 'smothered in feathers and pleasure'. She
triumphs in a final image where her vastness becomes beauty itself:
'Now she looked big enough to crack the roof of the god-hut, all
wild hair and feathers and triumphant breasts and blue eyes the size
of dinnerplates' (p. 291). When he discovers that she has no navel,
the only proof that she was born from an egg, he knows better than
to feel certain about anything and leaves the readers as doubtful as
the spectators of her show had always been.

Hybrids and freaks dominate the central part of Carter's novel,
depicting the baroque 'movable feast' of the circus: men dance with
animals; clowns mix comedy and tragedy, the human and the
diabolical; pigs are advisers and monkeys write contracts in their
own favour, thus gaining freedom; tigers fall in love with humans,
with *tearing* consequences, while Walser, the human *par excellence*
and a parodic reversal of the British view of 'quiet Americans',
makes a fool of himself as he learns how to juggle with his own
'strong' subjectivity. It is a reminder of the intricate plots of
vegetable, animal and human worlds represented in Max Ernst's
painting, and very close to the paroxysm of hellish and grotesque
cinematic forms in Tod Browning's *Freaks* and Ulrike Ottinger's
Freak Orlando.

With her irony, Carter is here asking for a total suspension of
disbelief from the reader as we have seen she does at the end of *Wise
Children*, the disbelief in this case being tied not so much to the
acceptance of the fantastic journeys in clownland as to the over-
turning of traditional assessments of female beauty, the erasure of
stereotypes of the feminine (a political goal of Carter's narrative
from the start).[36] Fevvers is the last in the gallery of hybrid bodies
that appeared in her short stories (often a rewriting or, as she herself
says, recycling of famous fables). The heroine of *Wolf-Alice* is the
result of a half-accomplished metamorphosis:

> Could this ragged girl with brindled lugs have spoken like we do
> she would have called herself a wolf, but she cannot speak,
> although she howls because she is lonely . . . Her panting tongue
> hangs out; her red lips are thick and fresh. Her legs are long, lean
> and muscular. Her elbows, hands and knees are thickly callused
> because she always runs on all fours.[37]

The girl in *The Company of Wolves* is not transformed into a wolf as
in Neil Jordan's film adaptation of the story, but she is not eaten by
the wolf either: 'All the better to eat you with. The girl burst out
laughing; she knew she was nobody's meat. She laughed at him full
in the face, she ripped off his shirt for him and flung it into the fire,
in the fiery wake of her own discarded clothing' (pp. 158–9).
Contrary to its model, the fable ends with the girl sleeping peacefully
'between the paws of the tender wolf' on Christmas night. Likewise
Winterson's Dog-Woman leads a symbiotic life with fleas and dogs,
and seems to be nearer animals than humans; Villanelle, the heroine
of *The Passion*, is a woman with webbed feet who can walk on the
Venetian lagoon and live without her heart.

They are half animals but also half devils. Like Ruth, Alice-Jael in
The Female Man is a she-devil too. She is part of a multiple
fluctuating ego and takes many shapes as she is 'the Woman Who
Has No Brand Name': 'Me with a new face, a puffy mask. Laid over
the old one in strips of plastic that hurt when they come off, a blond
Hallowe'en ghoul on top of the S.S. uniform' (p. 157). The 'I'
becomes a 'she', and this is how 'she' is objectified:

> Her laughter is horrid, a hard, screeching yell that ends in gasps
> and rusty sobbing, as if some mechanical vulture on a gigantic
> garbage heap on the surface of the moon were giving one forced
> shriek for the death of all organic life .´. . the ends of her fingers
> ragged under the long silvery nails, as sharp as knives . . . She has
> hairpin-shaped scars under her ears, too. (p. 159)

In a novel whose dominant mode is pastiche and parody, the author
winks here at popular icons of the female witch, ironically quoting
the stereotypes of a Disneyesque world.

· In other novels the monsters have a mythological or literary
reference of a more refined kind, leading to forms of high grotesque,
in Mary Russo's term. Metamorphosis and hybridity are always
linked to mythological figures, such as chimeras, mermaids and

amazons, which are mostly the result of the contamination of human with animal. Often the monsters are on the frontier between life and death: women vampires from Sheridan LeFanu's Carmilla to Anne Rice's Claudia; un-dead creatures like Toni Morrison's Beloved; half-dead but on the way to resurrection in Abel Ferrara's film *The Addiction* (1995), an ironic rendering of academic vampirism, in which female students spread the contagion throughout a whole department of human science in a North American university of the nineties. Needless to say, postmodern philosophies are the main carriers.

In Anne Rice's *Interview with the Vampire*, we meet the female companion of the monster once more, only this time she has not been destroyed at the outset as in Shelley's novel (it will take the whole book in a battle of mutual destruction between her and Lestat, her creator) and, as if realising Victor Frankenstein's prediction, she has appropriated her monstrous nature without flaws. This is what she tells Louis her lover, another victim of Lestat and a vampire with human flaws: 'Human nature. I have no human nature. And no short story of a mother's corpse and hotel rooms where children learn monstrosity can give me one. I have none. Your eyes grow cold with fear when I say this to you . . . I am your vampire self more than you are.'[38]

Hybrid sexuality, failed identity

These monsters can also be half women, half men. Sexual ambiguity is another irregularity or asymmetry in these hybrid beings rising against what Denise Riley calls 'the dreadful air of constancy of sexual polarity'.[39] The link between bisexuality and the hysterical woman has often been made; Freud, for instance, regarded her as at the same time man and woman and considered hysteria a polymorphous perversion. Catherine Clément points to hysteria (and sorcery) as an exit from sex roles:

> The hysteric's *bisexuality*, like the sorceress's *nature*, is doubtlessly greater if one leaves hysteria behind; departs from the roles helplessly denounced by the hysteric. Quits the show. Ends the circus in which too many women are crushed to death. Is done with the couple: perversion and hysteria, inquisitor and sorceress.[40]

Carter's *The Passion of New Eve* consistently develops the theme of hybrid sexuality. We find the coexistence of sexual opposites in three characters, the Great Mother, the ephebic star Tristessa, and Eve(lyn). The latter becomes Eve after the mutilation performed by the Great Mother within the process of femininisation of the world that she has undertaken: 'Woman has been the antithesis in the dialectic of creation quite long enough . . . I'm about to make a start on the femininisation of Father Time.'[41] Eve(lyn), after the anatomical and linguistic castration, becomes 'a man-made masterpiece of skin and bone, the technological Eve in person' (p. 146), but her new femininity is ambiguous, jarring, flawed; its incompleteness is revealed when she falls in love with *the* symbol of feminine charm itself, the Hollywood star Tristessa (Greta Garbo? Joan Crawford? Marlene Dietrich? Audrey Hepburn?). Their sexual union is not a lesbian conjunction as it would seem at first, or a simple inversion of the gender difference, as you would be inclined to believe once you learn that the perfect symbol of womanhood is actually a transsexual. It is rather the meeting – on both sides of a threshold – between two new entities, one female in which the male trace is ever present, the other a perfectly ambivalent icon, in which femininity triumphs through the constant recollection of an underlying male element.

Tristessa de St Ange – 'billed (do you remember?) as "The most beautiful woman in the world", who executed her symbolic autobiography in arabesques of kitsch and hyperbole' (p. 5) – appears as an elusive double from the start, in spite of being the apotheosis of the feminine in the most powerful mythography of our century, the filmic imaginary. Only after a long resistance does new Eve accept Tristessa's double nature, her coexistence of masculine and feminine which is Eve's own as well:

> Masculine and feminine are correlatives which involve one another. I am sure of that – the quality and its negation are locked in necessity. But what the nature of masculine and the nature of feminine might be, whether they involve male and female . . . that I do not know. Though I have been both man and woman, still I do not know the answer to these questions. Still they bewilder me. (pp. 149–50)

The Great Mother had foreseen that one day she would discover the manifold structures and forms of sexuality: in these alienated times it is impossible to say what unity in sexuality is and what is not. In the end the knowledge of such a unity leads to the vanishing of the frontiers of individual and sexual identity: 'Here we were at the beginning or end of the world and I, in my sumptuous flesh, was in myself the fruit of the tree of knowledge; knowledge had made me' (p. 146), and again, 'He and I, she and he, are the sole oasis in this desert' (p. 148).

On the contrary, Weldon's she-devil moves between two fixed stereotypes, between the mimicry of Mary's femininity and her own masculinity, and is in the end sadly and tragically trapped in the polarity: her new sexuality is only a political act, her new identity a sad joke, as the bitter ending says. Weldon's naturalistic mode, respectful of the prevailing English tradition, dominates here: Ruth's transformation is not brought about by magical or fantastical powers but by the numerous plastic operations she painstakingly undergoes to become the copy of Mary Fisher, to be assimilated to the other. Temporal and spatial coherence and psychological ver-isimilitude are respected. The narrative subject is quite firmly grounded in Ruth looking at Mary as the other although, within that, the prevailing third person mode shifts to first person: Ruth is alternately 'I' and 'she'. In the same way the parodic register acts as a distorting lens: the minute and realistic details are brought to excess, while paradox becomes the narrative economy and rhythm. The bodily metaphor interrupts the realistic surface and creates a parallel diegetic text. In *Puffball*, another of her novels, the 'events' internal to the menstruation cycles and to the successive phases of conception in Liffey's body intersect with the twists of the *fabula*, in a close narrative counterpoint. Naturalism is brought to excess, as in the descriptions of Ruth's operations.

Alice-Jael is a female man, as the title of Russ's novel says, and these are her first words:

I'll tell you how I turned into a man.
First I had to turn into a woman.
For a long time I had been neuter. (p. 133)

In the same novel, Janet Evason, though the espression of a matriarchal society and the incarnation of a female multiple ego, exhibits her bisexual nature in her name and in her self-presentation ('When I was thirteen I stalked and killed a wolf, alone, on North Continent above the forty-eighth parallel, using only a rifle . . . I've

worked in the mines, on the radio network, on a milk farm . . . At
thirty I bore Yuriko Janetson': p. 1) and ends with the same
paradoxical juxtaposition of female and male stereotypes: 'I love
my daughter. I love my family (there are nineteen of us). I love my
wife (Vittoria). I have fought four duels. I've killed 4 times' (p. 2).
The gender juxtaposition is linked to the fluctuation of the narrat-
ing/narrated subjects, in an ambiguous zone in which bodies and
sexualities do not find any definition. This is how the author says
goodbye to her readers, and to her five selves: 'We got up and paid
our quintuple bill; then we went out into the street. I said goodbye
and went off with Laur, I, Janet; I also watched them go, I, Joanna;
moreover I went off to show Jael the city, I Jeannine, I Jael, I myself'
(p. 212).
The question is: where am I? Where is my sexual identity? The
fragmentation of identities is also spatial and temporal dissemina-
tion. Whileaway, Janet's planet, is the future, but not our future;
Jeannine and Joanna belong to two different presents, Jael to a
'changeable' time and space. Narrative time crosses different moments and stages, while identity, point of view and narrating
subjectivity are incessantly transmigrating. At the same time, the
novel presents an insistent tender representation of lesbian love –
between young Laur and adult Janet – tied to some extent to more
stable subjectivities.

   Jeanette Winterson's *Written on the Body* is an extreme statement,
or rather refusal of one, on sexual ambiguity. Writing here *is* the
body of a woman, of beautiful, red-haired Louise, first love's body
and then death's body; so much so that the book is partly a novel
and partly an anatomical treatise. The ambiguity is in the narrator,
whose sex eludes the reader throughout the narration, here and there
giving a baffling suggestion in one direction or another, or in the
erotic descriptions lingering at times on caressing or penetrating, but
always moving in a disturbing balance between one sex and another,
in an intersticial zone. It is an intentional game but yet at the same
time it is not as it appeals to that indistinct zone that is in each of us.
The narrator might be female or male, but is never a phallic voice. It
is a weak 'I', lost, uncertain, making mistakes, suffering a trial
whose outcome is unclear. In opposition Louise though fatally ill
and unambiguously female is strong and sure, and the one who
without hesitation puts the love of the other to a test. Her body is
the one that is written upon, the passive end, but she is the one who

expresses her awareness: 'Who taught you to write in blood on my back? Who taught you to use your hands as branding irons? You have scored your name into my shoulders, referenced me with your mark . . . you tap a message on to my skin, tap meaning onto my body.'[42]

There is no proper ending to the novel, which brings the reader full circle, with Louise beginning the narration again. Her 'appearance' at the end, after the 'I' has passed the test – women's symbolic journey through a wood as in the old fable? – is perhaps an apparition (the play on these two words was inaugurated in *Hamlet*): she may have miraculously recovered or she may be a ghost. The trace left by the appearance and disappearance of an ambiguous body is the deferral of the writing itself.

> Written on the body is a secret code only visible in certain lights; the accumulations of a lifetime gather there. In places the palimpsest is so heavily worked that the letters feel like braille. I like to keep my body rolled up away from prying eyes. Never unfold too much. I didn't know Louise would have reading hands. She has translated me into her own book. (p. 89)

This quotation leads back to the discourse of writing and the female body that started this chapter.

Of grafting and difference

> . . . you see, sweet maid, we marry
> A gentler scion to the wildest stock,
> And make conceive a bark of baser kind
> By bud of nobler race: this is an art
> Which does mend nature, change it rather, but
> The art itself is nature.
> *The Winter's Tale*, IV, 3, 92–7

> the transformation from one element to another, from waste matter to best gold, is a process that cannot be documented. It is fully mysterious. (Jeanette Winterson)

The theme of grafting, which goes back to Hermione and Perdita and to Shakespeare's last plays, is present in *Sexing the Cherry*, starting with its title. It also refers to the meeting of identities, of bodies, of plants. The practice is polysemic in the novel and works at many levels (as it did in Shakespeare). It is about giving strength to the weak and about metamorphosis and transformation; it is also about postcoloniality and its condition of transplanting oneself elsewhere, or the elsewhere here; about de-spatialisation; about travels and love; about coming into existence without seed or parent; about artificial as well as natural creation. Finally it is about the hybridity of sexual identities.

The title comes from a minor incident in the plot, the sexing of a cherry tree that Jordan performs in order to practise the French art of grafting after bringing exotic seeds and pods back from the Bermudas. His mother doubts that the monster produced by the union of a Polstead Black and a Morello may have a sex.

> I tried to explain to her that the tree would still be female although it had not been born from seed, but she said such things had no gender and were a confusion to themselves.
> 'Let the world mate of its own accord,' she said, 'or not at all.'
> But the cherry grew, and we have sexed it and it is female. (p. 79)

This brief glimpse on sexual difference finds its only explicit correspondence in Fortunata's tale, describing Artemis torn between her female nature and her stubborn refusal of it, represented in her immense desire for hunting. The tale speaks of the impossibility for her of finding a unity between her two identities, or otherwise a third one. As alchemists say, 'the third is not given'. 'What would it matter if she crossed the world and hunted down every living creature so long as her separate selves eluded her?' (p. 131). After killing Orion, she realises she has crossed over the frontiers of common sense. 'The fiery circle surrounding her held all the clues she needed to recognize that life is for a moment contained in one shape then released in another' (p. 130).

Winterson, like Carter, does not have replies. In the end Jordan, who has been looking for the princess dancer Fortunata throughout the novel, from the seventeenth century to modern times, in finding her, becomes her. Winterson describes here the indistinct border in which sexual difference is no longer clear. Feminist theory has shown the limits and dangers of rigid sexual binaries. Perhaps the need to feel ourselves part of a separate half is still here. How far can we go in accepting that man and woman are everywhere, without fearing the return of old paradigms and supremacies? This is probably a time that has started and not yet completed, for which it is necessary to use the confused and difficult language of transition. Hélène Cixous has imagined the possibility in a utopian future of radical transformations in behaviours, mores, roles, political and libidinal economy – a real liberation from sexuality – and Audre Lorde one in which woman is the antithesis, the sharpened edge where difference meets but does not merge.

The female novels I have been re-reading in the last two chapters presenting the collapse of traditional barriers – between factuality and imagination, criticism and fiction, heroes or heroines – cannot be easily categorised as gender-specific, except as a memento of something that, while being slowly erased, still appears in its cancellation. While erasing and denying, these novels go on speaking in a female way about women.

Women's laughter

Voices, or rather cries, yells, shouts, come from the women monsters that have peopled the novels I have examined. These sounds have many resonances, starting from Bertha Mason's yells in *Jane Eyre*, 'sounds of the bottomless pit' as the exasperated Rochester defines them, to Alice-Jael's screeching harsh laughter in Russ's *The Female Man*. Laughter, as is well known, is the mark of excess and does not become woman, but of late it has been rescued for its upsetting, displacing value. In 'The Laugh of the Medusa', Hélène Cixous reminds her readers that women have been riveted to the horrifying myth of Medusa and that it is important for them to look at Medusa's face for history to change its meaning: 'You only have to look at the Medusa straight on to see her. And she's not deadly. She's beautiful and she's laughing.'[43]

This is perhaps what Angela Carter is doing placing Fevvers' sardonic laughter at the end of *Nights at the Circus*, in her final joke on the myth (yet another) of women's virginity: 'The spiralling tornado of Fevvers' laughter began to twist and shudder across the entire globe, as if a spontaneous response to the giant comedy that endlessly unfolded beneath it, until everything that lived and breathed, everywhere, was laughing' (p. 295). Another lingering sound is the cry that closes *Sula*:

> 'All that time, all that time. I thought I was missing Jude.' And the loss pressed down on her chest and came up into her throat. 'We was girl together,' she said as though explaining something. 'O Lord, Sula,' she cried, 'girl, girl, girlgirlgirl'. (p. 154)

It would be only too easy to close on this cry as a note of triumph if Toni Morrison had not reminded us that underneath it there are 'circles and circles of sorrow'.

Chapter 6

Alterity and the Female Traveller: Jane Bowles

[F]or me fiction is the stitch masking the wound, the gap between two shores. (Leila Sebbar)

Every journey conceals another journey. (Jeanette Winterson)

A complex refraction

Jane Auer Bowles, born in New York in 1917 of Jewish-Hungarian family, spent half her life in Tangier and died in a psychiatric institution at Malaga in 1973. She was a nomadic writer, in some ways a typical American intellectual, like – and at the same time unlike – other occidental women writers who, in the first half of this century, went to Europe, and particularly Paris, in search of their art and themselves.

From a very early age she moved between New York and Paris, California and Mexico, North and South America. In spite of this, her relationship to travelling is a mixed one, as is clear from her works. In the same way, love-hate, attraction-revulsion are the contradictory impulses that governed her relationship to writing, and brought about the writing block that was to afflict her. Both these areas of crisis intermingle deeply in her liaison with a woman from another culture and race and concur with the displacement of the self: 'writing is precisely working (in) the in-between, inspecting the process of the same and of the other without which nothing can live, undoing the work of death'.[1]

This itinerary gives shape, through claustrophobic interior close-ups, to a tormented unclear vision that could be considered an

133

aesthetic failure, in contrast with artistically perfect male visions. In novels and films, she has been represented as a fateful icon presaging ruin and death, in strict relation to the exotic background and her lesbian sexual identity. The last move in this play of complex refractions in 'the fantasmatics of cultural difference' is the gaze on the other looking at another who is looking elsewhere.

Most of the themes that emerge here connect to the previous chapters: both her works and life are a statement of displacement: the encounter with the other woman – in this case the racial other – once more confirms difference within sameness; monstrosity represents sexual and ethnic diversity; the female body splits apart (as in the Cronenberg film), erring from one gender to another; silence is tied to the block and disintegration of writing. The journey in and through sexual identity, a leitmotif of most of the writing I examine, is the metaphor for the crossing of an indistinct zone between masculine and feminine. The exploration of sexual ambiguity is crucial here, as for Jane Bowles travelling meant also facing her lesbian identity.

Finally the theme of madness and melancholia links up to death, which will become a voluntary death in the next chapter dealing with female melancholia in *Hamlet*.

Death and the female traveller: male visions

Two women with the same face, one in a sordid hotel room in New York, the other at the back of a car passing the frontier to the imaginary country of Annexia: both women place a glass on their heads as the target for a man's gun. In both cases the woman is hit and dies. The glass rolls to the ground without breaking.[2]

A country in Africa. A silent, absent woman, who does not remember her name ('everything's lost' is her only reply to all questioning), has no luggage or money but only a passport in the name of Katherine Moresby. A taxi takes her to an hotel where somebody is waiting to send her home. The colonial officer who is with her gets out of the taxi and enters the hotel; a few seconds later, when people come out to fetch her, they find it empty. Not too far off, a streetcar full of people can be seen slowly mounting the ascent towards the Arab district, the end of the line.[3]

Aicha Qandicha, the fierce blue-breasted goddess who hangs around springs and wells and steals men's souls . . . She appears to men, never to women who, however, are very afraid of her. She will call you from behind, often in the voice of your mother. If you turn around, you are lost as she is the most beautiful woman and once you look at her you have no power against her . . . 25 years ago 35 000 men in Morocco were said to be married to her. A lot of the people in Ber Rechid, the psychiatric hospital, are married to her.[4]

Jane Bowles travelled widely, but more than anything she was *observed* travelling by the male gaze. Paul Bowles, her husband, friend and fellow-traveller, was the participant observer, with other friends and writers such as William Burroughs, Truman Capote, Tennessee Williams and Gore Vidal. More recently that 'observing' eye has been transformed into a camera, it being in contemporary cinema that portraits of hers can be found. I am thinking here of Bernardo Bertolucci's *The Sheltering Sky*, based on Paul Bowles's novel of the same title, and of David Cronenberg's *Naked Lunch*, inspired by William Burroughs' novel. In the latter film the literary derivation is more oblique, and it refers to other works by Burroughs (in particular *Interzone* and *The Exterminator*), as well as to general aspects and themes drawn from his life.

The leitmotif of *Naked Lunch* is the process of writing and the problem of the authorial bloc, somewhat buried in the novel and made more explicit by Cronenberg.[5] This is infused with Cronenberg's cinematic aesthetics and sensibility, mainly his need to construct material, concrete 'creatures' out of the ghosts of the mind, with the help of special effects.[6] The fatal dangers connected to writing, the vision of imagination as a disease become physically present in the film: the giant centipedes, the Mugwumps, the Sex Blobs, the giant bugs mutating into typewriters and vice versa (all speaking through anus-like mouths) are potentially harmful creatures who represent, and at the same time defend, the dangers of imagination: 'If you accept . . . the Freudian dictum that civilization is repression, then imagination – and an unrepressed creativity – is dangerous to civilization. But . . . imagination is also an innate part of civilization. If you destroy it, you might also destroy civilization'.[7]

Further, Cronenberg insists that one of the differences between Burroughs and himself is that he is heterosexual and therefore finds the presence of female characters essential to his creativity. One of the changes in the film in fact is the dilation of the female figure who in Burroughs' novel is very tangentially present and thus summarily dispatched: 'In Cuernavaco or was it Taxco? Jane meets a pimp trombone player and disappears in a cloud of tea smoke . . . A year later in Tangier I heard she was dead.'[8] The person Burroughs is referring to can be identified as Jane Bowles, whom he had repeatedly met in Tangiers. Many years before her death, she is given as dead, under the dictates of his poetical vision and perhaps under the influence of the news of her serious illness. The sentence seems to suggest a moral judgement, surprising in an anti-conformist who keeps company with 'wild boys'. Even stranger is that her loose ways are depicted as heterosexual since Jane in her turn prefers 'wild girls': Helvetia, Nora, Cory, Frances, Martha, and the Arabian peasant Cherifa.

This distorted vision of Jane's sexual promiscuity is common to both Paul Bowles's novel and Bertolucci's film, where her extra-marital relations are heterosexual from the outset. Ethnic diversity, which in Burroughs is only hinted at, is underlined in *The Sheltering Sky*: 'The young Arab who had told her the name of the other bordj walked by as they sat on the floor eating. Kit could not help noticing how unusually tall he was, what an admirable figure he cut when he stood erect in his flowing white garment.'[9] Though denying that the novel is autobiographical, Bowles admits that his wife Jane has been the inspiration for the heroine. The plot revolves around Port and Kit, an American couple travelling in Africa with their friend Tunner, who eventually becomes Kit's lover. The Sahara is the great adventure with a bitter ending. Port dies from typhus and Kit joins a passing Arab caravan led by the attractive Belqassim, becoming his lover and slave. In the end, driven away by his wives' jealousy, she drifts to despair and ruin, and then finally to the 'disappearance' predicted by Burroughs.

In Bowles's novel, the most important thing for the heroine is to escape the Western world and what she has left behind.[10] This is the sense of her final flight: on hearing that Tunner is waiting for her at the hotel, she decides to lose herself in nothingness, the nothingness that is the Western signifier for the loss of the self: 'going native'. The desert, as the zeroing of the ego and/or a new beginning from zero, is the essential metaphor of this vision. Kit's voluntary annihilation starts very traditionally in her sexual enthralment to her Arab lover. Once more it is the woman who becomes the sign and symbol of such vision.

The attraction of ruin and death is often represented as female. Edward Šaid sees in this association one of the common traits of the various accounts of the Orient, spanning three centuries, different national viewpoints, and the building and collapse of empires.[11] As Mayda Yegenoglu notes, 'the process of Orientalisation of the Orient is one that intermingles with its feminisation'. She further stresses that 'the typography of femininity as enigmatic, mysterious, concealing a secret behind its veil is projected onto the iconography of the Orient'.[12] The novel and the film can be considered part of the historical and literary vision of the West's fatal attraction for the Arabian world, an essential aspect of the construction of the East that, from Rimbaud and T. E. Lawrence to cinema and cartoons, includes both the intellectual image found in the modernist avant-garde and the popular icon of the Arab in mass culture. In their representation of ethnic diversity, both Bowles and Bertolucci are not too distant from this icon. Deborah Root severely defines the film a 'colonialist nightmare' and a parody of desert adventure films, like *Lawrence of Arabia* and other spectacular versions of exotica.[13]

Again in Cronenberg's film the image of 'woman' is associated with death, though this time the image of the colonial African city is very much in the background. The female character is a double: Joan Lee, wife of the hero Bill, and Joan Frost, living in Tangier with her husband the writer Tom, appear in the first and the second part of the film respectively, both ending with the death of the woman, played by the same actress. This double character recalls two real figures: Joan Vollmer, William Burroughs' wife, killed by him in Mexico City in an accident similar to the one described in the film, and Jane Bowles, metaphorically also killed by Burroughs (at least in his novel). The film, inspired by the mythology of the American beat poets who were in Tangier with Burroughs in those years, places Jane/Joan at the centre of this group, though Jane was actually very tangential to it. There is no proof that the inspiration of this character goes back to Jane Bowles: Cronenberg does not acknowledge it in his first interview on the film but, on the other hand, there are many concrete details from her life, and Paul Bowles's *Conversations* are repeatedly used.

It is not important to verify how and where fiction draws from reality in this case, or anticipates it in the novels. It is almost as though this group of people were writing the scripts of their lives. In an unreal play from one dimension to the other, reality metamorphoses into fiction in temporal and spatial anticipation. The foreboding in Bowles's novels, mostly written before Jane's arrival in Africa, are an uncanny instance of this, just as the horrid prevision of Jane's death was in Burroughs. An even stranger coincidence occurs with the obsessive images of typewriters in Cronenberg's film, for, during the unhappy years of her illness, Jane became more and more dependent on them, due to her progressive inability to speak and write. The writing block is a further link, even though in the film it refers to male characters.

The actress Judy Davis is reminiscent, in her features, expressions and dahlia-shaped hair style, of photographs of Jane. The drugs and alcohol, the sexual promiscuity, this time openly bisexual, and the unconventional personality recall her, while contributing to an image of the *femme fatale* so dear to *maudite* literature. From the outset the female icon is related to drugs and to literary inspiration. The hero, Bill Lee, like Burroughs at one point, is a bug killer, an exterminator, and also 'the exterminator of all rational thought'. In the very first scene confronting the abominable speaking creatures, he finds himself without the essential insecticide powder. Soon after he discovers his wife in the act of injecting herself with it as she, like the creatures, has become addicted to the poison. From that moment the image of the giant bugs is linked to the woman in Bill's gesture of smearing the powder both on her mouth and on the animals' talking sphincters. Woman, writing and monstrosity are an inextricable triangle in Cronenberg's oneiric 'nightmare'.

There are further references to real events in Jane's life: her wanderings in the Casbah, her obstinate will to 'penetrate' the Moroccan world and culture (more than once she is suspected to be a spy from interzone – the spy story plot is essential to the film – and in Dillon's biography, Jane Bowles appears to refer to Tangier as 'interzone'), and, more importantly, her tie with a Moroccan woman she meets in the market: Cherifa, here called Fadela, is an important figure in the film, again a duplicitous icon alternating between feminine Arabian attire and masculine Western riding habit or colonial uniform. By representing magic, cruelty, transvestism and sexual ambiguity, she embodies crucial aspects of the film-maker's imaginary that have become dominant in the more recent *M Butterfly*. Fadela, divesting herself of her skin and coming out of her woman's body as Dr Benway (the actor Roy Scheider) – 'the manipulator of symbol systems' (Burroughs) – is a crucial image of this male/female split and the turning point in the film *Naked Lunch*. Here the tie between the two women is not foregrounded, as Joan and, in a different way, Fedela are seen as symbolical mediators of impotent, anguished male artists such as Burroughs/Bowles/Cronenberg.

Bill is William Tell. Both women's deaths are brought about by a re-enactment of the apple game: in both cases, once asked, she docilely places the glass on her head, he shoots and hits her, while the glass falls to the floor and remains intact.[14] But he is also Orpheus in search of his Eurydice, who loses her for turning back, while he is taking her from the dangerous interzone to the safety of a utopian world, but actually exchanges her for his newly found inspiration. In the second case, he is asked by the guards at the frontier of Annexia to prove he is a writer. Once he discovers that showing his pen is not enough, he exchanges it for a gun, turns around towards the back of the car where she has been sleeping and shoots her, after performing the usual ceremony.

Writing is connected to the elsewhere, to death and woman. Both plots in the film end with the writer in crisis killing the woman. He loves her but must kill her so his writing can exist: 'once in a lifetime, a man has to do a girl in', as T. S. Eliot's line goes. Only, in this case, 'once' is not enough.

A final image. San Francisco, May 1994

City Lights, San Francisco's famous bookstore, founded by Corso and Ferlinghetti in the 1950s, one of the intellectual centers of the city and monument to the poets of the Beat generation. On the first floor, a sort of sanctuary dedicated to the founding fathers, a picture representing five men on the beach at Tangier in 1959 can be seen. The five bodies – Kerouac and Orlovsky standing, Burroughs lying down, two Moroccan (wild) boys in the back-ground and Ginsberg behind the camera – seem organized around an empty centre, an absence, a ghost, the ghost of a woman haunting the modernist imagination.

The Moorish Lover

> I continue loving Tangier – maybe because I have the feeling of being on the edge of something that I will some day enter. (Jane Bowles)

Jane Bowles arrived in Tangier at the beginning of 1948 to join Paul, who soon after left for New York to write the music for Tennessee Williams' *The Glass Menagerie*. Jane's long letters to Paul in this first period describe the fascination that Africa held for her:

> The view of the Arab town from my window is a source of endless pleasure to me . . . Here there's the water and the sky and the mountains in the distance and all the blue in the Casbah; even in the white, there's lots of blue.The grain market is blue – blue and green.[15]

What charmed and magnetised her was the difficulty of penetrating that culture. It engaged her in a long and slow battle that never ended. Her acquaintance with two African women, and her attraction to one of them, is the emblematic initial *coup-de-foudre* and an essential part of that drive: 'Perhaps I shall be perpetually on the edge of this civilization of theirs. When I am in Cherifa's house I am still on the edge of it, and when I come out I can't believe I was really in it' (p. 85). The two women are Cherifa, who wears no veil and sells grain in the market, 'my little Cherifa, who is about twelve years younger than myself', and Tetum, described at first as 'the older "Mountain Dyke", that yellow ugly one':

> so God knows I'll probably stick around here forever, just for an occasional smile from Tetum or Cherifa. I wrote you how exciting it was to feel on the edge of something. Well, it's beginning to make me very nervous. I don't see any way of getting any further into it, since what I want is so particular (as usual); and as for forgetting them altogether, it's too late.[16] (p. 93)

Jane is obsessed by the grain market in which Cherifa has her stall, tormented by a social structure that she cannot quite understand, and by the tension of not being accepted. Her attitude towards the Arab world is mediated by the romantic possibilities she has found in it; all her letters express the difficulties of the relationship with Cherifa and of its beginnings with pressing anguish: 'I still have a dim hope that if I learned to speak Arabic she would be friendly maybe and I could sit in the hanootz with her when I chose to' (ibid.).

Soon her Arabic improves and so does her social life with the women in the market: Tatum, Zodelia, Cherifa and Quinza. She takes them to the doctor, gives them all her scarves and money, and in exchange gets to be called 'sister'. This good moment is accompanied by one of the rare joys about her writing, as she has finished *Camp Cataract*, 'the best thing I've ever done', soon followed by the pain for the impossibility of continuing to write attributed to the state of suspension she is in. Only in 1954 will Cherifa go and live with her, and even then her mysterious diversity still baffles and torments her, as she says in a long, unusually intimate, letter to her friends Natasha and Katharine:

> I waited and waited before writing because foolishly I hoped I could write you: 'I have or have not . . . Cherifa.' The awful thing is that I don't even know. I don't know what they do. I don't know how much they feel . . . So hard to know what is clever manoeuvring on her part, what is a lack of passion, and what is fear . . . She is terribly affectionate at times and kissing is heaven.[17] (pp. 177–8)

She describes moving forwards, and sometime backwards, in her cautious sexual approaches, as the threshold between tenderness and sex is unclear in the other culture, and she realises that Cherifa will yield mostly to please her rather than out of her own will. Also, she underlines how important it is to have enough money:

> I love this life and I'm terrified of the day when my money runs out. The sex thing aside, it is as if I had dreamed this life before I was born. Perhaps I will work hard to keep it. I cannot keep Cherifa without money, or even myself, after all . . . I think of her in terms of a long long time. How one can do this and at the same time fully realise that money is of paramount importance . . . I simply don't know . . . Yet they are not like we are. Someone behaving the same way who was not an Arab I couldn't bear.[18] (p. 180)

The period that follows is the happiest in her life as she feels more integrated in that world. In spite of occasional violent clashes with Cherifa, the tension is over but it all has a short life. At the age of forty, during Ramadan – which she always tried to observe, to Paul's dismay – Jane has a stroke of an uncertain nature, impairing her for the rest of her life. It marks a step forward in that slow and painfully conscious journey towards the writing block and the mental deterioration, a journey that overlaps with all her other journeys. It came ten years after her first arrival in Africa, towards the end of April 1957 (the events of her life seem to follow a ritualistic rhythm).

From that moment the slow decline in her health goes with the substantial deterioration of their *ménage*, which includes part of Cherifa's large family, and their maid Aicha with her child. This Arab 'family' does not exclude her husband, who is always in close proximity. Such coexistence is part of the extraordinary alchemy of her social life. It had already occurred with Jane's other lovers, particularly with Helvetia Perkins in New York at the onset of her marriage, but in this case it is more difficult because of the bad relationship between her two partners: Paul has accused Cherifa of manipulating and exploiting Jane and, after her death, like other mutual friends, of having slowly poisoned her.

In spite of the limits inherent in the relationship and added difficulties – its initial romanticism is soon submerged by the misunderstandings and the banalities of everyday life, the sexual liaison seems to be over after only two years, and Jane's interest in other women follows – their attachment uncannily survives. She goes on wanting to live with Cherifa who, in her turn, consents to going back to her, even between one hospitalisation and another. Jane must have felt a deep sense of guilt for isolating her from her own culture (a responsibility that she never evaded, providing for her until and after her death), but this cannot be the sole explanation. For Jane living in Tangier means being with Cherifa, and Cherifa is the essential condition for making Tangier a sort of home.

Many voices have been heard on their relationship, those of Paul and his companion Ahmed, of Jane's mother, and of Martha, a later lover, and they all speak of the very bad influence it had on Jane. Truman Capote's description of Cherifa as rough, old (!) and abrasive reflects the common view: 'The late Mrs. Bowles lived in an infinitesimal Casbah house . . . with her Moorish lover, the famous Cherifa, a rough old peasant woman . . . an abrasive personality only a genius as witty and dedicated to extreme oddity as Mrs Bowles could have abided.'[19] Cherifa's voice is hardly ever heard and if so, indirectly: in pictures there are a few rare images of a woman with a set, unsmiling face, in European clothes; in writings a few sentences and reactions always related by hostile onlookers. Absent from Jane's letters as she was illiterate, she is the one voiceless ghost in a highly literate world, demonised and described as a witch.[20]

The image of the witch or the malevolent goddess is a constant presence in African tales. The uncanny, the heart of darkness, is linked to the woman with magical powers, whether these are good (and then she has the power to heal, and is called a doctor) or bad (and then she is a witch). In Paul Bowles's interviews and diaries, Aicha Qandicha, a Moroccan version of Astarte, the fierce Stone-Age goddess appearing in one of the images I put at the beginning of this chapter, is often evoked. Cherifa, presented as the maid, is also recalled for her magical powers:

> this rather evil maid we had here gave her something . . . This maid was a horror. We used to find packets of magic around the house. In fact, in my big plant, in the roots, she hid a magic packet. She wanted to control the household through the plant. The plant was her proxy, or stooge, and she could give it orders before she left . . . A monster, a real monster. I could show you pictures of her that would freeze you.'[21]

Once again the equation of woman and monster appears.

Additions to the tale were provided by Paul's Moroccan partners, whose close relationship to Jane coexisted with hostility towards their fellow countrywoman. In a recent interview given to Soledad Alameda and published in *El Pais* in 1990, Paul irritatedly replies to the usual annoying questions about Jane that such practices are very common in Africa, and that in any case what really killed Jane was alcohol; but the bewitched plant comes up again (it reappears in Cronenberg's film too). Unexpectedly, however, in this case he remembers the vision he had of Cherifa the first time he saw her: 'There she was, in the big straw hat with ribbons that the farm women wear, in a red and white striped apron. She had very wild eyes . . . She said she was a saint, a virgin, that she had certificates to prove it.'[22]

'The bride is arriving' is a sentence that Cherifa is said to have pronounced when Paul and Ahmed send her away on Jane's return from the psychiatric hospital, as they believe it would be inadvisable for her to have Cherifa around; it is a sarcastic pronouncement, brutal and at the same time revealing a subaltern condition. This kind of 'witch' was colonised twice: as the other, mirror of unattainable desire; and as the mistress, the eternal third party, mistress in relation to the husband Paul, mistress in relation to the 'bride' Jane.

Towards silence

Much has been written on the contradictory impulse present in travelling: the pull between the reinforcement and the loss of identity, clarity and mystery, knowledge and its refusal. It is a spiral movement – like that of Don Quixote, the baroque hero – rather than the linear progress of most accounts of travel. The wanderings of the subversive and the rebel, of the sick and the mad have always been placed outside the genre.

It is the spiral dialectic of travelling, rather than the linearity of narrative, that is fundamental to Jane Bowles's writing. This is perhaps paradoxically why her work cannot be strictly defined as travel writing. In her only finished novel, *Two Serious Ladies*, and in her short stories, most of her characters are torn between the desire to go and the need for stability, between the necessity for and hate of travel, the compulsion to face the unknown and a substantial repulsion for it. The 'serious' ladies of the novel – the plot is made up of two parallel tales, linked only by the brief coming together of the two women at the beginning and at the end – are both travellers, but while Mrs Copperfield goes to Panama and stays there, Miss Goering only moves to an island not far from home, and then constantly escapes back to the mainland. Both reflect all the time on their contradictory attitudes to travelling. In both cases, travelling leads to romantic involvement. Christina Goering's minute movements are tied to tormented moral choices; she has created attachments from which she has fled, and has been on the threshold of absurd adventures with improbable men from which chance, or the blind fate that is guiding her, has mostly protected her.[23] Mrs Copperfield, whose first name (Frieda) is very rarely pronounced, meets a young woman named Pacifica in Panama.[24] She goes to live in the dubious Hotel Las Palmas owned by the bizarre Mrs Quill who becomes her friend, and eventually leaves her husband, of whom she is extremely fond, for Pacifica.[25]

For the two women, as for Jane Bowles herself, travelling (leaving the safe shelter of their culture and home) is a moral imperative; Miss Goering repeatedly expresses the pains of this conflict. As soon as her *ménage à quatre* is established she feels the urgency of leaving it.

> She decided that it was already necessary for her to take little trips to the tip of the island, where she could board the ferry and cross back over to the mainland. She hated to do this as she knew how upsetting it would be . . . 'It is not for fun that I am going,' said Miss Goering, 'but because it is necessary to do so.'[26] (p. 124)

The same contradiction – the urge to go and the need to stay – will tear apart other characters in the novel, mirroring the same division the young Jane must have felt in parting from the conventional rules of married life. In *Everything Is Nice*, the 'strangeness' and the charm of the blue Muslim town on the edge of the sea, where Jeanie meets Zodelia and the other Arab women, is strongly felt by Jeanie, but on the other hand she still clings to the old world and her life is split into two separate halves. In *A Guatemalan Idyll*, the American traveller (he is never identified in any other way) is torn between a revulsion for the other place and the many attractions it has for him. The sexual involvement with Senora Ramirez and the burgeoning romance with Senorita Córdoba are accompanied by a deep sense of guilt, followed by the relief of escaping to his old world.[27]

Even when there is no actual travel, there is a little movement, a transit, a day trip, a temporary distancing from your usual milieu, or the attempt at one, as in *A Stick of Green Candy* or *Plain Pleasures*. In the latter tale the reflection on travel is carried out by Alva Perry and her neighbour John Drake, who both love simple pleasures, like baking potatoes on a fire in the backyard; she talks about her restless sister Dorothy Alvarez.

> I warn Dorothy every time I see her that if she doesn't watch out her life is going to be left aching and starving on the side of the road and she's going to get to her grave without it. The farther a man follows the rainbow, the harder it is for him to get back to the life which he left starving like an old dog.[28]

Despite this, Alva decides to accept John's invitation to eat out, gets drunk and stays overnight at the hotel in a room offered by its seedy proprietor, thus taking on her sister's identity. On the following morning she will not remember anything except a great feeling of tenderness for her neighbour who, once left alone, has gone away in frustration. ' "John Drake", she whispered. "My sweet John Drake." '[29] At least for once, the trip has had an unequivocal liberating effect, though in a bizarre direction as Alva has probably slept with the wrong man. Both she and the reader do not know if that is the case: she does not remember anything on the following day, and Jane Bowles's reader is far from being omniscient; in fact, most of the time the reader is actually kept in utter darkness. Sex is an important element in all her works, though perversely signalled by its absence.

Even in her play, *In the Summer House* (1954), which takes place in southern California, there is a constant brooding on going away and travelling. Gertrude leaves for Mexico with her second husband, Mr Solares, but hates it and comes back to her daughter Molly. Lionel always dreams of getting away from the cocktail bar where he and Molly work, and will finally do it in order to free her from her past and her mother's dominance. Again he speaks about the difficulty of leaving, and, at the same time, the dread of staying:

> They are harder to leave, Molly, places that don't work out. I know it sounds crazy, but they are . . . I can explain it all in some other way. (*Indicates oyster-shell door*) Suppose I kept on closing that door against the ocean every night because the ocean made me sad and then one night I went to open it and I couldn't even find the door. Suppose I couldn't tell it apart from the wall any more. Then it would be too late and we'd be shut in here forever once and for all.[30]

This rupture – between the acceptance and the refusal of the journey, between heterosexual and homosexual love, and between other indistinct, inexpressible contradictions – is reflected in frag-mentary narrative structures, in the obscure language of a writer who is never afraid of appearing difficult to understand. Her strong elliptical style seems to be moving towards silence, constantly verging on it. King-Kok Cheung notes how in women's writing silences may be due to choice: 'silences – textual ellipses, nonverbal gestures, authorial hesitations (as against moral, historical, religious, or political authority) – can also be articulate. The art of silence, on the other hand, covers various "strategies of reticence" . . . used by women writers to tell the forbidden and name the unspeakable.'[31] In Jane Bowles's case, there is the refusal to appear as the voice of truth: 'To undercut narrative authority they frequently resort to such devices as dream, fantasy, and unreliable point of view; or even project their anxiety as authors onto demented characters' (ibid.).

The main tension in her narration comes from the split between the 'here and now' and the need to escape everyday life: that is, in the sudden alternating movement between abstract allegorical situations and minute, realistic details. This is one of the reasons why her works escape strict genre definitions, whether it is autobiography or travel writing. A good example of this is the disquieting relationship in *Two Serious Ladies* between Christina Goering and Miss Gamelon, her governess. Both are torn by trust and suspicion, affection and self-interest, and we are given a description of their jarring domesticity. It is in this juxtaposition that the original and peculiar character of her art lies; the difficulties reside precisely in the unresolved tension between the necessity and yet the impossibility of leaving everyday life.

Jane Bowles's writing is in many ways related to the events in her life but is never strictly autobiographical.[32] In *What does a Woman Want? Reading and Sexual Difference*, Shoshana Felman speaks of the impossibility for a woman to write her own autobiography. Jane has neither really written hers nor wanted to write it. She was always in search of an unreachable objective correlative that would make her experiences 'concrete' and objective, distancing them from herself. And yet her writing is related to her travels in so many ways. Jane took her first novel, *Le Phaeton Hypocrite*, written in French, to Paris to get it published and lost it there; many of her pages were either forgotten in a taxi or flew out of the window, according to what Paul says in one of his 'conversations': 'One time about 300 pages blew out the window, a novel she was writing in Mexico City.'[33]

She always wrote in utter solitude, except for the novel which was revised with her husband: this is mainly why she felt it was not what she had wanted it to be. From the start her relation to writing was extremely conflictual. In a short biography she dictated in 1968 for *World Authors*, she spoke of the torture that even writing school papers had for her: 'I always thought it the most loathsome of all activities, and still do. At the same time I felt even then that I had to do it.'[34] She ends the biographical sketch by connecting travel to writing again: 'From the first day, Morocco seemed more dreamlike than real. I felt cut off from what I knew. In the twenty years that I have lived here I have written only two short stories, and nothing else' (ibid.).

With few exceptions (Williams and Capote among them), her works met largely with bemused reactions, all of which added to her solitude. She herself had a detached, cold stance towards Carson McCullers, Djuna Barnes and other women writers, and was rarely acknowledged by them. Her attitude is surprising as women have an all-important role both in her works and in her life, and may be explained by her sense of exclusion. She expresses her bitterness in a letter to Paul: 'The more I get into it, which isn't very far in pages, the more frightened I become at the isolated position I feel myself in vis-à-vis of all the writers whom I consider to be of any serious mind' (p. 33).

In 1966, when the *Collected Works* were published, largely against her will, Carson McCullers wrote a congratulatory letter: 'your curious, slanted and witty style has always given me boundless delight. I am so pleased to know that a new and bigger audience can share my pleasure. Anyway, darling, bless you and thank you for your writing.'[35] Jane replied that had she known she would have asked her to write a blurb for the book. Then, according to the friend typing the letter for her, she was seized by emotion and fell silent.

As she said, after her arrival in Africa she only wrote two short stories; she also finished the play started in New York, and began an ambitious autobiographical novel, *Out in the World*, of which only notes and fragments remain. Her writing block coincided with her final encounter with the elsewhere that, in a mysterious correspondence with writing, is tinged with insecurity, confusion, uncertainty. Jane's conflictual relationship with writing – love–hate, acceptance–refusal, sense–nonsense – is reproduced in Mrs Copperfield's liaison with Pacifica which strangely anticipates Jane's with Cherifa, again with the curious inversion of the link between life and art.

All this is made more complex by the very intricate knot uniting Jane's writing to her husband's. Paul Bowles, a composer of considerable fame in the thirties and forties, gave up music for writing after collaborating with Jane in the revision of her novel: 'It was this being present at the making of a novel that excited me and made me want to write my own fiction.' In another interview he says, 'I got really interested in the whole process, and thought, I wish I had written this book.'[36] In 1964 he wrote and published *Up Above the World*, a title recalling that of the novel Jane would not be able to finish. She is out of the world, he is up above it and everyday life: that everyday life that prevented her from writing, as happens to many women writers, and that very same everyday life underlying, like a subterranean and unexpected vein, the great themes of sin and salvation that made her art so singular and genial.

The journey to perdition

> [W]ho is the other woman? How am I naming her? How does she name me? (Gayatri Chakravorty Spivak)

The ghost wandering in the male authorial universe around Jane Bowles is that of her lesbian identity, a ghost that she has never really faced herself. In her published letters, it is a subject never hidden but neither discussed, always touched upon tangentially, as in the first joking description of the women's reactions in her family (her father had died when she was 13):

> they all sat down and said what a wonderful girl I was . . . – and that I was a grand normal girl – and that this Lesbian business was just an adolescent phase . . . and that if only I didn't have such an analytical mind I certainly would throw it off . . .
> Aunt Flo suggested 130 men to straighten me out – Aunt Connie 135. (p. 14)

Sexual ambiguity, in Jane Bowles's works, is often associated with ethnic difference. Her novels deal with the uncertain and ambivalent relationship between two or more women, against the background of racial hybridity. This is the case of Mrs Copperfield and Pacifica in *Two Serious Ladies*, or Gertrude and Mrs Lopez, who is constituted as the 'positive other' in the play. The encounter between

Zodelia and Jeanie in *Everything Is Nice* stresses the hybridity in a curious inversion of roles and voices; the Arab woman gives a little histrionic show, imitating Jeanie telling a woman friend she has just met (a play of mirrors?) about her split life:

'Good-bye, Jeanie, where are you going?'

'I am going to a Moslem house to visit my Moslem friends, Betsoul and her family. I will sit in a Moslem room and eat Moslem food and sleep on a Moslem bed.'

'Jeanie, Jeanie, when will you come back to us in the hotel and sleep in your own room?'

'I will come back to you in three days. I will come back and sit in a Nazarene room and eat Nazarene food and sleep on a Nazarene bed. I will spend half the week with Moslem friends and the other half with Nazarenes.'[37]

This short delicate tale on a casual meeting between two women, a sort of interlude rather than a proper short story, touches the essence of Jane's life and writing, with her inability to live in either of the two worlds. As she says in the self-parody enacted by Zodelia, she will be living in neither place, neither in the concrete nor in the abstract, neither with the other nor without her. Zodelia/Cherifa miming the other, the Western woman, is only the inverted image of the writer who, in her tales, 'mimics' the other woman, the foreigner, whether Arabian, Mexican or Guatemalan, by recreating her in fiction.

The relationship is not always tied to ethnic diversity, as in the case of Gertrude and Molly in the play, or of the two 'serious ladies' in the novel, but it still has a hybrid, 'interzone' character. In her works the difficulty, and at the same time the absolute importance, of the relation between women is often a question of life and death. The younger sister in *Camp Cataract* will disappear behind the waterfall after she realises her sister is not returning home; Mrs Copperfield changes her life for another woman; Gertrude and Molly have both killed the other woman (the killing is ritual but also real) and are tied by a heritage going from mother to daughter. This is always associated to the travel theme: the difference between the two sisters in *Camp Cataract* is mainly due to the fact that one wants to go and the other wants to stay, that one can live without the other (in fact needs to live away from her) and the other cannot.

The inhumanity of those who travel and do not know any longer where their souls are is set against the impossibility of survival for those who stay. The independent and the dependent are probably one, in an ambiguous tie. The multi-layered, confused, contradictory relations between women constitute the risky, dark journey without a port of call, the unfillable gap between two shores.

This fascination for the elsewhere is ultimately tied to a death drive.[38] In *Everything is Nice* Jeanie, after Zodelia leaves, goes over to the wall where they had met and leans on it.

> Although the sun had sunk behind the houses, the sky was still luminous and the blue of the wall had deepened. She rubbed her fingers along it: the wash was fresh and a little of the powdery stuff came off. And she remembered how once she had reached out to touch the face of a clown because it had awakened some longing. It had happened at a little circus, but not when she was a child.[39]

Like the face behind the powder, the other always recedes into the shadow. Cherifa escapes her and never really yields to her. In the fiction, Pacifica invariably has some young boyfriend to go back to, and Zodelia and her group of women never abandon a condescending and incomprehensible irony towards her. In the end even for her, Muslim culture is a baffling mystery. For the other, one gives everything up including life. Of the other, one can die.

At the end of her novel, the two heroines meet again in a bar, after having gone their separate ways. Miss Goering sees Mrs Copperfield and Pacifica arrive elegantly dressed in black, one very emaciated and suffering from a rash, the other (whom she sees for the first time) very attractive. As Pacifica leaves, Mrs Copperfield confides how important this liaison is, how afraid she is of losing her, and how they will soon be going back to Panama to live together. To her friend who fears she has gone to pieces, she replies:

> I *have* gone to pieces, which is a thing I have wanted to do for years. I know I am as guilty as I can be, but I have my happiness, which I guard like a wolf, and I have authority now and a certain amount of daring, which, if I remember correctly, I never had before. (p. 197)

After her departure, Miss Goering can only hope to be able to lose herself as well. Paradoxically she discovers that salvation, her only interest in life, means going to pieces and leads to the undoing and loss of the self. It seems to be at one with its opposite, perdition:

> 'Certainly I am nearer to becoming a saint,' reflected Miss Goering, 'but is it possible that a part of me hidden from my sight is piling sin upon sin as fast as Mrs Copperfield?' This latter possibility Miss Goering thought to be of considerable interest but of no great importance. (p. 201)

The circle is perhaps closed

The circle is perhaps closed: in an oblique play between reflections of subalternity, Jane is the irreducible alterity associated with death by the male look. In this complex knot, as Cronenberg shows, woman must be sacrificed to the flame of male inspiration, consigned to absence and silence and made immortal. Jane, in turn, has constructed the mysterious unattainable other as the space of her desire, the exotic and the archaic as the site of her dream. The thread of lack and desire guides these relationships between gender, ethnicity and subalternity, constituting an alterity sited in obscurity and mystery.

> In absolute difference, the rhetoric of alterity locates a pure otherness waiting to be filled by the presence of our desires, a blank page awaiting our words, like the 'empty' wilderness – from the African *veldt* to the American West – waiting to be settled and domesticated, and brought into the redemptive time of our history.[40]

It could be said that Jane Bowles embodies the Westerner's gaze on the other culture, to exercise her power and impress her presence on the subaltern woman, ultimately to possess or try to possess her. She could be described as the accomplice of imperialist discourse, a discourse that, according to Homi Bhabha, does nothing but search, in the analysis of the other, for the construction (and constrictions) of a 'regime of truth'.[41]

Mayda Yegenoglu sees Western women as complicitous in the Orientalist vision and conducts a lengthy analysis of Lady Mary Watley Montagu's *Turkish Embassy Letters* to prove this and polemicise with Lisa Lowe (particularly her *Critical Terrains: French and British Orientalisms*), James Clifford, Mata Lani and others. She sees in this 'feminist' text a supplement to the male vision: 'The Western woman's descriptions of the harem and Oriental women, the supplement, this plus, by the very fact that it substitutes the lack of the Western subject, is also less than the original text.'[42] The opposition is between those who see in women's discourse a difference within male Orientalism – Lady Montagu identifies with Turkish women, adopts their clothes, admires their independence and accuses male accounts of being partial and false – and those who have seen in it merely a substantial re-affirmation of the Orientalist paradigm.[43]

My doubts centre on the possibility of establishing the position 'from which one speaks' and of fixing origins and points of view in an unreal discursive coherence that ignores the multiple and shifting sites occupied by the speaking subject. Jane Bowles may have occupied the role of the American intellectual looking for meanings and certainties, evasions and escapes, in the Oriental woman but she never distanced herself from the object that is at the centre of her desire, or found in it that self-assurance that the West pursues in its construction of the Orient. She herself is the object of the gaze, at one with the Arab woman as we can see in many of Cronenberg's *master*-ful shots. The presence of the homoerotic look is such as to make it difficult to distinguish the look of the observer from that of the observed. The difficulty of assigning clear and definite roles is one of the few and fundamental clarities that emerge from her writings. At the beginning of this chapter, I quoted Cixous on 'writing as working (in) the in-between' between the same and the other, and the quotation goes on to illustrate this lack of differentiation: 'to admit this is first to want the two, as well as both, the ensemble of the one and the other, not fixed in sequences of struggle and expulsion or some other form of death but infinitely dynamized by an incessant process of exchange from one subject to another'.[44]

So, it is with reluctance that I assign Jane to a part in a rigid script, as though a mere illustration of a paradigm. If, in these perceptive analyses, the Western vision of the East and of the elsewhere finds a common denominator in the objectification of the other and the constitution of the imperialist subject, then it must be said that Jane Bowles *lives* and seeks the encounter with alterity rather than containing it in analysis; for she locates in it the undoing and the deconstruction of the Subject, thereby transgressing the fixity of that paradigm and confusing its terms.

It is difficult to place her within the tradition that fixes in the East the stereotypes of corruption and mysticism, feminine exoticism and sexual insatiability, crowded markets and magic lore. She did not produce texts that can be included in that genealogy; this is why my emphasis has often fallen on her life as the textualisation of her relationship with the Arab world. Jane Bowles has not offered a 'supplement' to the male vision; after all, she was not the spy from the interzone. If at all, it is Paul Bowles with his numerous works on Africa who has supplemented her vision with an 'objectification' of the exotic other, however refined and proximate.

She has not confined her fascination for the 'other' woman to the dream alone, to the poetical vision of a black goddess or to an imaginary nymph of exoticism, in the manner of so many Western poets and artists. She lived out this experience in guilt and pleasure, in joy and pain, and drank its chalice to the last bitter drop.

The redemption of her 'little original sin' can perhaps be found in her feeling an integral part of the obscurity and the mystery she was searching for, ultimately in her illness and death. Margaret Dillon, in her biography, quotes a short poem written by Jane in a friend's album when she was twelve. It ends like this: 'there's nothing orriginal about me – But a little orriginal Sin'.[45] The sense of this original sin following her in her adult life – her diversity? the diversity of (from) the 'other'? – is here marked by spelling mistakes, those mistakes to which she faithfully returned in the second part of her life, due to her illness, as though to a fatal and unavoidable appointment. The journey towards silence had started with the interruption in writing; it proceeds to illiteracy, the last mimesis with the Other.

Chapter 7

The Empty Place of Melancholia: Female Characters in *Hamlet*

Women's melancholia is the subject of philosophical and psycho-analytical enquiry in feminist theory: Clément and Cixous, together but in different ways, have shown how melancholia can be appropriated through the dance of hysteria, through poetry and writing. Irigaray and Kristeva have investigated it, using and overturning the Lacanian paradigm: Irigaray in *Speculum of the Other Woman*, has spoken of woman's 'melancholic sexuality'; Christine Buci-Glucksmann in *Tragique de l'ombre* has equated the Shakespearean tragic hero, particularly Hamlet, to Pessoa and other contemporary figures who escape the laws of classical tragedy to inhabit a world of shadows and shades, a world of undecidability, that is often associated with women. Kristeva in *Black Sun* has outlined three figures of female depressives in the case studies of Hélène, Marie-Ange and Isabelle, and deconstructed the Western paradigm of the melancholic in four artists (Holbein, Nerval, Dostoevsky and Marguerite Duras).

Kristeva herself never speaks of *Hamlet* but her first words seem to evoke its hero: 'I am trying to address an abyss of sorrow, a noncommunicable grief that . . . lays claim upon us to the extent of having us lose all interest in words, actions, and even life itself.'[1] Hélène Cixous in *The Newly-Born Woman*, although never mentioning Ophelia, circles around her figure in the long poetical argument on dreams centred on the figure of Sleeping Beauty, not disdaining to femininise Hamlet's over-famous monologue as a mocking reply to Freud's interrogation on the essence of woman.

Other texts I have previously examined in this book exhibit this Shakespearean thread: the most obvious reference is Angela Carter in *Wise Children* (see Ch. 4 above), but *Nights at the Circus* recalls Shakespeare too, particularly *King Lear* and *A Midsummer Night's Dream*, though in a less overt way. *Hamlet* is evoked in a parodical recitation of another monologue by Walser, in the middle of one of his eventful performances at the circus. But rather than in the actual quotation, it is in the uncertainty of this character, in the wrench from his own identity and the painful trials he undergoes in the search of a lost subjectivity that the hero of the drama is recalled: 'when they parted company and Walser's very self, as he had known it, departed from him, he experienced the freedom that lies behind the mask, within dissimulation, the freedom to juggle with being' (p. 103).

The text itself proposes the inversion of gender and genre paradigms at the onset of modernity, expressing that statute of discontinuity that was the mark of an epoch. Gaps and absences, equivocations, dreams and visions are the substance of a theatre that can only represent a theatre. It is in this picture that Ophelia, a scanty character always seen as a dim mirror for Hamlet, can assuredly claim melancholy for herself.

On the other side, feminist analyses have found in Shakespearean criticism a fruitful field of enquiry, as if the confrontation with the 'father' of English letters were no less important than the one with more recent theoretical fathers, recurrent in feminist theory. The revision of the latter has sometimes been coupled with the former: Hilda Doolittle for instance has united Shakespeare and Freud in her confrontation-revisitation, 'remembering them differently'. As a fortunate title by Carol Thomas Neely indicates, remembering Shakespeare has become a condition for revising ourselves, which I hope absolves me for this sudden plunge into the past.[2]

Male melancholia

Melancholy emerges at the beginning of the modern era with the awareness of the loss of a geocentric and anthropocentric universe, the loss of the solace of the centre. It is tied to the metaphysics of doubt that emerges in the passage between Renaissance and baroque aesthetics, the disquieting end of the Tudor era and the beginning of an unknown age. For the Stuart era will be itself ambiguous, torn by contrasting issues in religion and politics, and also in aesthetics. Foucault observes that the statute of discontinuity is the most difficult to establish in the history of thought as it describes epistemological ruptures, gaps and absences in which 'the sign does not correspond to meaning any longer'. At the beginning of the seventeenth century similitude ceases to be the form of knowledge; it becomes rather the occasion of mistake. It is a time in which metaphors and allegories coordinate the space of language, a time of dreams and visions.[3]

In this mesh the melancholic finds the opportunity to re-centre himself, if not herself: the gaze of occidental man can again – though in a new awareness of his destiny – include the whole world, become encyclopaedic, reinterpret himself and the new world and re-direct the gaze upon himself. In *The Anatomy of Melancholy*, Robert Burton presents this universal gaze, a visual utopia, based on the 'Otacousticon', an optical device rendering the observer invisible and allowing that person to see and understand all.[4] The melancholic gaze observes the world from outside, 'comprises' it in all its external appearances. The omni-seeing melancholic is observed by the artistic and anatomical enquiry. He is at once object and subject of the look.[5] Like Robert Burton's panopticon, the omnivorous theatrical gaze shows the melancholic hero – from Richard II to Brutus and Hamlet – losing himself in the contemplation of loss; surrendering the correspondence between sign and sense, only to successively reconstitute himself in mourning, or in self-destruction. Hamlet denies memory in order to commit himself to it. He solves and dissolves at the same time.

The discovery of new lands and hemispheres, dramatically linked to this relativistic melancholy, will be assimilated to the old world through religion, economics and ideology. The other, at first perceived as monstrous, the being from beyond, is then rendered similar to the self in appropriation and conquest. The other of then, presented in the descriptions of the first explorers, is now among us, still carrying an irreducible difference. Today the emphasis on melancholy returns with the decline of that imperialism on which, in more or less direct ways, the whole of the Western world has founded its present shape. The melancholic look, from Nerval to Pessoa, from Dostoevsky to Beckett, observes the decline and the end of an epistemology, and recentres itself in that decline. There is a fascination for the baroque and the classics of melancholy. A whole poetical and critical tradition, especially French, follows this path. Freud, Jones, Lacan, and others in their wake, have paid obsessive attention to *Hamlet*; so has, in different ways, female post-Freudian thought in the works of Julia Kristeva, Jacqueline Rose, Shoshana Felman, Marjorie Garber and Christine Buci-Glucksmann.

The sun of melancholy, black and bright at the same time, is at the centre of Julia Kristeva's book on depression. The original conception of melancholy – Aristotle's *melaina kole*, later accepted by Ficino, Dürer and Burton – was associated with genius, with man's restless nature and with Saturn as the planet of spirit and thought, opposing the Christian vision that places the melancholic 'among those that are suspended' (Dante) in a limbo of exclusion and desire.

The simultaneous sense of loss and its refusal are fundamental to the Freudian notion of melancholy. *Hamlet* was probably written after Shakespeare had lost his young son Hamnet, and had not yet forgotten a young woman Katherine Hammlet who had drowned at Stratford, probably inspiring the circumstances of Ophelia's death. In *The Songlines* (1987), Bruce Chatwin speaks of his childhood in Stratford, of the walks with his aunt along the river not far from Shakespeare's funerary monument. She often took him to Weir Brake, a hazel wood on a slope, and to the spot where Shakespeare came to 'tryst' with a young lady, 'the very bank whereon the wild thyme blew'. Later on he will look on the place with different eyes: 'Much later, when I *had* read Mr Shakespeare's plays and *did* know what a tryst was, it struck me that Weir Brake was far too muddy and prickly for Titania and Bottom to settle on, but an excellent spot for Ophelia to take the plunge.'[6]

The enigma of femininity

How many times Shakespeare draws fathers and daughters, never mothers and daughters. (Ellen Terry)

'If the child is the father of man,' she asked, 'then who is the mother of woman?' Speaking of which, has it ever occurred to you to spare a passing thought as to the character of the deceased Mrs Lear? Didn't it ever occur to you that Cordelia might have taken after her mother while the other girls . . . (Angela Carter)

The obsessive critical enquiry on the enigma of *Hamlet* has concentrated on his inadequacy, on his ambiguity towards the task requested by his father's ghost, on his real or feigned 'madness', and, finally and most importantly, on his feelings towards Ophelia and his mother. The disquieting question that seems to be at the heart of all the others is: what ties him to the two women, suspicion or jealousy, hate or love, revulsion or attraction? Both Freudian and Lacanian psychoanalysis have repeatedly returned to the question.

At the beginning of the century Freud and Jones seemed to have found the key to the enigma in Hamlet's desire for his mother. Twenty years after his first observations on *Hamlet*, Freud returns to this inexplicable mystery, though not directly referring to the drama, and speaks of the union of *unheimlich* and of *heimlich* in the essay on *The Uncanny*.[7] What is the ghost in *Hamlet* – and the subconscious it represents – if not these two opposites, the evident and the hidden, the familiar and the unknown, the identity between mystery and truth, the enigma and its solution? What is closest becomes distant, and vice-versa; the familiar hides the horror, the intimate becomes interior, internal, hidden, buried. Ultimately the uncanny is the female womb, man's first home.[8]

Since then, the disquieting pervasive melancholy of this text has repeatedly been brought back to a female root. Janet Adelman, in her *Suffocating Mothers*, attributes Hamlet's anguish to pre-oedipal impulses which make it difficult for him to differentiate the male and the female elements within himself.[9] Patricia Parker defines *Hamlet* as 'one of the founding texts of psychoanalysis itself', linking it to the search for a secret that ultimately is the mystery of femininity.[10] Similarly, Thomas Docherty links the obscurity of John Donne's poetry and its transgressivity to a need for secrecy, the necessity of hiding from the public eye, due to his secret marriage to Anne More.[11] In both cases secrecy is related to woman.

This has repeatedly been noted for *Hamlet*, starting from T. S. Eliot's disapproval of the text. His criticism was associated with femininity and found its pivotal point in the 'negative and insignificant' character of Gertrude, who was unable to represent the cause of Hamlet's disgust adequately. From her the drama derives its inexplicable character, making it the 'Mona Lisa' of literature. This undecidability reverberates from the mother to the son.

The contamination of the son by the mother is attributed by Adelman to her psychic power:

her frailty unleashes for Hamlet, and for Shakespeare, fantasies of
internal malevolence, of maternal spoiling, that are compelling
exactly as they are out of proportion to the character we know,
exactly as they seem to reiterate infantile fears and desires rather
than an adult apprehension of the mother as a separate person.[12]

Hamlet seems to be infected by the female element. Psychoanalytic
criticism interprets his behaviour as being induced by the need to
dis-identify with the female, all his actions and thoughts being
attempts to free himself from the impure mother, from the corruption brought into the world by Eve's guilt.[13] In the last instance
femininity is the test of insufficiency, as Jacqueline Rose points out
in her essay on *Hamlet*, describing such an experience as 'the drama
of sexual difference in which the woman is seen as the cause of just
such a failure in representation, as something deficient, lacking or
threatening to the system.'[14]

In his essay on Leonardo, Freud expresses the suspicion that the
Mona Lisa smile represents the stirrings of his maternal memories,
formulating the hypothesis that the close relation to his mother may
have created the conditions of his homosexuality. He sees in that
smile the reproduction of a double meaning, 'the promise of
unbounded tenderness and at the same time sinister menace', which
might illuminate Hamlet's ambivalence towards his mother.[15] The
baffling smile painted on the face of that icon of ambiguous
femininity underlines the inscrutable essence of the character of
Gertrude that remains inarticulate and decentred: throughout the
drama we do not know what she thinks or feels, what she has done
or not done.

When *her* scene, the *closet scene*, comes at the end of the third act,
she is finally confronted by her son and her sin, but just when she is
going to turn her eyes into her very soul,[16] the ghost appears,
remaining invisible to her eyes, and her figure becomes again
marginal to the confrontation between father and son. Hamlet finds
her in the closet and leaves her there: she starts with a shameful
secret and ends with the burden of another.

Be thou assur'd, if words be made of breath,
And breath of life, I have no life to breathe
What thou hast said to me.

(III, 4, 197–99)

She is left with the male injunction to abstinence, with the warning against 'rank corruption'. Likewise, Ophelia had been warned by Laertes against 'the shot and danger of desire' and its 'contagious blastments' (see I, 3, 33–44). Both he and Polonius, in warning her, show their morbid lingering on the details of her intimacy with Hamlet: in trying to make her confess, they confess the sins of their imagination, in the double bind that always ties the two sides of confession. It will happen again in *Othello* where, in their imagining of Desdemona's guilt, both Iago and Othello play the role of voyeurs of her sexuality. In taking on the role of censor of his mother, Hamlet enters the incestuous bed more than once: 'in the rank sweat of an unseamed bed,/Stew'd in corruption, honeying and making love/Over the nasty sty' (III, 4, 92–4). Or again, when he is binding her to silence, he does so by unnecessarily conjuring another scene:

> Let the bloat king tempt you again to bed,
> Pinch wanton on your cheek, call you his mouse,
> And let him, for a pair of reechy kisses,
> Or paddling in your neck with his damn'd fingers,
> Make you to ravel all this matter out . . .
>
> (III, 4, 182–8)

The *incipit* to the sequel of images of corruption and death related to women had been given in the second scene of the second act, when Hamlet speaks to Polonius about his daughter: 'For if the sun breed maggots in a dead dog, being a good kissing carrion . . . have you a daughter? . . . Let her not walk i' th' sun: conception is a blessing; but not as your daughter may conceive' (II, 2, 183–9). Later, during the 'play within the play', Hamlet will unleash his censorious rage on Ophelia herself. The sombre gaze on death finds its object in the impurity of that uncanny place of origin that woman is.

Between male and female genres

Ham. A dream itself is but a shadow.
Ros. Truly, and I hold ambition of so airy and light a quality that it is but a shadow's shadow.

> (II, 2, 263–5)

The prince is the paradigm of the melancholy man.

> (Walter Benjamin)

The ambiguous position of the characters in the drama finds a correspondence in its suspension among different modes and genres. This suspension is reflected in the disregard – common in Shakespeare – for the classical rules. Polonius' comment, quoted at the beginning of Chapter 2, offers a parodic mimicry of the law of genre, in a spiral of fragmentation, combination and accumulation. The prince is a melancholy man. Mourning places Hamlet on the margins of the Aristolean partitions, in the shadow of the great genres.[17] In *The Origin of German Tragic Drama*, Benjamin defines the drama as a *Trauerspiel*, a play of sorrow and mourning, a genre where the Aristotelian theory of tragic effect is traversed by splits and differences.[18] The union of comedy and allegory can be seen in Rosencrantz and Guildenstern, the element of grotesque in Hamlet and Polonius. The same demonic grimace is visible behind the mourning of a prince and the mirth (in this case false) of the councillors. The drama is thus poised between a number of genres: revenge, crime or ghost story; political chronicle or domestic melodrama; and so is its hero, unable to decide in which of them he is going to act, whose *mise en scène* to perform, whose 'law' to follow. His rebellion against the law of the father in the end is also a refusal of the law of genre.

The references are mostly to male genres: in the last scene, there is Horatio's adventure story with its succession of chance events, fatal accidents, violent deeds, and then Fortinbras' war drama, giving a vision of Hamlet as a soldier to be buried with martial music and rites. But the last words in the play ('Take up the bodies: such a sight as this/Becomes the field, but here shows much amiss': V, 2, 309–400) ironically indicate the genre that was not, the hero that failed to be. Another genre, the revenge story to which *Hamlet* belongs by right, is transgressed and denied, through Hamlet's resistance and rebellion: 'Between Hamlet and the Ghost, there is not only a conflict of generations, but also a conflict of genres.'[19] Gertrude, like Jocasta, is a subsidiary to the plot of revenge and at the same time crucial. Femininity is again associated with the negation of a male genre.

The play is also a tale of 'crime and detection', but again it proposes both the genre and its trangression and enfeeblement: the hero is at once detective, victim and avenger; the snare neither uncovers guilt nor brings about the final dénouement, but marks a further deferring. The classical last scene, a fixed piece in which all the characters are summoned for the final confrontation, leads to an atonement–purgation, uniting the guilty and the innocent.

In this way the delay, or the deferment, spreads outside the narrative in a tunnel of echoes and resonances that push *Hamlet* out of its textual confine. The text goes on being deferred through time, becoming a fantasmatic trace, at times exhibited, at other times hidden or marginal, not more than a breath, a sigh. Dealing with memory, the unacceptable 're-memory' of the Ghost, the play becomes a trace of memory itself, an unceasing repetition and resonance: like a stone thrown into a pond it creates ripples in thought and literature. The re-writing of *Hamlet* by critics, philosophers and poets is endless; so, too, are popular reworkings in the theatre, the circus, music hall, popular fiction and cinema. The drama acts as the unconscious origin (in Freud's words as 'the navel of the dream'), the contact with the interior, the unknown: a subconscious scene that can only be approached through the incessant drive to repeat, remember and work through. As Foucault says, it is a theatre representing another theatre.

The thriller in particular is a modern genre that has developed after the play and in its wake. *Hamlet*, along with Oedipus, is considered among the prototypes of the detective story, often blatantly recalled both in the plot and the title. More frequently the figure of Hamlet is an influence and source of inspiration: a ghostly presence so diffused as to be untraceable. Hamlet and Horatio could be likened to Holmes and Watson, except that Hamlet is no Sherlock Holmes, with his swift apprehension of clues, his sure evaluation of good and evil, and the subsequent atonement (though even Holmes has his underside), but can be recognised in a later alternative version, in a long line of disillusioned lonely men in a society where evil triumphs and the wicked can never really be defeated; in other words, the detectives of the hard-boiled tradition.

The *summa* of this figure of delusion and defeat, of unfocused idealism and sceptical ideology, is Philip Marlowe lost in the Elsinore of Los Angeles. Chandler's most famous novel, *The Big Sleep* (1939), commencing from the title and atmosphere, is emblematic. It is about the link between Marlowe and a father figure, Colonel Sternwood, a dying man in a wheelchair, pained by the problems given him by his two daughters: 'his face was a leaden mask, with the bloodless lips and the sharp nose and the sunken temples and the outward-turning earlobes of approaching dissolution'. At the end of the novel the embittered hero leaves the scene after the unsatisfactory conclusion, but the rebellious daughters have been tamed and the time set right; the ghostly father can now be put at rest and the hero can now face the big sleep:

> You just slept the big sleep, not caring about the nastiness of how you died or where you fell. Me, I was part of the nastiness now . . . But the old man didn't have to be. He could lie quiet in his canopied bed, with his bloodless hands folded on the sheet, waiting. His heart was a brief, uncertain murmur. His thoughts were as grey as ashes. And in a little while he too . . . would be sleeping the big sleep.[20]

In Raymond Chandler, and in the whole hard-boiled tradition, the heroines occupy marginal, yet crucial, roles. In the final dénouement, their death becomes a necessity, a way to put things straight. Asked who killed Muriel at the end of *The Lady in The Lake*, Marlowe replies: 'Somebody who thought she needed killing, somebody who had loved her and hated her, somebody who was too much of a cop to let her get away with any more murders.'[21] The *femme fatale* is damned and damning for the lonely hero who is always ambivalent about her. Marlowe's bitterness in *The Big Sleep* is about the elusiveness of the good sister who has been his antagonist in trying to protect the bad one, Carmen Sternwood, the psychotic murderer who is the plot originator. The latter appears at first Ophelia-like, walking as if she were floating, minute and delicate, airy and beautiful, but 'she had little predatory teeth, as white as fresh orange pith and as shiny as porcelain. They glistened between her thin too taut lips. Her face lacked colour and didn't look too healthy' (p. 10).

The resemblance to an animal, or a vampire – recalling the female hybrids we have met up to now – then becomes evident: 'The gun pointed at my chest. Her hand seemed to be quite steady. The hissing sound grew louder and her face had the scraped bone look. Aged, deteriorated, become animal, and not a nice animal' (p. 210). They are evil and carriers of death (mostly to men) and are punished, as in Dashiel Hammett's *The Maltese Falcon*.

Among the many re-writings, *Hamlet* seems to have a special place in women's texts, particularly thrillers, although (as we have seen) when the text is not by women the reference is still to women.

The British author P. D. James inscribes these literary antecedents with a feminine twist, giving a sister to Hamlet by creating a woman detective with a Shakespearean name. Cordelia Gray has no father and identifies strongly with fatherless characters: with the victim of murder, for example, in *An Unsuitable Job for a Woman* (1980). *The Skull Beneath the Skin* (1982), a sort of Jacobean thriller stitched together with 'clues' from Webster and Shakespeare, is transversally referred to *Hamlet*, both in the title and in the plot hinging on the search for a father and the pursuit of an impossible revenge.[22] The novel takes place in a Shakespearean universe of the second degree, for the protagonist is an actress who specialises in Elizabethan and Jacobean theatre.

Ten years later Angela Carter set her last novel *Wise Children* in Shakespearean worlds of the second and third degree (see above, chapter 4), recalling *Hamlet* in the story of a 'hypothetical, disputed, absent father' (p. 227), and of two daughters in the impossible and unrequited search for what they realise in the end is a ghost. The ironic reference is to the Father of English letters, Shakespeare, and to the metamorphosis this entity undergoes through a genealogy of actors, among whom Estella Hazard is the only really great interpreter of the bard in the family. Though strictly not a thriller – the novel being a Shakespearean palimpsest reproducing the *mélange* of genres of his late plays – it speaks of women's troublesome search for a father figure, a *leitmotif* of most female thrillers, from Sara Paretsky to Ruth Rendell and P. D. James.

Finally, I would like to end with a reference to a famous television series of the late eighties, *Twin Peaks*, directed by David Lynch, a false 'whodunit' traversing many genres as in many of Lynch's films, above all *Blue Velvet*. The series commences with the discovery of Laura Palmer's body, and her murder is at the centre of the investigation and the tale. Once more, resemblances to *Hamlet* are easily found: there is the troubled detective Cooper with his reassuring Horatio in the person of the county sheriff, a demonic ghost Bob in the cellar, and the supernatural horror hiding behind the known and familiar: in this case middle-class American life in an apparently peaceful provincial town, and the beautiful wilderness of the surrounding scenario. The hero consigns his monologues to a tape-recorder with a woman's name (no, it is not Ophelia) and in the end, on getting closer to the murderer, will be faced by the horror lurking in his own subconscious. There is a ghost in the cellar, a sort of evil presence possessing the numerous characters who may (or may not) have committed the murder, but the real ghost hovering above it all is Laura herself and her enigmatic smile as it appeared weekly in the titles of the series. She is the unsolvable enigma, and detective Cooper finds his disquieting doubles both in the satanic Bob and in her. She is the core of the secret, the mystery that cannot be fathomed. In the end the thriller and the horror find the only possible escape in a grotesque fantasy that offers no conclusion: in Walter Benjamin's words, 'the stream continues on its course'.[23]

Thus in the end women – though scarcely present in the text – have found their way in the rewritings and re-echoing of *Hamlet*. Generic uncertainty and ambiguity is another mark of femininity in the play. We have seen male genres denied, transgressed, as if infected by the female element. Melancholy has placed it in a sort of limbo, outside the definite domains of classical genres which are there but distorted and displaced by a mourning exceeding definite causes and conscious explanations. As Benjamin noticed, Albrecht Dürer's *Melencolie* had anticipated many characters of the baroque. By no chance that mood and mode was represented by a woman.

The prince's mother

O wonderful son, that can so stonish a mother!

(III, 2, 329–30)

The infant king becomes unbearably sad before speaking his first words: it is his being separated without remedy, desperately from his mother that drives him to try and find her again, like all the other love objects, first in his imagination, and then in his words. (Julia Kristeva)

Hamlet can also be read as horror or ghost story. Today, there are other spectres, other spirits, the result of sophisticated special effects, artificial physio-biological creatures, the pastiche of organic and electronic images emitting dark humours and showing organs that are usually hidden from view. The horror lies, then and now, in bringing to light what ought to be hidden, what is underneath; the movement is from inside to outside, from the intimate and profoundly familiar to the strange and wonderful, from the self to the other, from the depth to the surface. Hamlet's mourning is hiding in the depth and cannot come to light, as he himself tells his mother: 'I have that within which passes show' (I, 2, 85). 'Within' and 'show' represent an essential polarity for Hamlet, between the space of appearances and its own interiority 'infected by ghosts'. Expression of this ambivalence is the tension pushing him to prepare the *mise-en-scène* of what is buried within him.

All his words and acts, from the moment in which the ghost appears, place emphasis on the secret and the hidden, on the terror that what is at the bottom might come to the surface: 'foul deeds will rise,/Though all the earth o'erwhelm them, to men's eyes' (I, 2, 256–7). He is obsessed, hypnotised by that mystery, by that 'undiscover'd country' where he might go on dreaming ('in that sleep of death what dreams may come?'), by that return to the origins that he refers to woman, to his mother, to the secret part of the feminine, and ultimately to death.

An insistent metaphor for this secret is women's habit of making-up their faces, the abhorred female masquerade that hides the skull, the image of death. Addressing Yorick's skull, he says: 'Now get you to my lady's chamber, and tell her, let her paint an inch thick, to this favour she must come' (V, 1, 187–8). He had already expressed his abhorrence of these feminine wiles in his attack against Ophelia in the nunnery scene: 'I have heard of your paintings too, well enough. God hath given you one face and you make yourselves another, you jig, you amble, and you lisp, you nickname God's creatures' (III, 1, 146–9). The emphasis on women's double nature is the centre of his suspicion, the true secret that is the object of the melancholy gaze. More directly Claudius had likened his guilt, his 'hidden' (it will go on being so as he succeeds in confessing it only to himself) guilt, to a whore's face:

Claudius. The harlot's cheek, beautied with plast'ring art,
Is not more ugly to the thing that helps it,
Than is my deed to my most painted word.

(III, 1, 51–3)

In '*Othello* and *Hamlet*: Dilation, Spying, and the "Secret Place" of Woman', Patricia Parker notes the many references made in the drama to women's private parts, as they were defined in contemporary anatomical treatises: 'too obscene to look upon' in the words of Helkiah Crooke in *Microcosmographia: A Description of the Body of Man* (1615).

> The orifice of the matrix or womb – in ways highly suggestive when placed beside the familiar Shakespearean euphemism for the female sexual orifice, the 'O' or 'nothing' printed in early Shakespeare texts as a graphically smaller 'o' – is described in this same medical text as 'like the letter, o, small and wondrous narrow,' yet capable of being 'more open' according to the woman's appetite.[24]

She underlines that the language of the 'closed' and the 'open', of a hidden 'matter' that could be dilated, opened and exhibited, contrasts female genitalia with the male's which is all exterior. However and in spite of the common anatomical practice of 'ocular inspection', this and other contemporary texts recommend caution and decorum, and stop on the threshold of the mystery: 'The sense of a female "privity" too "obscene" to be seen also lies behind the warnings against and simultaneous stimulation of the gaze in anatomical treatises aware of bringing before the eyes what otherwise would be lapped, folded, secret, hid.'[25] Lacan, in 'The hysterical question (II): What is a woman?', observes: 'The female sex has the character of an absence, of emptiness, of a hole, . . . an essential dissymmetry.'[26] Dora's problem is that she does not offer symbolic material, 'in fact she needs one'. Irigaray comments: 'Nothing to be seen is equivalent to having no thing. No being and no truth.'[27]

Woman is the basis for depression. Freud sees the impossible mourning for the maternal object everywhere; Kristeva stresses that melancholy, like mourning, masks aggressivity against the unobtainable object through a feeling of ambivalence:

> I love that object . . . but even more so I hate it; because I love it, and in order not to lose it, I embed it in myself; but because I hate it, that other within myself is a bad self, I am bad, I am non-existent, I shall kill myself. (p. 11)

Self-annulment and the matricide pulsion are sublimated in the deadly representation of women: the link established by Hamlet between Yorick and Gertrude, the images of corruption and/or decay associated with Ophelia, his frantic acceptance of mourning on her death, and only then. It is the moment in which Hamlet, through mourning, recognises his identity – 'This is I,/Hamlet the Dane' (III, 1, 251–2) – and the moment in which the real duel with Laertes happens. With his leap into Ophelia's grave, he appropriates her death, in this way accepting his own.

Repeatedly the maternal object becomes at one with 'matter', first with Rosencrantz and Guildenstern ('Therefore no more, but to the matter – my mother, you say': III, 2, 324–6), and again in his confrontation with her: 'Now, mother, what's the matter?' (III, 4, 8). In his journey towards 'his mother's closet', Hamlet progresses to 'the witches hour', in which graves are opened and infernal rites are performed, the symbolic matricide among them.

> *Hamlet.* . . . now could I drink hot blood,
> And do such bitter business as the day
> Would quake to look on: soft, now to my mother –
> O heart, lose not thy nature, let not ever
> The soul of Nero enter this firm bosom,
> Let me be cruel not unnatural.
> I will speak daggers to her, but use none.
>
> (III, 2, 393–9)

His journey towards that 'closed' place, emblem of the feminine, continues with the revisitation of the fathers' sins: King Hamlet 'with all his crimes broad blown, as flush as May', and Claudius in the 'incestuous pleasure of his bed'. The traumatic return to the past reopens the unhealed narcissistic wound; the point of arrival is the look into his mother's 'most secret parts'.

The whole drama, like the play-within-the-play staged by Hamlet himself, is constructed to bring to the surface what is closed and concealed. However, and in spite of Hamlet's apparent determination to disclose the hidden, there are secrets that will never unravel, as the ghost announces from the beginning. The play within the play, with all its calls for 'light', will not shed light on the unknown; death remains the undiscovered country, like the uncanny maternal womb. The dichotomy between being and seeming, the deep and the superficial is erased, they become one and the same: 'Seems, madam! nay it is, I know not "seems"' (I, 2, 76).

In *The Murders in the Rue Morgue*, Edgar Allan Poe, poet of the secret and the abyss, has spoken of the impossibility of distinguishing between depth and surface: 'There is such a thing as being too profound. Truth is not always in a well. In fact, as regards the most important knowledge, I do believe she is invariably superficial.'[28] In her essay on Lacan's seminar on *The Purloined Letter*, Shoshana Felman observes that the purloined letter is the metaphor of the identity between the two levels. The deepest secret lies close to the surface: 'the purloined letter . . . becomes itself . . . a symbol or a signifier of the unconscious, to the extent that it is destined "to signify the annulment of what signifies" – the necessity of its own repression, of the repression of its message.'[29] It is what Derrida, in a recent seminar, has called the secret without secret.[30]

Mary Russo refers a certain construction of femininity to an aesthetics of the superficial and the marginal and to the late Renaissance and baroque combination of depth and surface models of the body, in order to explain contemporary examples of female grotesque. 'The displacement of depth models of epistemology, architecture and the body by the play of surfaces offers interesting possibilities for re-configuring cultural identity and, for some postmodernist feminists, a way out of essentialist models of woman-as-body or woman-as-space.'[31]

As Irigaray puts it in her mimicry of Lacan, woman is lack, and in Shoshana Felman's words, 'lack' is itself signifying.[32] In *The Wake of Deconstruction*, Barbara Johnson insists on this lack when she is speaking of the interruption both in Mary Joe Frug's life and in the essay – in fact the sentence – she was writing.

> In my commentary, I wrote about this sentence, calling it 'the lesbian gap' and asking, 'How does this gap signify?' . . . '*How* does the gap signify?' raises the question of what it means to mean, raises meaning as a question, implies that the gap *has to be read*, but that it can't be presumed to have been intended.[33]

It is not a question of assuming a meaning, whatever it is, but rather of putting in doubt the concept of life as meaning.

The odd, the uncanny thing

What is the thing in itself? (Martin Heidegger)

Oph. I think nothing, my lord.
Ham. That's a fair thought to lie between maids' legs.
Oph. What is, my lord?
Ham. Nothing.

(III, 2, 115–19)

The feminine must be deciphered as interdict: within the signs or between them, between the realized meanings, between the lines.

(Luce Irigaray)

The melancholic subject looks on emptiness, nothingness, shadows. Women as lovers, women as mothers, are the objects of the gaze, the point of arrival of the return to the past and to the origins, as in Orpheus' backward journey. Ophelia, like Eurydice, is sent back to the depths by the male gaze and desire. The abyss is the zero of the female genitalia, the nothing that lies 'between maids' legs'.[34] In 'The Gaze, Always at Stake', Irigaray says: 'Nothing to be seen is equivalent to having no thing. No being and no truth.'[35] Around this nothing – or at least nothing that is penis-shaped – the gaze and the eye linger in horror.

Ophelia occupies this passive space. Shakespearean criticism has usually considered her as an empty vessel, a double of Gertrude in Hamlet's eyes, a mirror reflecting his melancholy and fatherly loss. 'Her speech is nothing' (IV, 1, 8) is her epitaph, that 'nothing' framing her in the whole play. She never symbolises her depression, like Freud's female patients. For her, humour is not a language, or melancholy a form of thought. She is kept at the margin, is left out of her brother's journeys, comes second in her father's warnings, and can only utter hesitant, doubtful interjections: 'do you doubt that?' or 'no more but so?'. Her drive to self-cancellation is clearly expressed : 'I do not know, my lord, what I should think' or 'I shall obey, my lord', with which her first apparition in Act I, Scene 3, ends. Like Gertrude, she is the guardian of the secret, and she is inhabited by it: ''Tis in my memory locked' (I, 3, 86–7). She is, by Laertes first, and by her father soon after, deprived of her own interpretation of things: 'My lord, he hath importun'd me with love/

In honourable fashion' (I, 3, 110–11). She pleads uselessly, and then renounces that love. In front of Hamlet's aggressive stance, she can only reply 'I think nothing, my lord.'[36]

Like Miranda, her chastity is tied to the destiny of others, her father first of all: 'Tender yourself very dearly,/Or . . . you'll tender me a fool' (I, 3, 107–9).[37] These others insert her in their plots, Polonius, Claudius and Hamlet, while her own plot remains empty or never exists. She can only express feelings of compassion and sympathy for the plight of others: for Hamlet's madness, and for her father's death (a madness and a death that become her own). Her disappearing act is the substance of her plot. Compassion is her main verbalization, alongside songs and poems of folly. Like the neurotic depressive described by Kristeva, she speaks little and then only through broken sentences; like them she will let herself go, towards death and self-destruction after introjecting the lost object: father, brother, lover.

Little by little she turns towards the inanimate, becoming water, leaves and flowers, in a halo of wet clothes: 'her garments, heavy with their drink,/Pulled the poor wretch from her melodious lay/To muddy death' (IV, 7, 182). Like Dürer's *Melencolie*, she is surrounded by things and objects, what Gertrude calls her weedy trophies: 'There with fantastic garlands did she come,/Of crow-flowers, nettles, daisies, and long purples' (IV, 7, 169–70).

Kristeva speaks of 'psychic emptiness' for the woman depressive, in the wake of André Green's work. She describes the feverish activity that masks the effect of castration following the loss of the erotic object. 'Even though a woman has no penis to lose, it is her entire being – body and especially soul – that she feels is threatened by castration' (p. 82). She becomes like a zombie: 'depression appears as the veil of a *blank perversion* – one that is dreamed of, desired, even thought through, but unmentionable and forever *impossible*. The depressive course . . . hollows out the painful psyche and stands in the way of experienced sex as shameful' (ibid.)

Like a beauty sleeping in her wood, 'she is intact, eternal, absolutely powerless' as Cixous says. Man's dream, or maybe woman's dream – as she knows she had to be in the grave, passive, unattainable, distant, in order to attract him: 'What does she want? To sleep, perchance to dream, to be loved in a dream, to be approached, touched, almost, to almost come (*jouir*). But not to come: or else she would wake up. But she came in a dream, once upon a time.'[38] She is the thing and at the same time she is not. She appears with the mark of erasure upon herself. Consigned to the pre-Raphaelite icon, she floats on the river, body on water, life without word, death without resurrection, like Holbein's Christ. Silence is the only sense of this character. Not much can be said of her: she did not yield to the talking cure, she could not be healed. Silence, emptiness and gaps are her essential signifiers.

The melancholia of a cold maid

>. . . and long purples
>That liberal shepherds give a grosser name,
>But our cold maids do dead fingers call them.
>
>(IV, 7, 168–70)

>Either woman is passive or she does not exist. What is left of her is unthinkable, unthought. Which certainly means that she is not thought, she does not enter into the opposition, that she does not make a couple with the father (who makes a couple with the son).
>(Hélène Cixous)

In his lifelong search to cure woman of herself, Freud found an object of resistance in the hysterical female body. Shoshana Felman reminds us that towards the end of his career Freud admits that he has not been able to solve the question of woman: 'The great question that has never been answered and which I have not been able to answer, despite my thirty years of research into the feminine soul, is "What does a woman want?"' In the book that takes its title from this question, Felman examines three male texts in which a woman must be cured but fails to be cured. Stéphanie and Paquita, in Balzac's two short stories 'Adieu' and 'The Girl with the Golden Eyes', and Irma, in Freud's dream, all resist male interpretation: 'the female knot of pain resists and undercuts the mastery – and the integrity – of psychoanalytic theory'.[39] On the other hand, Freud finds in the dream a point of resistance to his own interpretation of it, to his own self-analysis.[40]

In the same way both Gertrude and Ophelia are resistant to treatment: the melancholic in them does not reappropriate the gaze and cannot be appropriated by the gaze. Patricia Parker reminds us that anatomy stops in front of that secret; Burton's encyclopaedic look seems to be blind to women. Freud finds in his patient Irma, as later in Dora in *Fragment of an Analysis of Hysteria* (1901), the impenetrable object, and in female hysteria the illness that cannot be cured.[41] The three women in Irma's dream are united by being recalcitrant and rebellious to his treatment. Shakespeare shows Gertrude to be the origin of the rupture, and Ophelia its symptom. Both are beyond cure, assimilation or understanding.

This impenetrable core is revealed in the tie between the two women. It comes up unexpectedly at the end of the play and can only be explained through reference to the hidden. Gertrude expresses disquiet and fear at the description of Ophelia's mourning. At first she vehemently refuses to see her as if fearing that her mad look can penetrate her hidden secret. Here the image used for the display of what is hidden changes, the female secret becomes a liquid, fluid matter:

> *Queen.* Let her come in.
> (*aside*) 'to my sick soul, as sin's true nature is,
> 'Each toy seems prologue to some great amiss,
> 'So full of artless jealousie is guilt,
> 'It spills itself, in fearing to be spilt.'
>
> (IV, 5, 17–20)

It is the acceptance of her guilt that up to now she has tried to distance from herself: 'O Hamlet, speak no more/. . . O speak to me no more,/These words like daggers enter in mine ears,/No more sweet Hamlet' (III, 4, 88 and 94–6).

Soon after she will show an unexpected emotion in hearing of Ophelia's death, uniting her with her son in feelings of tenderness, as though through Ophelia she could finally acknowledge motherhood.

> *Queen (scattering flowers).* Sweets to the sweet.
>   Farewell!
> I hoped thou shouldst have been my Hamlet's wife:
> I thought thy bride-bed to have decked, sweet maid,
> And not have strewed thy grave.
>
> (V, 1, 236–39)

Again the stress is on liquidity: this time water is clearly signalled as a sort of exchange between them: 'Too much of water hast thou, poor Ophelia,/And therefore I forbid my tears' (IV, 7, 183–4).

The tie between women is very rare in Shakespeare, and even rarer is the representation of mothers and daughters, as Angela Carter stresses in her epigraph to *Wise Children* quoted above. There is no wife for Prospero, and Polonius' wife is never mentioned.[42] Ophelia, like Miranda, has no mother or sister, or woman friend. Miranda sees another woman only in her image in the mirror ('I do not know/ One of my sex, no woman's face remember,/Save from my glass, mine own': III, 1, 48–50). A reminder of this can be found in Irigaray's Alice who 'has light blue eyes. Her eyes have opened through the mirror . . . her violated eyes. Light blue and red. That know the right, the verso, and the overlapping.'[43]

Thus Ophelia's eyes 'open through the mirror'. In his mute apparition Hamlet turns to her as if to a mirror and from that moment his melancholy becomes her own. Her description of his distressful act is like Borges' infinite narrative regression, one of the many Chinese boxes in the play. She becomes reflection and deflection of male melancholia, the echo of its interrogations and doubts,[44] growing more and more verbal as she approaches her own annihilation. She gives her vision of Hamlet, of what he is not going to be: 'O! woe is me,/To have seen what I have seen, see what I see' (III, 1, 169–70). Like Gertrude, she is the repository of remembrance ('Nymph, in thy orisons/Be all my sins remembered'), and she does remember. When Hamlet denies having loved her, she replies: 'My honour'd lord, you know right well you did.' During the puppet scene, she faces his aggressiveness boldly, though she is only supposed to spy. She was told to remember, and differently from Hamlet she wields her remembrance, first of her lost love, later of her lost father, in order to appropriate her own past, and then to approach her death.

In Velasquez' *Las Meninas* Foucault notes that the subject has exited from the picture, or remains as an indirect, vague reflection in a mirror; a ghost, in fact. Instead women have moved to the centre of the picture: they were not supposed to be there, yet they have become the object of the gaze; at the same time they become subject themselves as part of the interrogative look gazing on the disappearing 'thing'. They have entered the picture and ironically given it a name. The name is that of the displaced subject, of what was not supposed to be there. Cixous and Clément have spoken of woman's appropriation of madness, of woman's hysteria as rebellion. Ophelia finds resistance and knowledge in the appropriation of melancholic nonsense and death. She sings of the loss of a father but also of virginity; she offers flowers for melancholy but also for sexuality. After all, she is the one who resolutely takes the plunge.

The Shakespearean female man: a short postfaction

Am I simulating? What? Whom? My mother, a woman, my father's wife? Woman? Or, rather: the ideal woman, the essence, which is to say, the model and the copy have struck up a relationship of impossible correspondence and nothing is conceivable as long as there is an effort to make one of the terms *be* an image of the other: *to make what is the same be what is not.* In order for everything to signify it is necessary to accept that I am not inhabited by duality but by an *intensity of simulation* that constitutes its own end, outside of whatever it imitates: what is simulated? Simulation. (Severo Sarduy)

How can we speak of Ophelia as a woman? She was interpreted by a young boy actor and was a mixture of masculine and feminine, in a certain sense (though obverse, as in a mirror), which again reflects Hamlet's ambiguity as regards male and female. We witness a trajectory of a floating female gender from Hamlet to Ophelia and back. It is not a question of hiding, or forgetting this circumstance; in fact it is very important to remember it. I do not wish to engage here on the discussion of how far Renaissance theatrical aesthetics was influenced by this circumstance: it would rather be a case of enquiring how ingrained this usage was in a culture whose imaginary had a space for androgyny and sexual ambiguity. More specifically, I wish to assert here that this element is an important part of this character, and of Gertrude's too.

Ophelia and Gertrude are about transvestism and cross-dressing as well. The cypher of their mystery lies very much in that. In her extensive study of cross-dressing, Marjorie Garber gives many examples of sexual ambiguity in real life, such as the famous case of Billy Tipton, a jazz musician who lived with a wife and three adopted children and was discovered to be a woman after death.

Both in real life and in fiction – whether novels, films or theatre and
entertainment – transvestism is representation, and all functional
and psychological interpretations are a way of explaining it away,
ignoring its intrinsic eroticism and its value as an autonomous
signifier, as a disrupting metaphor.[45] Whether the representation
is real or artistic, it brings us back to the question that Severo
Sarduy asks: 'What is gender, after all? What is a man or a
woman?'[46]

Notes and References

Chapter 1   Introduction: The Swing of Theory

1. R. Barthes, *Roland Barthes par Roland Barthes* (Paris: Editions du Seuil, 1980), p. 170: my translation.
2. At the same time some see feminism itself – with its belief in social progress, transformation and the binary structure of sexual difference – as one of the great metanarratives in decline. Derrida has advocated replacing the dualistic opposition with an indefinite series of differences, in an anti-dialectic movement: 'When we speak here of sexual difference, we must distinguish between opposition and difference. Opposition is two, opposition is man/woman. Difference on the other hand, can be an indefinite number of sexes . . . All that you can call 'gift' – love, jouissance – is absolutely forbidden, is forbidden by the dual opposition.': J. Derrida, 'Women in the beehive: A Seminar', in A. Jardine and P. Smith (eds), *Men in Feminism* (London: Methuen, 1987), p. 198.
3. In G. C. Spivak, *In Other Worlds. Essays in Cultural Politics* (London and New York: Methuen, 1987), p. 107.
4. L. Irigaray, 'The Power of Discourse', in *This Sex Which Is Not One*, transl. by C. Porter with C. Burke (Ithaca, NY: Cornell University Press, 1995), p. 76. Successive references in the text are to this edition.
5. 'A Literary Representation of the Subaltern', in *In Other Worlds*, p. 268. The two short stories, *Draupadi* and *The Breast-Giver*, are also included in Spivak's book.
6. S. Hall, 'Minimal Selves', in *The Real Me – Postmodernism and the Question of Identity* (London: ICA, 1987), p. 44.
7. G. Vattimo, *La fine della modernità* (Milano: Garzanti, 1985), p. 21: my translation; *The End of Modernity* (Oxford, Polity Press, 1988).
8. See S. Hall, 'When was the Postcolonial?' and I. Chambers, 'Signs of silence, lines of listening', in I. Chambers and L. Curti (eds), *The Postcolonial Question – Common Skies, Divided Horizons* (London and New York: Routledge, 1996). See also P. Hulme, 'Including America', *Ariel*, 26, 1 (1995).
9. This is probably due to the interesting ambiguities and chiaroscuri of Jameson's description. Differently from him, Baudrillard utters his dismayed outcry: in *Les stratégies fatales*, by calling the new regime of

178

the transpolitical 'this historical collapse, this coma, this disappearance of the real' (London: Pluto, 1990, p. 14). Iain Chambers observes: 'behind this science-fiction scenario I think we can hear the dying echo of the call for a now apparently impossible "authenticity" . . . We are left to wander alone, without direction, in the desert among the semiotic debris of dead meanings.': *Border Dialogues. Journeys in Postmodernity* (London and New York: Routledge, 1990, p. 89).

10. The development of cultural studies has been fraught with such oppositions (Thompson's argument on the 'poverty of theory' and his pragmatic attack on foreign-ness come to mind), but there have been other turns in earlier decades. See, among others, S. Hall, 'Cultural Studies and the Centre: Some Problematics and Problems', in S. Hall *et al.* (eds), *Culture, Media, Language* (London: Hutchinson and CCCS, 1980).

11. P. Anderson, 'Modernity and Revolution', *New Left Review*, 144 (1984), p. 113.

12. D. Hebdige, *Hiding in the Light* (London and New York: Routledge, 1988), p. 206.

13. Eagleton sees postmodernism as the betrayal of the revolutionary values implied by the historical avant garde and of the political project of the struggle for human emancipation. He invokes Brecht and Benjamin, who were isolated in a modernism crossed by 'antipolitical impulses': T. Eagleton, 'Capitalism, Modernism and Postmodernism', *New Left Review*, 152 (1985), p. 72.

14. F. Rella, 'Ho tanta nostalgia di Brecht e Lukacs', *Mercurio – La Repubblica*, 10 June 1989, p. 19.

15. F. Jameson, 'Postmodernism, or the Cultural Logic of Late Capitalism', *New Left Review*, 146 (1984) p. 82.

16. Stuart Hall and Fredric Jameson, 'Clinging to the Wreckage: A conversation', *Marxism Today*, Sept. 1990, p. 29.

17. J. Baudrillard, *America* (London & New York: Verso, 1989), pp. 59–60.

18. D. Hebdige, 'The Bottom Line on Planet One', *Ten.8*, 19 (1987), p. 29.

19. He later defends himself against this imputation, indirectly emphasising the guilty halo that has surrounded postmodernism in England. He does it in a subsequent essay, by recalling a personal crisis (see Hebdige, 'Some Sons and Their Fathers', *Ten.8*, 17, 1985), indirectly underlining the emotional character with which this intellectual *querelle* is curiously charged.

20. In an essay written in the mid-eighties, Angela McRobbie speaks of the breath of fresh air that this new sensibility has brought to Great Britain: its attention to the importance of representation, to the 'instantaneity of communication', to the fragmentation of experience, seems to her closer to the lived experience of women and young people than the unitary vision that is championed so nostalgically by many. She refers to de Beauvoir and Sontag, who have spoken of a dimension where public and private are joined and where pastiche, parody and 'camp' show a subversive potential: 'Postmodernism and Popular Culture', *Postmodernism* (London: ICA, 1986).

21. The crucial role that popular culture has played in postmodernism is often mentioned in the debate as the main basis for contention. Jameson and Hebdige have used such urban temples as shopping centres, hotels and youth magazines as their main examples. In his *Uncommon Cultures,* Collins has spoken at length of the convergence of culturalists and feminists with the postmodernist vision of a non-monolithic concept of mass culture (London: Routledge, 1989, pp. xiv and 20). Andreas Huyssen was the first to point out more consciously that postmodernity had the merit of overcoming the modernist division between high and popular art. See *After the Great Divide – Modernism, Mass Culture and Postmodernism* (London, Macmillan, 1986), p. viii.
22. D. Hebdige, *Hiding*, p. 207.
23. P. Waugh, *Feminine Fictions – Revisiting the Postmodern* (London and New York: Routledge, 1989), p. 6.
24. L. Hutcheon, *The Politics of Postmodernism* (London and New York: Routledge, 1989), p. 167. She speaks above all of the possibilities offered by postmodern parodical strategies to feminist artists.
25. L. J. Nicholson (ed.), *Feminism/Postmodernism* (New York and London: Routledge, 1990), p. 5.
26. *Signs*, 12, 4 (Summer 1987), respectively p. 622 and p. 643.
27. S. J. Hekman, *Gender and Knowledge – Elements of a Postmodern Feminism* (London: Polity Press, 1990), p. 175.
28. R. Braidotti, *Patterns of Dissonance* (Cambridge: Polity Press, 1991), p. 15.
29. Ibid., p. 14.
30. Ibid., p. 9.
31. bell hooks, *Ain't I a Woman – Black Women and Feminism* (London: Pluto, 1982), p. 124.
32. Ibid., respectively pp. 12 and 195.
33. Barbara Smith, 'Toward a Black Feminist Criticism', in *The New Feminist Criticism – Essays on Women, Literature, Theory* (London: Virago, 1986), p. 170.
34. Ibid., p. 174. This separation parallels the one that Showalter's *A Literature of Their Own* proposes for women's writing (see Chapter 4), though Smith points out that for Showalter black literature is another literary subculture as if 'being Black and female are mutually exclusive' (ibid., p. 172).
35. M. Barrett, *Women's Oppression Today* (London: Verso, 1980), p. 48.
36. Ibid., respectively pp. 114 and 258. In more recent times, she takes Foucault into account, rearticulating his microphysics of the body and power in a feminist perspective. See M. Barrett *The Politics of Truth* (Cambridge: Polity Press, 1992).
37. Women's Studies Group/CCCS, *Women Take Issue – Aspects of Women's Subordination* (London: Hutchinson in association with the CCCS, University of Birmingham, 1978), p. 11. Angela McRobbie noticed this absence particularly in the work done on youth subcul-

tures, and she concentrated on this 'missing dimension' (p. 96) in her 'Working class girls and the culture of femininity', her first study of teenage girls' culture. She further explored these silences in 'Settling accounts with subcultures: a feminist critique', in T. Bennett *et al.* (eds), *Culture, Ideology and Social Process* (London: Batsford with the Open University Press, 1981).

38. J. Winship, 'A woman's world: "Woman" – an ideology of femininity', *Women Take Issue*, p. 134.

39. Ibid., p. 137.

40. See respectively C. Weedon, *Feminist Practice and Poststructuralist Theory* (Oxford: Blackwell, 1987), p. 165 and S. Lovibond, 'Feminism and Postmodernism', in R. Boyne and A. Rattansi, *Postmodernism and Society* (London: Macmillan, 1990).

41. 'Feminist politics must be founded on the ackowledgement of the oppression that determines women's existence; subjectivity is not only an aesthetic factor but also a demand for change': E. Wilson, *Hallucinations* (London: Radius/Hutchinson, 1988), p. 20.

42. P. Waugh, *Feminine Fictions*, p. 6.

43. See respectively L. Hutcheon, *A Poetics of Postmodernism – History, Theory, Fiction* (London and New York: Routledge, 1988), p. 231, and *The Politics of Postmodernism*, p. 168.

44. See respectively A. Huyssen, 'Mapping the Postmodern', in L. Nicholson (ed.), *Feminism/ Postmodernism* (New York and London: Routledge, 1990), p. 250; and C. Owens, 'The Discourse of Others: Feminists and Postmodernism', in H. Foster (ed.), *The Anti-Aesthetic* (Port Townsend, WA: Bay Press, 1985), p. 61.

45. See Waugh, *Feminine Fictions*, p. 27.

46. 'Deconstruction's Other: Trinh T. Minh-ha and Jacques Derrida', *Diacritics*, 25, 2 (Summer 1995), p. 112.

47. J. Baudrillard, *Fatal Strategies*, transl. P. Beitchman and W.G.J. Niesluchowski (London: Semiotext(e)/Pluto, 1990), p. 124. There are different positions among male critics stressing the important role of feminism as a component of postmodernism. Andreas Huyssen and Craig Owens, among the American scholars of postmodernity, and Iain Chambers, among the British, are some of those who try to develop their critical discourse in a dialogue with feminist theoretical elaborations.

48. This sonnet deals with lust, the hell against which men are powerless, without any specific gender reference, though Alessandro Serpieri notes that it is not by chance that it appears in the 'dark lady' section of the sonnets: W. Shakespeare, *Sonetti*, ed. by A. Serpieri (Milano: Rizzoli, 1991), p. 740.

49. J. Derrida, 'Women in the Beehive: A Seminar', p. 194.

50. A. Jardine, *Gynesis – Configuration of Woman and Modernity* (Ithaca and London: Cornell University Press, 1985), p. 207. In her postfaction, Alice Jardine, who has dedicated her book to French feminist thought, directs her questions to women critics such as Cixous, Kristeva and Irigaray as well.

51. T. de Lauretis, *Technologies of Gender – Essays on Theory, Film, and Fiction* (Bloomington and Indianapolis: Indiana University Press, 1987).
52. G. C. Spivak, 'Displacement and the Discourse of Woman', in M. Krupnik (ed.), *Displacement, Derrida and After* (Bloomington: Indiana University Press, 1983), p. 169.
53. R. Braidotti, 'Commento alla relazione di Adriana Cavarero', in M.C. Marcuzzo and Anna Rossi-Doria (eds), *Alla ricerca delle donne – Studi femministi in Italia* (Turin: Rosenberg & Sellier, 1987), respectively p. 189 and pp. 198–9: my translation.
54. A. Cavarero *et al.*, *Diotima – Il pensiero della differenza sessuale* (Milano: La Tartaruga, 1987), pp. 180–1: my translation. The risk here is that of substituting the essentiality of the one with that of the two. See T. de Lauretis's interesting discussion of Italian feminist theory in 'The Essence of the Triangle or, Taking the Risk of Essentialism Seriously', in Naomi Schor and Elizabeth Weed (eds), *the essential difference* (Bloomington and Indianapolis: Indiana University Press, 1994).
55. M. Wittig, 'The Mark of Gender', in N.K. Miller (ed.), *The Poetics of Gender* (New York: Columbia University Press, 1986), p. 67; she continues: 'Gender then must be destroyed. The possibility of its destruction is given through the very exercise of language. For each time I say 'I', I reorganize the world from my point of view and through abstraction I lay claim to universality. This fact holds true for every locutor' (ibid.).
56. The exploration of lesbian identity as a way of overcoming the opposition active/passive is central in many female autobiographies. Elizabeth Wilson in *Mirror Writing* (London: Virago, 1982) speaks of a new bodily economy beyond gender boundaries.
57. *In Other Worlds*, p. 77.
58. T. de Lauretis (ed.), *Feminist Studies/Critical Studies* (Bloomington: Indiana University Press, 1986), p. 14.
59. J. Kristeva, *Eretica dell'amore* (Turin: La Rosa), 1979, p. 88: my translation. In 'Women's Time', she examines the development of the women's movement, speaking for some of its aspects of 'inverted sexism' and warning against 'playing with fire': 'What can identity, even 'sexual identity', mean in a new theoretical and scientific space where the very notion of identity is challenged?': in T. Moi (ed.), *The Kristeva Reader* (Oxford: Basil Blackwell, 1986), p. 209.
60. R. Braidotti, *Patterns of Dissonance*, p. 238. Braidotti does not go quite so far as Spivak, who denounces Kristeva's 'ferocious Western Europeanism' (among other things) in her interview with Ellen Rooney ('In a word. *Interview*' in *the essential difference*). The same dissociation can be found in Naomi Schor's negative comments on Toril Moi's Kristevian positions in 'This Essentialism Which Is Not One: Coming to Grips with Irigaray', in *the essential difference*.
61. See, among others, Libreria delle Donne di Milano, '*Più donne che uomini*' (More Women than Men), *Sottosopra*, 1983.

62. '*É accaduto non per caso*', *Sottosopra*, January 1996, p. 1. The title of the document 'It happened not by chance' comes from Lidia Storoni Mazzolani recalling that in history and mythology women from Helen and Cassandra, Euriclea and Andromache, Antigone and Electra, have been weavers of history and life. 'It has happened without intention, but not by chance' (p. 8). If the era of patriarchy has ended (this is the title of the first section of the document), the authors ask the question whether patriarchy ever coincided with male sexuality and say that maybe now feminism can enter a political relation with those men who experience a free sense of male difference.
63. R. Braidotti, 'Commento alla relazione di Adriana Cavarero' p. 192.
64. J. Rose, *Sexuality in the Field of Vision* (London: Verso, 1986), p. 15.
65. Mary Russo, 'Female grotesque: carnival and theory', *Center for Twentieth Century Studies, Working Paper no. I* (Autumn 1985), p. 12.
66. 'Another Look, Another Woman: Retranslations of French Feminism', in Lynn Huffer (ed.), *Yale French Studies*, 87 (1995). All the references in the text are to this edition. This issue comes after the influential 'Feminist Readings: French Texts/American Contexts' (*Yale French Studies* 62) and the two essential volumes 'Post-colonial Conditions: Exiles, Migrations, and Nomadisms' (*Yale French Studies* 81 and 82).
67. One third of the volume – 'Other Realities, Other Fictions' – is in fact devoted to translations of works by Luce Irigaray, Nicole Brossard, Maryse Condé, Assia Djebar and Sarah Kofman (to whose memory 'Another Look' is dedicated).
68. She notes that 'commentary like Gilbert's seems simply not to have noticed the resistance Cixous's texts pose to this kind of appropriation' (p. 72). The 'untranslatability' of her work is underlined by Mary Lydon's article in the same issue, 'Retranslating no Re-reading no, rather: Rejoicing (with) Hélène Cixous'.
69. *the essential difference*, p. xvii.
70. Ibid., p. 51.
71. Gayatri Chakravorty Spivak, 'In a Word. *Interview*', p. 157.
72. Trinh T.M., *Woman Native Other – Writing Postcoloniality and Feminism* (Bloomington and Indianapolis: Indiana University Press, 1989), p. 120.
73. L. Erdrich, *The Bingo Palace* (London: HarperCollins/Flamingo), 1995, p. 269.

Chapter 2   D for Difference: Gender, Genre, Writing

1. S. Neale, *Genre* (London: British Film Institute, 1980), p. 48. The play between repetition and difference has been the recurrent feature of many generic definitions, but often the emphasis is placed on the lack of creativity and originality, echoing Benedetto Croce's diffidence on the subject. See below.

2. C. McArthur calls it 'an agreed code between film-maker and audience': *Underworld USA* (London: Secker & Warburg, 1972), p. 64.

3. T. O'Sullivan, *et al.* (eds), *Key Communications Terms* (London and New York: Methuen, 1983), p. 98.

4. Monique Wittig in 'The Mark of Gender' discusses the slide from nature to culture: 'American feminists use gender as a sociological category, making clear that there is nothing natural about this notion, as sexes have been artificially constructed into political categories – categories of oppression.' In N. K. Miller (ed.), *The Poetics of Gender* (New York: Columbia University Press, 1986), p. 64.

5. J. Derrida, 'The Law of Genre', in W. J. T. Mitchell (ed.), *On Narrative* (Chicago and London: Chicago University Press, 1981), p. 52. Further references in the text will be to this edition.

6. See Neale, *Genre*, p. 7.

7. *Genres in Discourse*, trans. by C. Porter (Cambridge: Cambridge University Press, 1990), p. 18.

8. In *L'évolution des genres dans l'histoire de la littérature* (1890), François Brunetière maintained that genres 'are born, grow and die' like every individual, and within that they live an internal dynamics of subdivisions and transformations.

9. B. Croce, *Estetica* (Bari, Laterza, 1958), p. 43. He believed that any true artistic expression violates an established genre, and opposed any normative theory of literary genres, stressing that it is a mistake to deduct the expression from the concept, and in the substituting element (genre) find the laws for what is being substituted (the work of art). Cf. pp. 41 ff.

10. For Genette the most important innovation lies in the interest for the modal interpretation of generic forms: '*Les genres peuvent traverser le modes (Oedipe raconté reste tragique), peut-être comme les oeuvres traversent les genres.*' 'Genres, "types", modes', *Poètique*, 32: 'Genre', p. 421). As to the Aristotelian triad, he notices that everybody, including James Joyce and Hélène Cixous, forgets that Aristotle had not mentioned poetry.

11. F. Jameson, *The Political Unconscious – Narrative as a Socially Symbolic Act* (London: Methuen, 1981), pp. 140–1.

12. A. Cranny-Francis, *Feminist Fiction – Feminist Uses of Generic Fiction* (Oxford: Polity Press, 1990), p. 17.

13. Ibid., pp. 18–19.

14. Gender differences are linked to genre demarcations both in reception studies and in popular culture analyses; some examples are E. A. Flynn and P. P. Schweickart's *Gender and Reading* (1986), J. Radway's influential *Reading the Romance* (1984), D. Longhurst's *Gender, Genre and Narrative Pleasure* (1989), and R. Dyer's analyses of film and Hollywood genres, apart from the works on television that will be discussed in the next chapter. It is impossible to forget the important role that Tania Modleski's *Loving With a Vengeance* (1982) has had in this discourse.

15. W. Benjamin, 'The Storyteller', in H. Arendt (ed.), *Illuminations*, trans. Harry Zohn (London: Collins/Fontana, 1973), p. 87. He refers to Don Quixote as an example of the 'perplexity of living', whose spiritual greatness and boldness come from being deprived of any spark of wisdom. He quotes Georg Lukàcs (who in *Theory of the Novel* sees the novel as the shape of 'transcendental unrootedness' and the only artistic form containing time) and contrasts 'the perpetuating remembrance of the novelist as contrasted with the short-lived reminiscences of the storyteller': ibid., p. 98).
16. L. M. Silko, *Ceremony* (Harmondsworth: Penguin, 1986), p. 2.
17. In a talk in Naples, '*Letteratura e giornalismo*' (Naples: The British Council), 24 November 1994.
18. Cf. J. Batsleer, T. Davies, R. O'Rourke and C. Weedon, *Rewriting English. Cultural Politics of Gender and Class* (London: Methuen, 1985), pp. 89 et seq.
19. On this point see P. Craig and M. Cadogan, *The Lady Investigates – Women Detectives and Spies in Fiction* (Oxford, Oxford University Press, 1986).
20. Cf. E. Tennant, *Two Women of London – The Strange Case of Ms Jekyll and Mrs Hyde* (London: Faber, 1989), p. 121. The following quotations are referred to this edition. Tennant has since produced more revisions of male literary classics, among them the beautiful *Faustine* (London: Faber & Faber, 1992).
21. A. Byatt, *Possession – A Romance* (London: Vintage, 1991); R. Tremain, *Restoration* (London: Sceptre, 1991; Hamish Hamilton, 1990). Further references in the text are to these editions.
22. M. Forster, *The Lady's Maid* (Harmondsworth: Penguin, 1991; Chatto & Windus, 1990). Her biography of Barrett Browning was very popular and received The Royal Society Literature Award in 1988.
23. A. S. Byatt, *Iris Murdoch* (London: Longman, 1976), p. 38. The coexistence of prose, poetry and dialogue could be found, before Brooke-Rose and Russ, in Murdoch's *An Accidental Man* (1971).
24. C. Brooke-Rose, *Textermination* (London: Carcanet, 1991). Further references in text are to this edition.
25. In her novel *Between*, she had been less sceptical on women as a possible hope in an age dominated by 'masculine upwards myths'. See S. R. Suleiman, *Risking Who One Is – Encounters with Contemporary Art and Literature* (Cambridge and London: Harvard University Press, 1994), pp. 169 ff.
26. 'Angela Carter intervistata da Lidia Curti', *Anglistica*, XXXV, 2–3 (1992), p. 10.
27. P. Highsmith, *Ripley's Game* (Harmondsworth: Penguin, 1980), p. 8. Further references in the text are to this edition.
28. Cf. P. D. James, *Innocent Blood* (London: Sphere Books, 1988), p. 295. Further references in the text are to this edition.
29. 'Celebrity and Celebrities', in 'Stack of the Artist of Konroo Project', 1995, unpublished.

30. L. Irigaray, *This Sex Which Is Not One* (Ithaca: Cornell University Press, 1995), p. 60. The discourse on female mimesis is recurrent in this work; the warning against the dangers of mimicry for women, 'the erasure of sexual difference into the self-representative systems of a male subject', is developed in the conversation called 'The Power of Discourse'.

Chapter 3   The Lure of the Image: Fe/male Serial Narratives

1. J. Stacey, 'Desperately Seeking Difference', in L. Gamman and M. Marshment (eds), *The Female Gaze – Women as Viewers of Popular Culture* (London: Verso, 1988), p. 112.
2. J. Lesage, 'Artful Racism, Artful Rape – Griffiths' *Broken Blossoms*', in C. Gledhill (ed.), *Home is Where the Heart Is – Studies in Melodrama and the Woman's Film* (London: British Film Institute, 1987), p. 250.
3. T. Modleski, *Loving With a Vengeance: Mass-Produced Fantasies for Women* (London: Methuen, 1982), p. 14.
4. G. Greer, *The Female Eunuch* (London: Paladin, 1971), p. 170.
5. In K. Davies, J. Dickey and T. Stratford (eds), *Out of Focus. Writings on Women and the Media* (London: The Women's Press, 1987), p. 140.
6. See above, Ch. 1, note 37.
7. Rosalind Coward, 'Come back Miss Ellie: on character and narrative in soap operas', *Critical Quarterly*, 28, 1–2 (1986), p. 171.
8. The padded shoulders of the notorious *Dynasty* women have been easy targets but there is also a sarcastic attitude to those who, like me, deal with such matters: 'No medium outside of TV is quite so beset with scholarly analysis based solely on its lowest achievements. Ever read a Leavisite purge of Zane Grey? No. So just what is it on TV that so attracts the tracts? . . . In the Career Person Eighties, bookshelves on the Left creak under countless analyses of *Dallas*, *Crossroads*, etc. NEW IMPROVED SEMIOLOGICAL ARIELS!': I. Penman, 'The fog that is Fallon', *The Face*, April 1986.
9. Cf. D. Hobson, *Crossroads – The Drama of a Soap Opera* (London: Methuen, 1982), p. 36.
10. See C. Brunsdon, 'The role of soap opera in the development of feminist television scholarship', in R. C. Allen (ed.), *To Be Continued . . . Soap Operas around the World* (London and New York: Routledge, 1995), pp. 52 ff. This essay, an informed analysis of feminist work on women and the media, confronts the problem of why feminists have been so interested in soap opera, and traces the historical and theoretical context of their analyses, from the mid-seventies to the early nineties.
11. U. Eco, interview with J. Le Goff on *Nouvel Observateur*, reprinted in *la Repubblica – Mercurio*, 24 February 1990.

12. 'Fictions everywhere, all pervasive, with consumption obligatory by virtue of this omnipresence, a veritable requirement of our social existence': S. Heath, *The Sexual Fix* (London: Macmillan, 1982), p. 85.

13. The loss of memory is used in many soaps as a device to start the plot (and the plots) all over again. The best example goes back to *Dynasty* with Blake's loss of memory that makes him think he is still married to his arch-enemy Alexis, while erasing all memory of his present marriage to Krystle.

14. Cf. Hobson, *Crossroads*, pp. 23–4. She refers to the uproar caused in the British press and among the viewers by the sacking of the actress interpreting the role of Meg; the equivalence of soap opera and real life is also underlined by Rosalind Coward who refers the construction of the parallel lives of characters and actor to an effect of immediacy and reality on otherwise highly conventionalised narratives: 'Come back Miss Ellie', p. 173.

15. This CBS series of the early eighties dealt with Washington political intrigues, and was followed by others in this vein. The action was centred on men's competitions and struggles for the White House, with references to McCarthyism and to more recent events of the Kennedy and post-Kennedy era. But politics was subordinate to the hate and love plots involving two rival families, as usual represented by two powerful maternal figures. The show has known a particular fortune on Italian television in the mid eighties, second only to *The Bold and the Beautiful* in the nineties. I have written on the transcodification and the reception of American soaps in Italy in 'Imported utopias', in Z. Baransky and R. Lumley (eds), *Culture and Conflict in Post-War Italy. Essays in Popular and Mass Culture* (London: Macmillan, 1990).

16. G. Vidal, *Duluth* (New York: Ballantine Books, 1983), p. 280.

17. C. R. Stimpson, 'Gertrude Stein and the Transposition of Gender', in N. K. Miller (ed.), *The Poetics of Gender* (New York: Columbia University Press, 1986), p. 3.

18. 'A Desire of One's Own: Psychoanalytic Feminism and Intersubjective Space', in T. de Lauretis (ed.), *Feminist Studies/Critical Studies* (Bloomington, Indiana University Press, 1986), p. 97.

19. Lesage, 'Artful Racism', p. 235.

20. M. A. Doane, 'The "Woman's Film" – Possession and Address', in Gledhill, *Home is Where the Heart is*, pp. 174–5.

21. I have always considered this identification unconvincing as Hollywood melodrama is frequently most 'unrealistic', or a clever blending of naturalistic narration and psychic fantasy.

22. *The Desire to Desire – The Woman's Film of the 1940s*, (Bloomington and Indianapolis: Indiana University Press, 1987), p. 17.

23. In *The Bold and the Beautiful*, the hero Ridge is the sex object: whenever possible his women (and particularly Brooke) get him to undress, and, what with sauna, swimming pool, shower or a massage, he appears half-naked most of the time. Dylan, a later entry in the series, exhibits his good looks in a strip-tease club, or in private parties, in order to pay for his university fees; in doubt whether to accept a

generous offer by a rich lady for an extension of his favours, he finally resists, refusing to be used as 'a sexual toy'. Here 'man's image' seems to have been substituted for the overexploited female image; the same happens in *NYPD Blue*, with a more conscious intent to subvert chauvinist stereotypes.

24. In observing the likeness between this character and Sue Ellen in *Dallas*, Christine Geraghty in *Women and Soap Opera – A Study of Prime Time Soaps* (Cambridge, Polity Press, 1991), pp. 50 ff., notes that the centrality of women in soaps is based on their intense investment in personal relationships.

25. Luce Irigaray, *An Ethics of Sexual Difference* (Ithaca, New York: Cornell University Press, 1993), p. 37. This is also the source of the epigraph at the beginning of this section.

26. Ibid., p. 70.

27. After nearly two thousand episodes, there has been a surprising truce with the long historical shot on the embrace between Stephanie in her sick bed (she is being slowly poisoned by Sheila) and Brooke who, against all wisdom, has come to rescue her. But, soon enough, the battle is resumed.

28. C. Moraga, 'From a Long Line of Vendidas: Chicanas and Feminism', in T. de Lauretis, *Feminist Studies*, p. 176.

29. L. Irigaray, *An Ethics of Sexual Difference*, p. 102.

30. Ibid., respectively pp. 104 and 105.

31. The actresses who played the 'angels' are now often seen in television movies; Farah Fawcett in particular has created a transversal role tied to her image and acting, rather than to particular movies, as the victimised woman successfully rebelling and taking a stand against the extraordinarily wicked men she happens to meet.

32. C. Brunsdon, 'The role of soap opera', p. 58. Annette Kuhn speaking of *Dallas* and *Dynasty*, *Coronation Street* and *Eastenders*, has said that 'in a society whose representations of itself are governed by the masculine, these genres (soap opera and melodrama) at least raise the possibility of female desire and female point of view': A. Kuhn, 'Women's Genres', *Screen*, 25, 1 (1984), p. 28. The same opinion has been expressed by Pam Cook, Christine Geraghty and Tania Modleski in stressing either intuition and emotivity or tolerance and passivity. Even those critics who had some doubts in relation to prime-time soap, such as Ien Ang and Peter Buckman, did not on the whole deny a female specificity to soap opera. On the other hand, increasing attention has been given to masculinity in television fiction.

33. According to John Caughie, 'Rhetoric, pleasure, and "art television"', *Screen*, 22, 4 (1981), these distancing elements are the features of art television, though I would recall the whole Chandler tradition of detective stories within popular fiction; it was also one of the surprising charms of *Magnum* and of the television adaptation of *Nero Wolfe*. There have been few examples of a female 'voice over'.

34. The differences lay among American, British or Australian productions; between daytime and prime time; from straight versions of a

format to its conscious parody or reversal. A good example of this reversal is given by Lynda La Plante's *Widows*, a short British serial that has attracted the attention of feminist critics. See G. Skirrow, '*Widows*', in M. Alvarado and J. Stewart (eds), *Made for Television: Euston Films Limited* (London: British Film Institute, 1985) and 'Women/Acting/Power', in H. Baher and G. Dyer (eds), *Boxed In: Women and Television* (London: Pandora, 1987).

35. The interesting treatment of black people was noted by Christine Geraghty with regard to *Eastenders* ('East Enders', *Marxism Today*, August 1985); later she writes on blacks in soaps in *Women and Soap Opera*, pp. 140 and ff. See also Stuart Hall, 'The Whites of Their Eyes: Racist Ideology and the Media', in M. Alvarado and J. O. Thompson (eds), *The Media Reader* (London: British Film Institute, 1990). He enumerates the various stereotypes of black characters in film and television, and observes: 'Blacks are still the most frightening, cunning and glamorous crooks (and policemen) in NY cop series. They are the fleet-footed, crazy-talking under-men who connect Starsky and Hutch to the drug-saturated ghetto' (p. 16).

36. Ien Ang and Jon Stratton, 'The end of civilization as we knew it: *Chances* and the postrealist soap opera', in Allen, *To Be Continued*, p. 125. Tessa Perkins, commenting on *South of the Border* and *Making Out*, maintains that they 'celebrate aspects of femininity – a celebration of excess. I think *Making Out* is vulgar and that's wonderful. They have an immense energy that maybe soaps are now lacking': R. Brunt, K. Jones, T. Perkins, 'A Conversation about Contemporary Television', *Women, a cultural review*, 2, 1 (Spring 1991), pp. 9–10. In the same conversation, Karen Jones says: 'Are soaps the subconscious of patriarchy? . . . That's why there are no solutions and the characters endlessly go around in circles in discussions' (p. 7). Further on, she observes that soap and crime series are two arenas where moral questions are debated.

37. This was the case in two forgotten British series, *Juliet Bravo* and *The Gentle Touch*, and the more popular *Cagney and Lacey*. This series of the eighties, though in many ways a conventional cop series, dealt with female friendship and with issues such as rape, incest, abortion, pornography, violence against women, and breast cancer, attracting much feminist commentary. See B. Alcock and J. Robson, 'Cagney and Lacey revisited', *Feminist Review*, 35 (Summer 1990); L. Gamman, 'Response: More Cagney and Lacey', *Feminist Review*, 37 (Spring 1991), and, above all, Julie D'Acci, *Defining Women: The Case of Cagney and Lacey* (Chapel Hill, NC: University of North Carolina, 1994). Lucy Gamman insists on the importance of homoerotic imagery in the series.

38. Jean Darblay in *Juliet Bravo* was often seen at home with a husband assuming the role normally assigned to women within (and without) the genre; the same can be said for Mary Beth Lacey talking in bed to her unemployed husband about her work, a partial reversal of the set scene between Joyce and Furillo in bed at the close of *Hill Street Blues*.

39. See I. Ang, *Watching Dallas* (London: Methuen, 1985) and T. Lovall, 'Ideology and *Coronation Street*', in R. Dyer, C. Geraghty, M. Jordan, T. Lovell, R. Paterson. J. Stewart, *Coronation Street* (London: British Film Institute, 1981).

Chapter 4   Hybrid Fictions . . .

1. J. Wicke and M. Ferguson (eds), *Feminism and Postmodernism* (Durham and London: Duke University Press, 1994), p. 2. They speak of the need the one has for the other: 'Feminist theory and practice . . . now require an understanding of the transformations of postmodernity, while a postmodern politics entails feminism as a cutting edge of its critique' (p. 4).
2. M. Russo, *the female grotesque: risk, excess and modernity* (London: Routledge, 1995), p. 65.
3. See J. Flax, *Thinking Fragments – Psychoanalysis, Feminism and Postmodernism in the Contemporary West* (Berkeley, CA: University of California Press, 1990), p. 14.
4. Ibid., pp. 12–13.
5. G. C. Spivak, *In Other Worlds. Essays in Cultural Politics* (London and New York: Methuen, 1987), p. 107 and p. 268.
6. J. A. Flieger, 'Entertaining the Ménage à Trois: Psychoanalysis, Feminism, and Literature', in *Feminism and Psychoanalysis*, ed. by R. Feldstein and J. Roof (Ithaca, NY and London: Cornell University Press, 1989), p. 186. In this essay the author also stresses the many pitfalls that may be in store for a feminist literary critic (see pp. 188–9).
7. *Speculum of the Other Woman*, trans. by Gillian C. Gill (Ithaca, NY: Cornell University Press, 1992), p. 167.
8. A. Rich, 'When We Dead Awaken', in *On Lies, Secrets, and Silence – Selected Prose 1966–1978* (London: Virago, 1980), p. 35.
9. *An Atlas of the Difficult World – Poems 1988–1991* (New York and London: W. W. Norton, 1991), respectively pp. 3, 42, 44. For a perceptive insight on *Eastern War Time*, see Homi Bhabha, in 'Unpacking my library . . . again', in I. Chambers and L. Curti (eds), *The Postcolonial Question – Common Skies, Divided Horizons* (London and New York: Routledge, 1996).
10. B. Christian, *Black Feminist Criticism – Perspectives on Black Women Writers* (Oxford and New York, Pergamon Press, 1985), p. ix.
11. See C. Belsey and J. Moore (eds), *The Feminist Reader – Essays in Gender and the Politics of Literary Criticism* (London: Macmillan, 1989), pp. 1–20. They remind us that such forerunners as Mary Wollstonecraft, George Eliot, Virginia Woolf and Q. D. Leavis had already looked at them, if not always with indulgent eyes.
12. J. Miller, *Seductions – Studies in Reading and Culture* (London: Virago, 1990), p. 6.
13. See O. Kenyon, *Women Novelists Today – A Survey of English Writing of the Seventies and the Eighties* (Brighton: Harvester Press, 1988), p. 12.

14. S. M. Gilbert and S. Gubar, *The Madwoman in the Attic – The Woman Writer and the Nineteenth-Century Literary Imagination* (New Haven and London: Yale University Press), p. 43. According to them, women authors need a continuity with those female writers who can provide an alternative model for their rebellion. This was also said in opposition to the oedipal revolt that, according to Harold Bloom, is necessary for the male writer to express his genius. The male 'anxiety of influence' becomes for women 'anxiety of authorship', a tradition of isolation, illness, alienation, inadequacy, which female writing must get rid of. See pp. 46–53.

15. B. Guy-Shetfall, 'Black Feminist Perspective on Transforming the Academy', in *Theorizing Black Feminisms*, ed. by S. M. James and A. P. A. Busia (London and New York: Routledge, 1993), p. 77.

16. B. Christian, *Black Feminist Criticism*, p. x.

17. T. Moi, *Sexual/Textual Politics: Feminist Literary Theory* (London and New York: Methuen 1985), p. 8. In *A Literature of Their Own* (London: Virago, 1991), Showalter had made a polemical attack against modernist writers who, in her opinion, have ignored female sensations, intimacy and physicality. Her critique of Woolf and of her idealisation of androgyny is very harsh: 'Androgyny was the myth that helped her evade confrontation with her own painful femaleness and enabled her to choke and repress her anger and ambition . . . Full "femaleness" and full "maleness" were equally dangerous' (pp. 264–6).

18. See M. L. Broe and A. Ingram (eds), *Women's Writing in Exile* (Chapel Hill and London: University of North Carolina Press, 1989), pp. 5–6. Stein was racist and classist, Woolf an elitist; the feminist revision of the canon is guilty of the exclusion of those writers who use traditional forms. The book deals with the 'elsewhere' of those British writers – whether black and Asian immigrants, or white women coming from the ex-colonies like Doris Lessing, Christina Stead and Jean Rhys – for whom home is no more home than England: 'exile is both at home and at Home' (p. 7).

19. I. Chambers, *Migrancy, Culture, Identity* (London and New York: Routledge, 1994), pp. 134–5.

20. M. Russo, *The Female Grotesque*, pp. 96–7.

21. H. Cixous, 'Sorties: Out and Out: Attacks/Ways Out/Forays', in H. Cixous and C. Clément, *The Newly Born Woman* (Minneapolis: University of Minnesota Press, 1986), p. 90. All references in the text are to this edition.

22. Postmodern fiction brings to mind Canadian, North American or French writers, hardly ever British names. In a review of Kathy Acker's *In Memoriam to Identity*, Suzanne Moore regrets that 'in Britain we like writers to write what is already known in a way that we can know it even more. That is good writing. If writers must start mucking about with the muddle of language itself then we'd prefer them to be men': 'Nerve Endings', in *Marxism Today*, Sept. 1990, p. 45.

23. Z. Fairbairns, S. Maitland, V. Miner, M. Roberts, M. Wandor, *Tales I Tell My Mother – A Collection of Feminist Short Stories* (London/West

Nyack: The Journeyman Press, 1978). 'I do not believe there is such a thing as a "feminist" language . . . Our language is in the use we make of it to call to the surface our submerged history and to express our feminist point of view on the world in which we live', notes Wandor (p. 9), and Valerie Miner adds: 'These stories suggest that the personal is political, that narrative includes therapy and propaganda' (p. 62).

24. Palmer deals with this particularly in 'Sisterhood', the last chapter of *Contemporary Women's Fiction – Narrative Practice and Feminist Theory* (New York and London: Harvester Wheatsheaf, 1989), pp. 125–59.

25. bell hooks, 'Writing Autobiography', in R. R. Warhol and D. Price Herndl (eds), *Feminisms – An Anthology of Literary Theory and Criticism* (New Brunswick, NJ: Rutgers University Press, 1991), p. 1038.

26. Quoted in J. Taylor, ' "Memoirs" was made of this', in *Notebooks, Memoirs, Archives – Reading and Rereading Doris Lessing*, ed. by J. Taylor (London: Routledge & Kegan Paul, 1982), p. 227. References from the novel are from *The Memoirs of a Survivor* (London: Picador, 1974).

27. Spark's heroine, Caroline Rose, is one of the many characters in search of an author who, according to Brian McHale, people postmodern novels: *Postmodernist Fiction* (New York and London: Methuen, 1987), pp. 64 ff.

28. As Derrida says after Heidegger, creation is to be written under the sign of erasure. In 'Freud et la scène de l'écriture', *L'écriture et la différence* (Paris: Editions du Seuil, 1967), writing is seen as life marked by self-cancellation. Metanarration stresses the 'falsity', the non-existence of fiction and its unavoidable end, while affirming its necessity and function. McHale speaks of narrative self-erasure in the case of Beckett, Pynchon, Robbe-Grillet and Spark.

29. '[O]r with his pencil or with his stick or/or light light I mean/never there he will never/never anything/there/any more . . .' (S. Beckett, *Malone Dies* (Harmondsworth: Penguin, 1962), p. 144.

30. V. Woolf, *To the Lighthouse* (London: Dent, 1962), p. 242. As Gayatri Spivak says in her essay on the novel ('an attempt to articulate a woman's vision of a woman'), the appropriation of language by the woman artist, in contrast with the rationality of western philosophy, leads to the reunion with the mother. '*To the Lighthouse* reminds me that the womb is not an emptiness or a mystery, it is a place of production.' ('Unmaking and making in *To the Lighthouse*', in *In Other Worlds*, p. 45).

31. *Expletives Deleted* (London: Chatto & Windus, 1992), p. 2.

32. *Breaking the Sequence – Women's Experimental Fiction*, introduced and edited by E. G. Friedman and M. Fuchs (Princeton, NJ: Princeton University Press, 1989).

33. R. Coward, 'The True Story of How I Became My Own Person', in *Female Desire – Women's Sexuality Today* (London: Paladin, 1984), p. 185.

34. J. Winterson, *Oranges Are Not The Only Fruit* (London: Vintage, 1991), pp. 91–2. All references in the text are to this edition.
35. *Postmodernist Fiction*, p. 37.
36. See *The Passion* (Harmondsworth, Penguin, 1988), pp. 43 and 62; all references in the text are to this edition.
37. T. Morrison, *Beloved* (New York: Signet Books, 1987), p. 336. All references in the text are to this edition.
38. H. K. Bhabha, *The Location of Culture* (London and New York: Routledge, 1994), p. 17.
39. See *Boating for Beginners* (London: Minerva, 1991), p. 68.
40. *Sexing the Cherry* (London: Vintage, 1989), p. 104. All references in the text are to this edition.
41. *Wise Children* (London: Chatto & Windus, 1991), p. 232. All references in the text are to this edition.

Chapter 5   . . . and Monstrous Bodies in Contemporary Women's Writing

1. M. Russo, *The Female Grotesque: Risk, Excess and Modernity* (London: Routledge, 1995), p. 1.
2. J. Rose, *Sexuality in the Field of Vision* (London: Verso, 1986), pp. 90–1.
3. L. Irigaray, 'Questions', *This Sex Which is Not One*, trans. by G. C. Gill (Ithaca, NY: Cornell University Press, 1995), p. 134.
4. 'The Power of Discourse', *This Sex*, p. 79.
5. 'I write woman: woman must write woman. And man, man': 'The Laugh of the Medusa', in R. R. Warhol and D. Price Herndl (eds), *Feminisms – An Anthology of Literary Theory and Criticism* (New Brunswick, NJ: Rutgers University Press, 1991), p. 335.
6. H. Cixous, 'Sorties', in H. Cixous and C. Clément, *The Newly Born Woman* (Minneapolis: University of Minnesota Press, 1986), p. 90.
7. J. Gallop, 'The Monster in the Mirror: the Feminist Critic's Psychoanalysis', in R. Feldstein and J. Roof (eds), *Feminism and Psychoanalysis* (Ithaca, NY, and London: Cornell University Press, 1989), pp. 15 ff. She is commenting on the special issue of *Yale French Studies*, 62, *Feminist Readings*, in which the collective of women editors define themselves as a seven headed monster.
8. Gallop, 'The Monster', p. 21. She asserts that feminism must celebrate the beauty of such 'monsters'; after recalling feminist analyses of the 'mirroring self' in *Jane Eyre* and *Wide Sargasso Sea*, she regrets that Western feminism tends to project its theories on Third World women, and quotes from Spivak's essay in *Yale French Studies*, 62, p. 179: 'I see no way to avoid insisting that there has to be a simultaneous other focus: not merely who am I? but who is the other woman?' (p. 24).
9. '[R]eaders of Mary Shelley's novel had frequently expressed the feeling that a young girl's fascination with the idea of monstrousness was somehow monstrous in itself': Barbara Johnson, 'My Monster/My Self', in *A World of Difference* (Baltimore and London: The Johns Hopkins University Press, 1987), p. 150.

10. D. Dinnerstein, *The Mermaid and the Minotaur* (New York: Harper Colophon, 1976), p. 5.
11. 'Author's Introduction to the Standard Novels Edition' (1831), in Mary Shelley, *Frankenstein or The Modern Prometheus*, ed. with an intro. by M. Hindle (Harmondsworth: Penguin, 1992), p. 5 and 10. All references in the text are to this edition.
12. Ibid. This sentence anticipates the torments Jane Bowles went through a century later, linking the two authors in a female writing block that is rarely spoken of. See Chapter 6.
13. B. Johnson, 'My Monster', p. 154.
14. M. Kelly, 'Re-Presenting the Body: On "Interim" Part I', in J. Donald (ed.), *Psychoanalysis and Cultural Theory* (London: Macmillan, 1991), pp. 61–2.
15. Russo, *The Female Grotesque*, p. 70.
16. In 'Introduction' to Cixous and Clément, *The Newly Born Woman*, p. xi. Her introductory essay and particularly this term has been under attack (see Ch. 1).
17. Cixous, *'Coming to Writing' and Other Essays* (Cambridge and London: Harvard University Press, 1991), respectively pp. 4, 12 and 20.
18. Cixous, 'Sorties', p. 97. Maggie Humm says: 'The body is given its full sign in Cixous's neologisms and syntactical turmoil. Her writing is often associational, built up of permutations of letters, puns, slips of the tongue and other forms of subjectivity': *Border Traffic – Strategies of Contemporary Women Writers* (Manchester: Manchester University Press, 1991), p. 21.
19. Cixous, *Coming to Writing*, p. 83. Jane Gallop notes that the term *écriture féminine* (by now used to indicate French feminist theory) evokes a physicality tied to the sinful image Paris has for Americans, especially for those women writers who in the thirties went there in search of their art: 'Ecriture féminine, not only female but somehow French, a passage from the phallic paradigm to oral sex': Gallop, *Around 1981* (London: Routledge, 1992), p. 42.
20. A. Banti, *Artemisia*, trans. by S. D'Ardia Caracciolo (Lincoln: University of Nebraska Press, 1988), p. 10. All references in the the text are to this edition. There is a later edition published in England (London: Serpent's Tail, 1995), with the same translation.
21. Artemisia's earlier life is lived in the shadow of two men, both painters: her father Oratio, with whom she has a baffling relationship – she will be able to relate to him only when he is dying – and Agostino Tassi who raped her when she was barely more than a child. She finds her independence when as an adult she becomes a recognised painter herself. But, in Banti's vision, the moment of freedom, from her past, from the fear of men, from the bonds of her condition, comes when she puts her last touch to the painting of *Judith and Holofernes*, and the conclusion is a sort of rite. Holofernes gives her the independence from men, but at the same time will always stand between her and men. 'At that time I was painting Holofernes. I feel I have reached the truth, an inexpressible truth, as I form these words on Artemisia's lips': p. 42. A

man had taken her freedom from her, her gaze and representation of another man – actually of that man's head – gives it back to her. She is now free from rage.

22. Trinh T. Minh-ha, *Woman Native Other – Writing Postcoloniality and Feminism* (Bloomington and Indianapolis: Indiana University Press, 1989), p. 28. All references in the text are to this edition.

23. A. Carter, *Nights at the Circus* (London: Chatto & Windus, 1984), p. 217.

24. G. Anzaldúa, *Borderlands/La Frontera* (San Francisco: Aunt Lute, 1987), p. 73.

25. Ibid., p. 75.

26. Shelley, *Frankenstein*, p. 160. Julia Kristeva has spoken of the fears tied to female reproductive power in *Pouvoirs de l'horreur – Essai sur l'abjection* (Paris: Éditions du Seuil, 1980).

27. *The Madwoman in the Attic* (New Haven and London: Yale University Press), p. 43. In reality what women writers discover is the yearning 'toward that sane and serious self concealed on the other side of the mirror . . . the real self buried beneath the 'copy' selves.'

28. C. Brontë, *Jane Eyre* (Oxford: Oxford University Press, 1989), p. 295.

29. G. C. Spivak, 'Three Women's Texts and a Critique of Imperialism', in *Critical Inquiry*, 12, 1 (Autumn 1985), pp. 247 and 249. She regrets that Western feminism reproduces those axioms: 'A basically isolationist admiration for the literature of the female subject in Europe and Anglo-America establishes the high feminist norm' (p. 243).

30. B. Smith, among others, has spoken of a possible lesbian feminist reading of *Sula* in *The New Feminist Criticism* (London: Virago, 1986).

31. T. Morrison, *Sula* (London: Grafton Books, 1982), p. 131. All references in the text are to this edition.

32. See J. Russ, *The Female Man* (London: The Women's Press, 1985); F. Weldon, *The Cloning of Joanna May* (London: Fontana/Collins, 1989) and *The Life and Loves of a She-Devil* (London: Hodder & Stoughton, 1983); A. Carter, *The Passion of New Eve* (London: Virago, 1977). All references in the text are to these editions.

33. A. Carter, *Nights at the Circus*. All references in the text are to this edition.

34. Cixous, 'The Laugh of the Medusa', p. 344.

35. *Sexing the Cherry* (London: Vintage, 1989), p. 24. All references in the text are to this edition.

36. In her review of *Jane Eyre*, Carter shows how Charlotte Brontë and her heroine defy all the limits and conventions of a traditional framework. 'Charlotte Brontë's fiction inhabits the space between passion and repression. She knows she must not have the thing she wants; she also knows it will be restored to her in her dreams': *Expletives Deleted*, p. 169. She compares Jane to Teresa Hawkins in Christina Stead's *For Love Alone*, and to Lessing's early heroines.

37. In *The Bloody Chamber* (Harmondsworth: Penguin, 1979), p. 160. Like other heroines, she questions the mirror for her identity: 'The moonlight spilled into the Duke's motionless bedroom from behind a cloud

and she saw how pale this wolf, not-wolf who played with her was. The moon and mirrors have this much in common: you cannot see behind them.' (p. 165). *The Company of Wolves* is also contained in this collection.

38. A. Rice, *Interview with the Vampire* (London: Warner Books, 1996), p. 130.
39. In *Am I that Name? – Feminism and the Category of 'Women' in History* (London, Macmillan, 1988), Denise Riley argues against the monotony of the concept of 'men' and 'women': 'the apparent continuity of the subject of "women" isn't to be relied on . . . "being a woman" is also inconstant, and can't provide an ontological foundation' (p. 2).
40. 'The Guilty One', in Clément and Cixous, *The Newly Born Woman*, p. 56.
41. Carter, *The Passion of New Eve*, p. 67. In the interview she gave me in Naples (The British Council, 23 October 1990), she said that the process of socialisation transforming Evelyn into Eve is not a very convincing one: 'If I were able to construct such a programme, believe me I would market it. It would be out there on the stands, it would be compulsory in all secondary schools for young men': *Anglistica*, XXXV, 2–3(1992), p. 9.
42. *Written on the Body* (London: Vintage, 1993), p. 89. All references in the text are to this edition.
43. Cixous, 'The Laugh of the Medusa', p. 342.

Chapter 6   Alterity and the Female Traveller: Jane Bowles

1. H. Cixous, 'The Laugh of the Medusa', in R. R. Warhol and D. Price Herndl (eds), *Feminisms – An Anthology of Literary Theory and Criticism* (New Brunswick, NJ: Rutgers University Press, 1991), p. 340.
2. From *Naked Lunch*, a film by David Cronenberg, produced by J. Thomas, with Peter Weller, Judy Davis (Joan Lee and Joan Frost), Ian Holm, Julian Sands and Roy Scheider, 1991, based on the book by William S. Burroughs. The music is by Howard Shore.
3. From *The Sheltering Sky*, a film by Bernardo Bertolucci, with Debra Winger and John Malkovich, 1989, based on the book by Paul Bowles. The music is by Ryuichi Sakamoto. Paul Bowles appears as the narrator.
4. See P. Bowles, *Conversations*, ed. G. D. Caponi (Jackson: University Press of Mississippi, 1993), pp. 79 and 104.
5. 'I wanted it to be about writing: the act of writing and creating something that is dangerous to you': Chris Rodley (ed.), *Cronenberg on Cronenberg* (London and Boston: Faber & Faber, 1992), pp. 164–5.
6. 'If it were just a question of mutilating bodies that way that hack-and-slash movies often do, I wouldn't find extreme imagery interesting . . . *Shivers* did start with a dream I had about a spider that emerged from a woman's mouth . . . The very purpose was to show the unshowable,

to speak the unspeakable. I was creating certain things that there was no way of suggesting because it was not common currency of the imagination. It had to be shown or else not done': ibid.

7. Ibid.
8. W. Burroughs, *The Naked Lunch* (London: Corgi Books, 1969), pp. 37–8. That pimp and trombone player (probably Mexican) must be a Western obsessive image for the white woman's seducer. It moves from high to popular culture as well as across genres. Italian consumers of both popular journalism and television saw 'the monster' resurrected in the recent case around the disappearance of a young Italian tourist, Ylenia Carrisi, in Spring 1994 – only this time it was New Orleans and he was Jamaican. His image filled Italian screens with a frequency similar to that of O. J. Simpson on U.S. screens more or less at the same time. In this case the uproar was linked to her being the daughter of the quite famous (at least in Italy) pop music couple, Al Bano and Romina Power (the Hollywood actor's daughter), and the accusations were prompted by her father first of all.
9. P. Bowles, *The Sheltering Sky* (New York: Vintage Books, 1977; first published 1949), p. 190.
10. 'They would spare no effort in seeking her out, they would pry open the wall she had built and force her to look at what she had buried there': ibid., p. 320.
11. 'The Oriental was linked thus to elements in Western society (delinquents, the insane, women, the poor) having in common an identity best described as lamentably alien': Edward Said, *Orientalism* (Harmondsworth: Penguin, 1978), p. 270.
12. M. Yegenoglu, 'Supplementing the Orientalist Lack: European Ladies in the Harem', *Inscriptions 6: 'Orientalism and Cultural Differences'*, 1992, respectively pp. 48 and 49.
13. D. Root, 'Misadventure in the Desert: *The Sheltering Sky* as Colonialist Nightmare', ibid., p. 95, n. 2. The essay comments on the association of the exotic with sexuality: 'Irrationality, savagery, violence, chaos and death: the "native" man brings these to the white woman, yet for Bowles it is also Kit's sexuality that is her enemy, something that is at some level 'alien' and destructive to her as the "native"': ibid., p. 89. This point, with the one made by Yegenoglu about the Oriental woman as the symbol of the secret and the obscure, finds a correspondence in Jane Bowles's description of her Arab lover.
14. It seems that in reality the game was even more risky and cruel, and somewhat closer to the model since there may have been a child involved; a version goes that William Burroughs did not place an apple (or a glass) on his wife's head but their infant child, named William after his father. Thus he was at one and the same time aiming at himself and at his progeny, the 'apple' of his eye. This is how the fatal accident was related, or at least interpreted, by William Burroughs Junior, a drug addict and alcoholic who died an early death. I owe this information to Richard Wohlfeiler, a friend of his while he lived in Santa Cruz.

15. *Out in the World – Selected Letters of Jane Bowles 1935–1970*, ed. by M. Dillon (Santa Barbara: Black Sparrow Press, 1985), pp. 81–2. All references in the text are to this edition.
16. Tetum is the 'husband' in a small harem, first accepted as a necessary complement to Cherifa, then loved in spite of the cynical initial description and, once her liaison with Cherifa is established, slowly forgotten.
17. In this group of letters, Jane Bowles occasionally falls into the opposition 'they' and 'us', which has been a linguistic marker for the estrangement of the 'other', along class, race or sexual lines.
18. Jane was always quite clear on financial matters, not unlike most of her characters. Miss Goering in *Two Serious Ladies* is particularly aware that money is the main mediatory link between her and the 'other' but is never put off by that.
19. Quoted in M. Dillon, *A Little Original Sin. The Life and Work of Jane Bowles* (London: Virago, 1988), p. 286.
20. Malek Alloul in *The Colonial Harem* (Minneapolis: University of Minnesota Press, 1986) observes that the Oriental look is always neglected. The book collects the postcards representing Algerian women, sent by the French from Algeria during 30 years of colonial presence, and underlines the absence of photographic traces of the gaze of the colonised.
21. P. Bowles, *Conversations*, pp. 82–3.
22. Ibid., p. 222.
23. There is the feeling that it is all decided for her, even the way she must invariably accept men's approaches; men are for her a threat that cannot be avoided, like the rumble of thunder or a low dark cloud getting close: 'she felt for one desolate moment that the whole thing had been prearranged and that although she had forced herself to take this little trip to the mainland, she had somehow at the same time been tricked into taking it by the powers above . . . . She noticed with a faint heart that the man had lifted his drink from the bar and was coming towards her': J. Bowles, *Two Serious Ladies*, in *The Collected Works of Jane Bowles*, with an introduction by Truman Capote (New York: The Noonday Press – Farrar, Straus & Giroux, 1966), p. 144. All references in the text are to this edition.
24. Mrs Copperfield has other bizarre encounters with women in the streets of Panama before being approached by Pacifica, and they all underline the ethnic diversity, after which neither colour nor race is ever mentioned again in the novel.
25. This is one of the many instances in which the female couple or pair extends to a third party, and the binary relation becomes a triangular one. In *In The Summer House*, both mother and daughter are at the centre of more than one triangle.
26. Once she decides to leave Andy with whom she lives in an inexplicably harmonious ménage, Miss Goering realises that however fond she is of him, her only interest lies elsewhere: 'For several days it had been quite clear to Miss Goering that Andy was no longer thinking of himself as a bum. This would have pleased her greatly had she been interested in

reforming her friends, but unfortunately she was only interested in the course that she was following in order to attain her own salvation': ibid., p. 159.

27. 'The traveller was lying on his bed, consumed by a feeling of guilt. He had never done anything like this before . . . He felt like a two-headed monster, as though he had somehow slipped from the real world into the other world, the world that he had always imagined as a little boy to be inhabited by assassins and orphans, and children whose mothers went to work': J. Bowles, *A Guatemalan Idyll*, in *Collected Works*, p. 349. In this case the swing is tipped in favour of the security of home and the portrait is probably satirical. Elements of parody are often present in her minor characters, especially men, and not unusual in her heroines; in the latter case parody is always veined with pathos.

28. J. Bowles, *Plain Pleasures*, in *Collected Works*, p. 302. He, too, has a restless brother – characters in Bowles often have an alter ego, sometime two – and contrary to him he feels that 'if a man leaves home he must leave for some very good reason – like the boys who went to construct the Panama canal or for any other decent reason': ibid., p. 303.

29. Ibid., p. 312.

30. *In the Summer House*, in *Collected Works*, pp. 272–3.

31. King-Kok Cheung, *Articulate Silences. Hisaye Yamamoto, Maxine Hong Kingston, Joy Kogawa* (Ithaca and London: Cornell University Press, 1993), p. 4.

32. *Everything Is Nice* is probably the closest she gets to autobiography, as, apart from the white woman's name, Jeanie, it describes her first encounter with the group of Arabian women in Tangier. Tetum appears with her own name, 'an old lady in a dress made of green and purple curtain fabric. Through the many rents in the material she could see the printed cotton dress and the tan sweater underneath . . . her bony cheeks were tattooed with tiny blue crosses': *Collected Works*, p. 317.

33. P. Bowles, *Conversations*, p. 27.

34. Quoted in M. Dillon, *A Little Original Sin*, p. 397. The description of her solitary battles is frequent in her letters and in the accounts given by Paul and her many close friends. Truman Capote, in his introduction to the *Collected Works*, writes: 'both her language and her themes are sought after along tortured paths and in stone quarries: the never realised relationships between her people, the mental and physical discomforts with which she surrounds and saturates them – every room an atrocity, every urban landscape a creation of neon-dourness' (p. viii).

35. Quoted in Dillon, *A Little Original Sin*, p. 382.

36. P. Bowles, *Conversations*, respectively pp. 124 and 187.

37. *Collected Works*, p. 314. This is certainly inspired by Cherifa's talent for mimicry: 'She was always getting dressed in costumes and doing imitations of American and Europeans or other Moroccans that she knew': Dillon, *A Little Original Sin*, p. 273. In this play of mirrors, Jane's great mimic and mimetic ability must be taken into account as

well. Capote, who describes it in his introduction ('the stiff-legged limp, her spectacles, her brilliant and poignant ability as a mimic': pp. vii–viii), reproduced it in the character of Mary O'Meaghan in his *Among the Paths of Eden.*

38. This is certainly not related to the legend describing her life companion as casting a spell on her. There is a solar and loving image of Cherifa and the other Muslim women in her letters, and of Zodelia and Pacifica in her fiction. In *Two Serious Ladies*, shortly after their first casual encounter, Pacifica takes Mrs Copperfield to her hotel room and this is how their 'romance' starts: ' "Now we rest a little while, yes?" The girl lay down on the bed and motioned to Mrs Copperfield to lie down beside her. She yawned, folded Mrs Copperfield's hand in her own, and fell asleep almost instantly. Mrs Copperfield thought that she might as well get some sleep too. At that moment she felt very peaceful': p. 50.

39. In *Collected Works*, p. 320.

40. I. Chambers, 'Signs of silence, lines of listening', in I. Chambers and L. Curti (eds), *The Post-Colonial Question – Common Skies, Divided Horizons* (London and New York: Routledge, 1996), pp. 57–8.

41. See H. K. Bhabha, 'The Other Question: Stereotype, Discrimination and the Discourse of Colonialism', in *The Location of Culture* (London and New York: Routledge, 1994).

42. Yegenoglu, 'Supplementing the Orientalist Lack', p. 54. It is strange that, in referring to Derrida's notion of the supplement, she does not consider that rather than compensate for a lack in phallogocentrism it overloads and swamps its logic. The knowledge of what is 'hidden behind the veil' is not an indifferent addition and may be upsetting to the Orientalist vision. On the ambivalence of the veil see Trinh T. Minh-ha, 'Not You/Like You: Post-colonial Woman and the Interlocking Questions of Identity and Difference', *Inscriptions*, 3/4 (1988), p. 73.

43. In this logic Montagu's letters are unavoidably implicated in 'the imperialist and masculinist act of cultural translation and Subject constitution', Yegenoglu, 'Supplementing the Orientalist Lack', p. 63. On the other hand, in *The Predicament of Culture* (Cambridge, MA: Harvard University Press, 1988), p. 258, James Clifford, in reviewing Edward Said's *Orientalism*, polemicises an 'intertextual unity, designed to emphasise the systematic and invariant nature of the Orientalist discourse'. For a discussion of attitudes on female Arab dress, see Vron Ware, 'Defining forces: 'race', gender and memories of empire', in Chambers and Curti, *The Postcolonial Question*, pp. 150–4.

44. Cixous, 'The Laugh of the Medusa', p. 340.

45. Quoted in Dillon, *A Little Original Sin*, p. 7.

Chapter 7   The Empty Place of Melancholia: Female Characters in *Hamlet*

1. Julia Kristeva, *Black Sun – Depression and Melancholia* (New York: Columbia University Press, 1989) p. 3.

2. C. T. Neely, 'Remembering Shakespeare, Revising Ourselves', in M. Novy (ed.), *Women's Re-visions of Shakespeare* (Urbana and Chicago: University of Illinois Press, 1990).

3. See *The Order of Things – An Archaeology of the Human Sciences* (London: Tavistock Publications, 1974) p. 65.

4. The gaze, both active and passive, is associated with the anatomical exam: 'my purpose and endeavour is . . . to anatomise this humour of melancholy, through all its parts and species'; and, soon after: 'I have anatomised my own folly': R. Burton, *The Anatomy of Melancholy* (London: Chatto & Windus, 1924), pp. 72 and 73.

5. Christine Buci-Glucksmann notes the importance of vision and appearance: 'In this great theatre of the abominable uncovering and putting on stage the melancolic gaze, virtue is nothing but a "bonum théâtral", men are admired only for their appearance and not for their being': *Tragique de l'ombre, Shakespeare et le maniérisme* (Paris, Galilée, 1990), p. 27: my translation.

6. B. Chatwin, *The Songlines* (London: Picador, 1987), p. 10.

7. The 1919 essay does not deal with *Hamlet* but uses it as a subtext. Cf. Marjorie Garber, *Shakespeare's Ghost Writers* (London: Methuen, 1987), p. 127. Freud had dealt with Hamlet first in a letter to Fliess in 1897, then in the famous formulation of the Oedipus complex in *The Interpretation of Dreams* (1899), and later in a manuscript called *Psychopathic Characters on the Scene* (c. 1905), eventually published after his death.

8. 'It often happens that neurotic men declare that they feel that there is something uncanny about the female genital organs. This *unheimlich* place, however, is the entrance to the former *Heim* (home) of all human beings, to the place where each one of us lived once upon a time and in the beginning': *The Uncanny*, in *The Standard Edition*, XVII (London: The Hogarth Press, 1955), p. 245. Freud concludes: 'In this case, too, then, the *unheimlich* is what was once *heimisch*, familiar; the prefix 'un' is the token of repression.' Luce Irigaray comments: 'while "heimisch" as a mother, woman would remain "un" as a woman. Since woman's sexuality is no doubt the most basic form of the *unheimlich*': 'Another "Cause" – Castration', in R. R. Warhol and D. Price Herndl (eds), *Feminisms – An Anthology of Literary Theory and Criticism* (New Brunswick, NJ: Rutgers University Press, 1991), p. 411.

9. 'I . . . emphasize preoedipal motives, in which phantasies of merger with and annihilation by the mother are prior to genital desire for her, and in which the strong father is needed more as an aid to differentiation and the establishment of masculine identity than as a superego protecting against incestuous desire': J. Adelman, *Suffocating Mothers – Fantasies of Maternal Origin in Shakespeare's Plays* (New York and London: Routledge, 1992), p. 247.

10. '*Othello* and *Hamlet*: – Dilation, Spying, and the "Secret Place" of Woman', in *Representations*, 44 (Autumn 1993), p. 79.

11. Cf. T. Docherty, *John Donne, Undone* (London: Methuen, 1986), pp. 5ff.

12. Adelman, *Suffocating Mothers*, p. 16. Further on, in an interesting and accurate analysis, Adelman shows the many associations Hamlet, and Shakespeare, make between the 'rank corruption' of female sexuality and the sexualised maternal body, which is the unweeded garden at the centre of Hamlet's melancholy. The equation of death with sex is tied to the impure mother, who from Aristotle onwards has been seen as the main carrier of mortality, the one giving the body in opposition to the spirit provided by the father.

13. Adelman shows the transfer of agency from male to female that Hamlet performs, displacing the blame for the murder from Claudius to Gertrude. 'And the play itself is complicit with Hamlet's shift of agency: though the degree of her literal guilt is never specified, in the deep fantasy of the play her sexuality itself becomes akin to murder': Adelman, *Suffocating Mothers*, p. 25.

14. J. Rose, *Sexuality in the Field of Vision* (London: Verso, 1986), pp. 126–7. She remarks that the ambiguity of the text, its aesthetic inadequacy, its 'excess', all leading to an image of the feminine, are the repetition of the psychic experience described by Freud in his essay on the Hamlet-like Leonardo da Vinci, written nine years before Eliot's essay.

15. S. Freud, 'Leonardo da Vinci and a Memory of Childhood' (1910), in *The Standard Edition*, vol. XI (London: The Hogarth Press, 1957), p. 115. In the androgynous figures appearing in many of his paintings, 'Leonardo has denied the unhappiness of his erotic life and triumphed over it in his art, by representing the wishes of the boy, infatuated with his mother, as fulfilled in this blissful union of the male and female natures' (p. 118). It is interesting to notice how close Eliot goes to the notion of the unconscious in his descriptions of Hamlet's failures and displacements. His essay, always quoted for the notion of objective correlative, in fact invokes the hidden and the inexpressible: 'We should have, finally, to know something which is by hypothesis unknowable . . . We should have to understand things which Shakespeare did not understand himself': 'Hamlet', in *Selected Essays* (London: Faber & Faber, 1953), p. 146.

16. 'And there I see such black and grainèd spots/As will not give their tinct' . . . 'These words like daggers enter in mine ears': William Shakespeare, *Hamlet*, ed. by J. D. Wilson (Cambridge: Cambridge University Press, 1972), III, 4, 90–1 and 96. All references in the text are to this edition.

17. Buci-Glucksmann speaks of the passage to a new tragical mode, more Latin, more modern, '*un tragique de l'ombre*', infected with ghosts. See '*Tragique de l'Ombre*', p. 31.

18. *The Origin of German Tragic Drama* (London: Verso, 1990), pp. 136–7.

19. Garber, *Shakespeare's Ghost Writers*, p. 172.

20. R. Chandler, *The Big Sleep* (Harmondsworth: Penguin, 1971), respectively pp. 13 and 220. All references in the text are to this edition.

21. R. Chandler, *The Lady in the Lake* (Harmondsworth: Penguin, 1966), p. 232.
22. P. D. James, *The Skull beneath the Skin* (London: Faber & Faber, 1982.
23. Walter Benjamin, *The Origin of German Tragic Drama*, p. 135. He is observing that the Trauerspiel has no proper ending.
24. P. Parker, '*Othello* and *Hamlet*', p. 65.
25. Ibid., p. 66.
26. J. Lacan, *Il seminario – Libro XIX* (Turin: Einaudi, 1983).
27. *Speculum of the Other Woman*, trans. by C. C. Gill (Ithaca, NY: Cornell University Press, 1992), p. 48.
28. E. A. Poe, *Tales of Mystery and Imagination* (London: Wordsworth Classics, 1993), p. 113. As in the case of the purloined letter, and also in the terrible murder of two women in Rue Morgue, it will be discovered that 'there were . . . no secret issues' (p. 120). As in a game of chess, 'what is only complex, is mistaken (a not unusual error) for what is profound' (p. 95).
29. S. Felman, *Jacques Lacan and the Adventure of Insight – Psychoanalysis in Contemporary Culture* (Cambridge, MA, and London: Harvard University Press, 1987), p. 42.
30. '*Le secret, le témoignage, la responsabilité*', Istituto di Studi Filosofici, Napoli, 23–27 May 1994.
31. M. Russo, *The Female Grotesque: Risk, Excess and Modernity* (London: Routledge, 1995), p. 27.
32. 'What *can* be read (and perhaps what *should* be read) is not just meaning but the lack of meaning; that significance lies not just in consciousness but, specifically, in its disruption; that the signifier can be analysed in its effects without its signified being known': S. Felman, *Jacques Lacan*, p. 45.
33. Barbara Johnson, *The Wake of Deconstruction* (Cambridge, MA, and Oxford: Basil Blackwell, 1994), p. 38.
34. In Lacan's analysis, after Ophelia is put aside as Hamlet's object of love ('I loved you, once'), she becomes the phallus, refused by the subject as the symbol of a life that he condemns, and he recalls that among the flowers surrounding her in death, there are the 'dead men's fingers', the *Orchis mascula*, connected to mandrake and to the phallic element. Cf. J. Lacan, 'Desire and the interpretation of desire in *Hamlet*', *Yale French Studies*, 55–6 (1978).
35. Irigary, *Speculum*, p. 48.
36. Except that in this case the reply is double-edged: on one level compliant with her submissive and tame character, on another speaking out of character and taking up Hamlet's wanton reference. The link between 'nothing' and the female genitals recurs in *Twelfth Night*.
37. In *The Tempest* the obsession with the themes of lust and fertility is even greater, starting with Gonzalo's terrible metaphor: 'the ship. . . as leaky as an unstanched wench' (I, 1, 46–7). Evil here is embodied in Sycorax' beastly sexuality successively inherited by Caliban, and seen

as the main threat to Miranda's much discussed chastity. The metaphors range from rape to conjugal legality, and are centred on the island, a male fantasy icon of fecundity. Gonzalo's ideal of a 'benign exploitation' is directed both to the island and Miranda.

38. H. Cixous and C. Clément, *The Newly Born Woman* (Minneapolis: University of Minnesota Press, 1986), respectively pp. 66 and 67. The figure of Sleeping Beauty is present in some of the novels I have examined, above all among Angela Carter's female freaks in *Nights at the Circus*.

39. S. Felman, *What Does a Woman Want? Reading and Sexual Difference* (Baltimore and London: The Johns Hopkins University Press, 1993), p. 4.

40. The dream is related in Ch. 2 of *The Interpretation of Dreams*. It is what he calls the navel of the dream, its impenetrable core: 'There is at least one spot in every dream at which it is unplumbable – a navel, as it were, that is its point of contact with the unknown': S. Freud, *The Interpretation of Dreams* (New York: Modern Library, 1950), p. 111, note 1). Garber discusses at length this concept and defines *Hamlet* 'as origin – or marker of the unknowability of origins, what Freud called the navel of the dream': *Shakespeare's Ghost Writers*, p. 158.

41. In his dream, Freud associates Irma, the hysteric patient resisting his treatment, to two other rebel women, one of which is his wife. It is precisely this that constitutes the point of resistance, the hindrance in his self-analysis. As Felman comments, the navel of Irma's dream is the mystery of femininity, which is not focused on one woman but on a cluster of women, 'a knot . . . which points not to the identifiability of any given feminine identity but to the inexhaustibility, the unaccountability, of female difference': *What Does a Woman Want?*, p. 115.

42. According to Abraham, the ghost of illegitimacy haunts the Polonides as well. Cf. M. Vitale, 'Romanzo familiare e fantasmi amletici', in L. Curti (ed), *Ombre di un'ombra* (Naples: Istituto Universitario Orientale, 1994).

43. Irigaray, 'The mirror, on the other side', *This Sex Which Is Not One*, trans. by C. Porter with Carolyn Burke (Ithaca, NY: Cornell University Press, 1995), p. 5.

44. This again brings us back to Ophelia as simply a spy for things, a mere reflection, the abject. She is told by Polonius to spy on Hamlet, and is repeatedly spied on both by him and by her father. Technically, for most of her appearances, she is under a man's gaze, and the spectator is always looking at her through the look of others.

45. '[T]he compelling force of transvestism in literature and culture comes . . . also from its instatement of metaphor itself, not as that for which a literal meaning must be found, but precisely as that without which there would be no such thing as meaning in the first place': M. Garber, *Vested Interests – Cross-Dressing and Cultural Anxiety* (New York and London: Routledge, 1992), p. 390. She sees the appropriation of transvestism in the service of a humanist 'progress narrative' at work in Shakespearean criticism, and above all in Stephen's Greenblatt's

readings. Her encyclopaedic book moves from Peter Pan to Red Riding Hood, from Rudolph Valentino and Arab mores to Freud's Wolf-Man, finally seeing transvestism as a re-enactment of the primal scene.

46. Severo Sarduy, 'Copy/Simulacrum', in *Written on a Body*, trans. by Carol Maier (New York: Lumen Books, 1989), p. 2, originally published as *Escrito sobre un Cuerpo* (1969).

Bibliography

Adelman, Janet, *Suffocating Mothers – Fantasies of Maternal Origin in Shakespeare's Plays* (New York and London: Routledge, 1992).

Alcock, Beverly and Jocelyn Robson, 'Cagney and Lacey revisited', *Feminist Review*, 35 (Summer 1990).

Alloul, Malek, *The Colonial Harem* (Minneapolis, University of Minnesota Press, 1986).

Anderson, Perry, 'Modernity and Revolution', *New Left Review*, 144 (1984).

Ang, Ien, *Watching 'Dallas'* (London: Methuen, 1985).

Ang, I. and Jon Stratton, 'The end of civilization as we knew it: *Chances* and the postrealist soap opera', in Robert C. Allen (ed.), *To Be Continued . . . – Soap Operas around the World* (London and New York: Routledge, 1995).

Anzaldúa, Gloria, *Borderlands/La Frontera: The New Mestiza* (San Francisco: Spinsters/Aunt Lute, 1987).

Baher, Helen and Gillian Dyer (eds), *Boxed In: Women and Television* (London: Pandora, 1987).

Banti, Anna, *Artemisia*, trans. by Shirley D'Ardia Caracciolo (Lincoln, University of Nebraska Press, 1988).

Barrett, Michèle, *Women's Oppression Today* (London: Verso, 1980).

Barrett, M., *The Politics of Truth* (Cambridge: Polity Press, 1992).

Barthes, Roland, *Roland Barthes by Roland Barthes*, trans. by Richard Howard (New York: Hill and Wang, 1977).

Batsleer, Janet, Tony Davies, Rebecca O'Rourke and Chris Weedon, *Rewriting English. Cultural Politics of Gender and Class* (London, Methuen, 1985).

Baudrillard, Jean, *America* (London and New York: Verso, 1989).

Baudrillard, J., *Fatal Strategies* (London: Pluto, 1990).

Beckett, Samuel, *Malone Dies* (Harmondsworth: Penguin, 1962).

Belsey, Catherine and Jane Moore (eds), *The Feminist Reader – Essays in Gender and the Politics of Literary Criticism* (London: Macmillan, 1989).

Benjamin, Jessica, 'A Desire of One's Own: Psychoanalytic Feminism and Intersubjective Space', in Teresa de Lauretis (ed.), *Feminist Studies/ Critical Studies* (Bloomington, Indiana University Press, 1986).

Benjamin, Walter, 'The Storyteller', in H. Arendt (ed.), *Illuminations*, trans. by Harry Zohn (London: Collins/Fontana, 1973).

Benjamin, W., *The Origin of German Tragic Drama* (London: Verso, 1990).

Bhabha, Homi K., *The Location of Culture* (London and New York: Routledge, 1994).

Bhabha, H.K., 'Unpacking my library . . . again', in Iain Chambers and Lidia Curti (eds), *The Postcolonial Question – Common Skies, Divided Horizons* (London and New York: Routledge, 1996).

Bowles, Jane, *The Collected Works*, with an introduction by Truman Capote (New York: The Noonday Press – Farrar, Strauss and Giroux, 1966).

Bowles, J., *Out in the World – Selected Letters 1935–1970*, ed. by M. Dillon (Santa Barbara: Black Sparrow Press, 1985).

Bowles, Paul, *The Sheltering Sky* (New York: Vintage Books, 1977).

Bowles, P., *Conversations*, ed. by G. D. Caponi (Jackson: University Press of Mississippi, 1993).

Braidotti, Rosi, 'Commento alla relazione di Adriana Cavarero', in Maria Cristina Marcuzzo and Anna Rossi-Doria (eds), *Alla ricerca delle donne – studi femministi in Italia* (Turin: Rosenberg & Sellier, 1987).

Braidotti, R., *Patterns of Dissonance* (Cambridge: Polity Press, 1991).

Broe, Mary Lynn and Angela Ingram (eds), *Women's Writing in Exile* (Chapel Hill and London: University of North Carolina Press, 1989).

Brooke-Rose, Christine, *Textermination* (London, Carcanet, 1991).

Brontë, Charlotte, *Jane Eyre* (Oxford: Oxford University Press, 1989).

Brossard, Nicole, 'The Textured Angle of Desire', *Yale French Studies*, 87 (1995).

Brunsdon, Charlotte, 'The role of soap opera in the development of feminist television scholarship', in R. C. Allen (ed.), *To Be Continued . . . Soap operas around the world* (London and New York: Routledge, 1995).

Brunt, Rosalind, Karen Jones, Tessa Perkins, 'A conversation about Contemporary Television', *Women, a cultural review*, 2, 1 (Spring 1991).

Buci-Glucksmann, Christine, *Tragique de l'ombre, Shakespeare et le maniérisme* (Paris: Galilée, 1990).

Burroughs, William, *The Naked Lunch* (London: Corgi Books, 1969).

Burton, Robert, *The Anatomy of Melancholy* (London: Chatto & Windus, 1924).

Byatt, Antonia S., *Iris Murdoch* (London: Longman, 1976).

Byatt, A.S., *Possession – A Romance* (London: Vintage, 1991).

Carter, Angela, *The Passion of New Eve* (London: Virago, 1977).

Carter, A., *The Bloody Chamber* (Harmondsworth: Penguin, 1979).

Carter, A., *Nights at the Circus* (London: Chatto & Windus, 1984).

Carter, A., *Wise Children* (London, Chatto & Windus, 1991).

Carter, A., *Expletives Deleted* (London, Chatto & Windus, 1992).

Caughie, John, 'Rhetoric, pleasure, and "art television"', *Screen*, 22, 4 (1981).

Cavarero, Adriana, 'L'elaborazione filosofica della differenza sessuale', in Maria Cristina Marcuzzo e Anna Rossi-Doria (eds), *Alla ricerca delle donne – studi femministi in Italia* (Turin: Rosenberg & Sellier, 1987).

Cavarero, A. (et al.), *Diotima – Il pensiero della differenza sessuale* (Milan: La Tartaruga, 1987).

Chambers, Iain, *Border Dialogues. Journeys in Postmodernity* (London and New York: Routledge, 1990).

Chambers, I., *Migrancy, Culture, Identity* (London and New York: Routledge, 1994).

Chambers, I., 'Signs of silence, lines of listening', in Iain Chambers and Lidia Curti (eds), *The Postcolonial Question – Common Skies, Divided Horizons* (London and New York: Routledge, 1996).

Chandler, Raymond, *The Lady in the Lake* (Harmondsworth: Penguin, 1966).

Chandler, R., *The Big Sleep* (Harmondsworth: Penguin, 1971).

Chatwin, Bruce, *The Songlines* (London: Picador, 1987).

Cheung, King-Kok, *Articulate Silences. Hisaye Yamamoto, Maxine Hong Kingston, Joy Kogawa* (Ithaca, NY, and London: Cornell University Press, 1993).

Christian, Barbara, *Black Feminist Criticism – Perspectives on Black Women Writers* (Oxford and New York: Pergamon Press, 1985).

Cixous, Hélène and Catherine Clément, *The Newly Born Woman*, intro. by Sandra M. Gilbert, trans. by Betsy Wing (Minneapolis: University of Minnesota Press, 1986; Manchester, Manchester University Press, 1987).

Cixous, H.,'Coming to Writing' and Other Essays*, ed. by Deborah Jenson, intro. by Susan Rubin Suleiman, trans. by Sarah Cornell, Deborah Jenson, Anne Liddle and Susan Sellers (Cambridge and London: Harvard University Press, 1991).

Cixous, H., 'The Laugh of the Medusa', in Robin R. Warhol and Diane Price Herndl (eds), *Feminisms – An Anthology of Literary Theory and Criticism* (New Brunswick, New Jersey: Rutgers University Press, 1991).

Clifford, James, *The Predicament of Culture – Twentieth-Century Ethnography, Literature, and Art* (Cambridge: Harvard University Press, 1988).

Collins, James, *Uncommon Cultures* (London: Routledge, 1989).

Coward, Rosalind, *Female Desire – Women's Sexuality Today* (London: Paladin, 1984).

Coward, R., 'Come back Miss Ellie: on character and narrative in soap operas', *Critical Quarterly*, 28, 1–2 (1986).

Craig, Patricia and Mary Cadogan, *The Lady Investigates – Women Detectives and Spies in Fiction* (Oxford: Oxford University Press, 1986).

Cranny-Francis, Anne, *Feminist Fiction – Feminist Uses of Generic Fiction* (Oxford: Polity Press, 1990).

Croce, Benedetto, *Estetica* (Bari: Laterza, 1958).

Curti, Lidia, 'Genre and gender', *Cultural Studies*, 2, 2 (May 1988).

Curti, L., 'Imported utopias', in Zygmund Baransky and Robert Lumley (eds), *Culture and Conflict in Post-war Italy. Essays in popular and mass culture* (London: Macmillan, 1990).

Curti, L., 'Angela Carter intervistata da Lidia Curti', *Anglistica* XXXV, 2–3 (1992).

Curti, L. (ed.), *Ombre di un'ombra – Amleto e i suoi fantasmi* (Naples: Istituto Universitario Orientale, 1994).

D'Acci, Julie, *Defining Women: The Case of Cagney and Lacey* (Chapel Hill, NC: University of North Carolina Press, 1994).

Davies, Kath, Julienne Dickey and Teresa Stratford (eds), *Out of Focus. Writings on Women and the Media* (London: The Women's Press, 1987).

de Certeau, Michel, *The Practice of Everyday Life* (Berkeley: University of California Press, 1988).

de Lauretis, Teresa (ed.), *Feminist Studies/Critical Studies* (Bloomington: Indiana University Press, 1986).

de Lauretis, T., *Technologies of Gender – Essays on Theory, Film, and Fiction* (Bloomington and Indianapolis: Indiana University Press, 1987).

de Lauretis, T., 'The Essence of the Triangle or, Taking the Risk of Essentialism Seriously', in Naomi Schor and Elizabeth Weed (eds), *The Essential Difference* (Bloomington and Indianapolis: Indiana University Press, 1994).

Derrida, Jacques, *Writing and Difference* (Chicago: Chicago University Press, 1978; originally published in French in Paris: Editions du Seuil, 1967).

Derrida, J., 'The Law of Genre', in W. J. T. Mitchell (ed.), *On Narrative* (Chicago and London: Chicago University Press, 1981).

Derrida, J., 'Women in the Beehive: A Seminar', in Alice Jardine and Paul Smith (eds), *Men in Feminism* (London: Methuen, 1987).

Dillon, Margaret, *A Little Original Sin. The Life and Work of Jane Bowles* (London, Virago, 1988).

Dinnerstein, Dorothy, *The Mermaid and the Minotaur* (New York: Harper Colophon, 1976).

Doane, Mary Ann, *The Desire to Desire – The Woman's Film of the 1940s* (Bloomington and Indianapolis: Indiana University Press, 1987).

Doane, M. A., 'The "Woman's Film" – Possession and Address', in Christine Gledhill (ed.), *Home is Where the Heart Is – Studies in Melodrama and the Woman's Film*, (London: British Film Institute, 1987).

Docherty, Thomas, *John Donne, Undone* (London: Methuen, 1986).

Eagleton, Terry, 'Capitalism, Modernism and Postmodernism', *New Left Review*, 152 (1985).

Eco, Umberto, 'Interview with J. Le Goff', *la Repubblica – Mercurio*, 24 February 1990.

Eliot, T.S., 'Hamlet', in *Selected Essays* (London: Faber & Faber, 1953).

Erdrich, Louise, *The Bingo Palace* (London: HarperCollins/Flamingo, 1995).

Fairbairns, Zoe, Sarah Maitland, Valerie Miner, Michèle Roberts and Micheline Wandor, *Tales I Tell My Mother – A Collection of Feminist Short Stories* (London/West Nyack: The Journeyman Press, 1978).

Felman, Shoshana, *Jacques Lacan and the Adventure of Insight – Psychoanalysis in Contemporary Culture* (Cambridge, MA, and London: Harvard University Press, 1987).

Felman, S., *What Does a Woman Want? Reading and Sexual Difference* (Baltimore and London: The Johns Hopkins University Press, 1993).

Flax, Jane, 'Postmodernism and Gender Relations in Feminist Theory', *Signs*, 12, 4 (Summer 1987).

Flax, J., *Thinking Fragments – Psychoanalysis, Feminism and Postmodernism in the Contemporary West* (Berkeley, CA: University of California Press, 1990).

Flieger, Jerry Aline, 'Entertaining the Ménage à Trois: Psychoanalysis, Feminism, and Literature', in Richard Feldstein and Judith Roof (eds), *Feminism and Psychoanalysis* (Ithaca, NY, and London: Cornell University Press, 1989).

Flitterman, Sandy, 'Thighs and whiskers', *Screen*, 26, 2 (1985).

Forster, Margaret, *Lady's Maid* (Harmondsworth: Penguin, 1991).

Foucault, Michel, *The Order of Things – An Archaeology of the Human Sciences* (London: Tavistock Publications, 1974).

Freud, Sigmund, *The Interpretation of Dreams*, trans. by A. A. Brill (New York: Modern Library, 1950).

Freud, S., 'The Uncanny', *The Standard Edition*, XVII (London: The Hogarth Press, 1955).

Freud, S. 'Leonardo da Vinci and a Memory of Childhood' (1910), *The Standard Edition*, XI (London: The Hogarth Press, 1957).

Friedman, Ellen G. and Myriam Fuchs (eds), *Breaking the Sequence – Women's Experimental Fiction* (Princeton, NJ: Princeton University Press, 1989).

Gallop, Jane, 'The Monster in the Mirror: the Feminist Critic's Psychoanalysis', in Richard Feldstein and Judith Roof (eds), *Feminism and Psychoanalysis* (Ithaca, NY, and London: Cornell University Press, 1989).

Gallop, J., *Around 1981 – Academic Feminist Literary Theory* (London: Routledge, 1992).

Gamman, Lucy, 'Response: More Cagney and Lacey', *Feminist Review*, 37 (Spring 1991).

Garber, Marjorie, *Shakespeare's Ghost Writers* (London: Methuen, 1987).

Garber, M., *Vested Interests – Cross-Dressing and Cultural Anxiety* (New York and London: Routledge, 1992).

Genette, Gerard, 'Genres, "types", modes', *Poètique* 32 (1977).

Geraghty, Christine, 'East Enders', *Marxism Today*, August 1985.

Geraghty, C., *Women and Soap Opera – A Study of Prime Time Soaps* (Cambridge: Polity Press, 1991).

Gilbert, Sandra M. and Susan Gubar, *The Madwoman in the Attic – The Woman Writer and the Nineteenth-Century Literary Imagination* (New Haven and London: Yale University Press, 1984).

Greer, Germaine, *The Female Eunuch* (London: Paladin, 1971).

Guy-Shetfall, Beverly, 'Black Feminist Perspective on Transforming the Academy', in Stanlie M. James and Abena P. A. Busia (eds), *Theorizing Black Feminisms* (London and New York: Routledge, 1993).

Hall, Stuart, 'Cultural Studies and the Centre: Some Problematics and Problems', in S. Hall, Dorothy Hobson, Andrew Lowe and Paul Willis (eds), *Culture, Media, Language* (London: Hutchinson and CCCS, 1980).

Hall, S., 'Minimal Selves', in *The Real Me – Postmodernism and the Question of Identity* (London: ICA, 1987).

Hall, S., 'The Whites of Their Eyes: Racist Ideology and the Media', in Manuel Alvarado and John O. Thompson (eds), *The Media Reader*, (London: British Film Institute, 1990).

Hall, S., 'When was the Postcolonial?', in Iain Chambers and Lidia Curti (eds), *The Postcolonial Question – Common Skies, Divided Horizons* (London and New York: Routledge, 1996).

Hall, S. and F. Jameson, 'Clinging to the Wreckage: A conversation', *Marxism Today*, Sept. 1990.

Heath, Stephen, *The Sexual Fix* (London: Macmillan, 1982).

Hebdige, Dick, 'Some Sons and Their Fathers', *Ten.8*, 17 (1985).

Hebdige, D., 'The Bottom Line on Planet One', *Ten.8*, 19 (1987).

Hebdige, D., *Hiding in the Light* (London and New York: Routledge, 1988).

Hekman, Susan J., *Gender and Knowledge – Elements of a Postmodern Feminism* (London: Polity Press, 1990).

Highsmith, Patricia, *Ripley's Game* (Harmondsworth: Penguin, 1980).

Hobson, Dorothy, *Crossroads – The Drama of a Soap Opera* (London: Methuen, 1982).

hooks, bell, *Ain't I a Woman – Black Women and Feminism* (London: Pluto, 1982).

hooks, b., 'Writing Autobiography', in Robin R. Warhol and Diane Price Herndl (eds), *Feminisms – An Anthology of Literary Theory and Criticism* (New Brunswick, NJ: Rutgers University Press, 1991).

Huffer, Lynne (ed.), 'Another Look, Another Woman: Retranslations of French Feminism', *Yale French Studies*, 87 (1995).

Hulme, Peter, 'Including America', *Ariel*, 26, 1 (1995).

Humm, Maggie, *Border Traffic – Strategies of Contemporary Women Writers* (Manchester: Manchester University Press, 1991).

Hutcheon, Linda, *A Poetics of Postmodernism – History, Theory, Fiction* (London and New York: Routledge, 1988).

Hutcheon, L., *The Politics of Postmodernism* (London and New York: Routledge, 1989).

Huyssen, Andreas, *After the Great Divide – Modernism, Mass Culture and Postmodernism* (London: Macmillan, 1986).

Huyssen, A. 'Mapping the Postmodern', in L. Nicholson (ed.), *Feminism/Postmodernism* (New York and London: Routledge, 1990).

Irigaray, Luce, *Speculum of the Other Woman*, transl. by Gillian C. Gill (Ithaca, NY: Cornell University Press, 1992).

Irigaray, L., *This Sex Which Is Not One*, transl. by Catherine Porter with Carolyn Burke (Ithaca, NY: Cornell University Press, 1995).

Irigaray, L., 'Another "Cause" – Castration', in Robin R. Warhol and Diane Price Herndl (eds), *Feminisms – An Anthology of Literary Theory and Criticism* (New Brunswick, New Jersey: Rutgers University Press, 1991).

Irigaray, L., 'The Question of the Other', in *Yale French Studies*, 87 (1995).

Irigaray, L., *An Ethics of Sexual Difference*, Ithaca (New York: Cornell University Press, 1993).

James, P.D., *The Skull beneath the Skin* (London: Faber & Faber, 1982).

James, P.D., *Innocent Blood* (London: Sphere Books, 1988).

Jameson, Fredric, *The Political Unconscious – Narrative as a Socially Symbolic Act* (London: Methuen, 1981).

Jameson, F., 'Postmodernism, or the Cultural Logic of Late Capitalism', *New Left Review*, 146 (1984).

Jardine, Alice, *Gynesis – Configuration of Woman and Modernity* (Ithaca, NY, and London: Cornell University Press, 1985).

Johnson, Barbara, *A World of Difference* (Baltimore and London: The Johns Hopkins University Press, 1987).

Johnson, B., *The Wake of Deconstruction* (Cambridge, MA, and Oxford: Basil Blackwell, 1994).

Kamuf, Peggy, 'To Give Place: Semi-Approaches to Hélène Cixous', *Yale French Studies*, 87 (1995).

Kelly, Mary, *Re-Presenting the Body: On 'Interim' Part I*, in J. Donald (ed.), *Psychoanalysis and Cultural Theory* (London: Macmillan, 1991).

Kenyon, Olga, *Women Novelists Today – A Survey of English Writing of the Seventies and the Eighties* (Brighton: Harvester Press, 1988).

Kristeva, Julia, *Eretica dell'amore* (Turin: La Rosa, 1979).

Kristeva, J., *Pouvoirs de l'horreur – Essai sur l'abjection* (Paris: Éditions du Seuil, 1980).

Kristeva, J. 'Women's Time', in T. Moi (ed.), *The Kristeva Reader* (Oxford: Basil Blackwell, 1986).

Kristeva, J., *Black Sun – Depression and Melancholia*, trans. by Leon S. Roudiez (New York: Columbia University Press, 1989).

Kuhn, Annette, 'Women's Genres', *Screen*, 25, 1 (1984).

Lacan, Jacques, 'Desire and the interpretation of desire in *Hamlet*', *Yale French Studies*, 55–6 (1978).

Lacan, J., *Il Seminario – Libro XIX* (Turin: Einaudi, 1983).

Lesage, Julia, 'Artful Racism, Artful Rape – Griffith's Broken Blossoms', in Christine Gledhill (ed.), *Home Is Where the Heart Is – Studies in Melodrama and the Woman's Film* (London: British Film Institute, 1987).

Lessing, Doris, *The Memoirs of a Survivor* (London: Picador, 1974).

Libreria delle Donne di Milano, '*Più donne che uomini*', *Sottosopra*, January 1983.

Libreria delle Donne di Milano, '*È accaduto non per caso*', *Sottosopra*, January 1996.

Lonzi, Carla, *Sputiamo su Hegel* (Milan: Scritti di Rivolta Femminile, 1974).

Lovell, Terry, 'Ideology and *Coronation Street*', in R. Dyer, C. Geraghty, M. Jordan, T. Lovell, R. Paterson, J. Stewart, *Coronation Street* (London: British Film Institute, 1981).

Lovibond, Sabina, 'Feminism and Postmodernism', in Roy Boyne and Ali Rattansi, *Postmodernism and Society* (London: Macmillan, 1990).

Lydon, Mary, 'Retranslating no, Re-reading no, rather: Rejoicing (with) Hélène Cixous', *Yale French Studies*, 87 (1995).

McArthur, Colin, *Underworld USA* (London: Secker and Warburg, 1972).

McHale, Brian, *Postmodernist Fiction* (New York and London: Methuen, 1987).

McRobbie, Angela, 'Working class girls and the culture of femininity', in Women's Studies Group (eds), *Women Take Issue – Aspects of Women's Subordination* (London: Hutchinson and CCCS, 1978).

McRobbie, A., 'Settling accounts with subcultures: a feminist critique', in Tony Bennett, Graham Martin, Colin Mercer and Janet Woollacott (eds), *Culture, Ideology and Social Process* (London: Batsford with the Open University Press, 1981).

McRobbie, A., 'Postmodernism and Popular Culture', *Postmodernism* (London: ICA, 1986).

Miller, Jane, *Seductions – Studies in Reading and Culture* (London: Virago, 1990).

Modleski, Tania, *Loving With a Vengeance: Mass-Produced Fantasies for Women* (London: Methuen, 1982).

Moi, Toril, *Sexual/Textual Politics: Feminist Literary Theory* (London and New York: Methuen, 1985).

Moore, Suzanne, 'Nerve Endings', *Marxism Today*, Sept. 1990.

Moraga, Cherríe, 'From a Long Line of Vendidas: Chicanas and Feminism', in Teresa de Lauretis (ed.), *Feminist Studies/Critical Studies* (Bloomington: Indiana University Press, 1986).

Morrison, Toni, *Sula* (London: Grafton Books, 1982).

Morrison, T., *Beloved* (New York: Signet Books, 1987).

Mulvey, Laura, *Visual and Other Pleasures* (London: Macmillan, 1989).

Neale, Stephen, *Genre* (London: BFI, 1980).

Nicholson, Linda J. (ed.), *Feminism/Postmodernism* (New York and London: Routledge, 1990).

Novy, Marianne (ed.), *Women's Re-visions of Shakespeare* (Urbana and Chicago: University of Illinois Press, 1990).

O'Sullivan, T. *et al.* (eds), *Key Communications Terms* (London and New York: Methuen, 1983).

Owens, Craig, ' The Discourse of Others: Feminists and Postmodernism', in Hal Foster (ed.), *The Anti-Aesthetic* (Port Townsend, WA: Bay Press, 1985).

Palmer, Paulina, *Contemporary Women's Fiction – Narrative Practice and Feminist Theory* (New York and London: Harvester Wheatsheaf, 1989).

Parker, Patricia, ' "Othello" and "Hamlet" – Dilation, Spying, and the "Secret Place" of Woman', *Representations* 44 (Autumn 1993).

Penman, Ian, 'The fog that is Fallon', *The Face*, April 1986.

Pinkola Estés, Clarissa, *Women Who Run with the Wolves, Contacting the Power of the Wild Woman* (London: Rider, 1992).

Poe, Edgar Allan, *Tales of Mystery and Imagination* (London: Wordsworth Classics, 1993).

Rapaport, Hermann, 'Deconstruction's Other: Trinh T. Minh-ha and Jacques Derrida', *Diacritics*, 25, 2 (Summer 1995).

Rasy, Elisabetta, *La lingua della nutrice* (Rome: edizioni delle donne, 1978).

Rella, Franco, 'Ho tanta nostalgia di Brecht e Lukács', *Mercurio – La Repubblica*, 10 June 1989, p. 19.

Rice, A. *Interview with the Vampire* (London: Warner Books, 1996).

Rich, Adrienne, *On Lies, Secrets, and Silence: Selected Prose, 1966–1978* (London: Virago, 1980).

Rich, A., *An Atlas of the Difficult World – Poems 1988–1991* (New York and London: Norton, 1991).

Riley, Denise, *Am I that Name? – Feminism and the Category of 'Women' in History* (London: Macmillan, 1988).

Rodley, Chris (ed.), *Cronenberg on Cronenberg* (London and Boston: Faber & Faber, 1992).

Root, Deborah, 'Misadventure in the Desert: *The Sheltering Sky* as Colonialist Nightmare', *Inscriptions 6: 'Orientalism and Cultural Differences'*, 1992.

Rose, Jacqueline, *Sexuality in the Field of Vision* (London: Verso, 1986).

Russ, Joanna, *The Female Man* (London: The Women's Press, 1985).

Russo, Mary, 'Female grotesque: carnival and theory', *Center for Twentieth Century Studies, Working Paper no. I* (Autumn 1985).

Russo, M., *The Female Grotesque: Risk, Excess and Modernity* (London: Routledge, 1995).

Said, Edward, *Orientalism* (Harmondsworth: Penguin, 1978).

Sarduy, Severo, *Written on a Body*, translated by Carol Maier (New York: Lumen Books, 1989).

Schor, N., 'This Essentialism Which Is Not One: Coming to Grips with Irigaray', in Naomi Schor and Elizabeth Weed (eds), *The Essential Difference* (Bloomington and Indianapolis: Indiana University Press, 1994).

Shakespeare, William, *Hamlet*, ed. by J. D. Wilson (Cambridge: Cambridge University Press, 1972).

Shakespeare, W., *Sonetti*, ed. by Alessandro Serpieri (Milan: Rizzoli, 1991).

Shelley, Mary, *Frankenstein or The Modern Prometheus*, ed. with an intro. by Maurice Hindle (Harmondsworth: Penguin, 1992).

Showalter, Elaine, *A Literature of Their Own* (London: Virago, 1991).

Silko, Leslie Marmon, *Ceremony* (Harmondsworth: Penguin, 1986).

Skirrow, Gillian, '*Widows*', in Manuel Alvarado and John O. Thompson (eds), *Made for Television: Euston Films Limited* (London: British Film Institute, 1985).

Skirrow, G., 'Women/Acting/Power', in Helen Baher and Gillian Dyer (eds), *Boxed In: Women and Television* (London: Pandora, 1987).

Smith, Barbara, 'Toward a Black Feminist Criticism', in *The New Feminist Criticism – Essays on Women, Literature, Theory* (London: Virago, 1986).

Spivak, Gayatri Chakravorty, 'Displacement and the Discourse of Woman', in M. Krupnik (ed.), *Displacement, Derrida and After* (Bloomington: Indiana University Press, 1983).

Spivak, G. C., 'Three Women's Texts and a Critique of Imperialism', *Critical Inquiry*, 12, 1 (Autumn 1985).

Spivak, G. C., *In Other Worlds. Essays in Cultural Politics* (London and New York: Methuen, 1987).

Stacey, Jackie, 'Desperately Seeking Difference', in L. Gamman and M. Marshment (eds), *The Female Gaze – Women as Viewers of Popular Culture* (London: Verso, 1988).

Stimpson, Catherine R., 'Gertrude Stein and the Transposition of Gender', in Nancy K. Miller (ed.), *The Poetics of Gender* (New York: Columbia University Press, 1986).

Suleiman, Susan Rubin, *Risking Who One Is – Encounters with Contemporary Art and Literature* (Cambridge, MA, and London: Harvard University Press, 1994).

Taylor, Jenny, ' "Memoirs" was made of this', in J. Taylor (ed.), *Notebooks, Memoirs, Archives – Reading and Rereading Doris Lessing* (London: Routledge & Kegan Paul, 1982).

Tennant, Emma, *Two Women of London – The Strange Case of Ms Jekyll and Mrs Hyde* (London: Faber & Faber, 1989).

Todorov, Tristan, *Genres in Discourse*, trans. by Catherine Porter (Cambridge: Cambridge University Press, 1990).

Tremain, Rose, *Restoration* (London: Sceptre, 1991).

Trinh T. M., 'Not You/ Like You: Post-colonial Woman and the Interlocking Questions of Identity and Difference', *Inscriptions*, 3/4 (1988).

Trinh T. M., *Woman Native Other – Writing Postcoloniality and Feminism* (Bloomington and Indianapolis: Indiana University Press, 1989).

Trinh T. M., 'Other than myself/my other self', in George Robertson, Melinda Mash, Lisa Tickner, Jon Bird, Barry Curtis and Tim Putnam (eds), *Travellers' Tales – Narratives of Home and Displacement* (London and New York: Routledge, 1994).

Vattimo, Gianni, *The End of Modernity* (Oxford: Polity Press, 1988).

Vidal, Gore, *Duluth* (New York: Ballantine Books, 1983).

Ward Jouve, Nicole, *White Woman Speaks with Forked Tongue – Criticism as Autobiography* (London: Routledge, 1991).

Ware, Vron, 'Defining forces: "race", gender and memories of empire', in Iain Chambers and Lidia Curti (eds), *The Postcolonial Question – Common Skies, Divided Horizons* (London and New York: Routledge, 1996).

Waugh, Patricia, *Feminine Fictions – Revisiting the Postmodern* (London and New York: Routledge, 1989).

Weedon, Chris, *Feminist Practice and Poststructuralist Theory* (Oxford: Basil Blackwell, 1987).

Weldon, Fay, *The Life and Loves of a She-Devil* (London: Hodder & Stoughton, 1983).

Weldon, F., *The Cloning of Joanna May* (London: Fontana/Collins, 1989).

Wicke, Jennifer and Margaret Ferguson (eds), *Feminism and Postmodernism* (Durham, NC, and London: Duke University Press, 1994).

Wilson, Elizabeth, *Mirror Writing. An Autobiography* (London: Virago, 1982).

Wilson, E., *Hallucinations* (London: Radius/Hutchinson, 1988).

Winship, Janice, 'A woman's world: "Woman" – an ideology of femininity', in Women's Studies Group (eds), *Women Take Issue – Aspects of Women's Subordination* (London: Hutchinson and CCCS, 1978).

Winterson, Jeanette, *The Passion* (Harmondsworth: Penguin, 1988).

Winterson, J., *Sexing the Cherry* (London: Vintage, 1989).

Winterson, J., *Boating for Beginners* (London: Minerva, 1991).
Winterson, J., *Oranges are not the Only Fruit* (London: Vintage, 1991).
Winterson, J., *Written on the Body* (London: Vintage, 1993).
Wittig, Monique, 'The Mark of Gender', in Nancy K. Miller (ed.), *The Poetics of Gender* (New York: Columbia University Press, 1986).
Woolf, Virginia, *To the Lighthouse* (London: Dent, 1962).
Woolf, V., *A Room of One's Own* (London: The Hogarth Press, 1974).
Yegenoglu, Mayda, 'Supplementing the Orientalist Lack: European Ladies in the Harem', *Inscriptions 6: 'Orientalism and Cultural Differences'*, 1992.

Index

217

Silko, L. M.   xi
   Ceremony   x, xvi, 28, 38, 185
   generic transgression   xii, 30
Skirrow, G.   189
Smith, B.   11
   *The New Feminist
      Criticism . . .*   180, 195
   'Toward a Black Feminist
      Criticism . . .'   12, 180
Smith, P.   178
soap operas *see* television
socialism, feminism and   13
Sontag, S.   179
Sottosopra   22, 182–3
Spark, M.   94, 192
   The Bachelors   92
   The Comforters   91–2, 192
   The Hothouse by the East River   93
   Robinson   41
Spivak, G. C.   149
   'Displacement and the Discourse
      of Woman'   18, 182
   essentialism   21, 26
   'Explanation and Culture:
      Marginalia'   3
   'In a word . . .'   26, 182, 183
   In Other Worlds   3–4, 21, 22, 82,
      178, 182, 190, 192
   postmodernism   11, 16
   'Three Women's Texts . . .'   118,
      195
   women's studies   5
Stacey, J.   56–7, 186
Stead, C.   191, 195
Stein, G.   62, 94, 191
Stevenson, R. L.   40, 41
Stewart, J.   189
Stimpson, C.   62–3, 187
Stratford, T.   58, 186
Stratton, J.   74, 189
Stubbs, P.   86

Taylor, J.   192
television
   gender and genre   30, 39, 71–9,
      184; borders   79;
      contamination   73–4;
      hybridity   73–4

movies   73, 77–8
serials   xii–xiii, xv, 39, 54–79;
   crime/police   189; *Cagney
   and Lacey*   71, 75, 77–8,
   189; *Cassie and
   Company*   71; *Charlie's
   Angels*   71, 75; feminism
   and   189; gender and
   genre   74–5, 76, 77–9; *The
   Gentle Touch*   189; *Hill
   Street Blues*   75–6; *Juliet
   Bravo*   79, 189;
   Magnum   188; moral
   questions in   189; *Nero
   Wolfe*   188; *NYPD
   Blue*   76, 188; *Prime
   Suspect*   75; *Starsky and
   Hutch*   74, 189;
   Widows   189; doubles
   in   60–2; feminism
   and   58–9, 186, 189;
   Gabriela   64; gender and
   genre   71–7, 184; hospital;
   ER   73; identification
   with   63–4; identity
   in   59–62; *Law and
   Order*   73; melodrama   55,
   60, 65; *Moonlighting*   73;
   My Little Solitude   61;
   novels and   49; 'reality'   1;
   Remington Steele   73; *The
   Rich Also Cry*   70; situation
   comedies; *Absolutely
   Fabulous*   75; soap
   operas   54–79; aesthetics
   of   72; Aids in   73   ; *All
   My Children*   69; *The Bold
   and the Beautiful*   55, 60, 62,
   67–8, 69–70, 72, 77, 187–8;
   Brookside   69, 72–3;
   Capitol   55, 61, 62, 65–7,
   187; *Chances*   74; contract
   killing in   73; *Coronation
   Street*   76, 188; *A Country
   Practice*   74;
   criticism   57–9;
   Crossroads   58;
   Dallas   55–6, 60, 69, 74, 76,